"The Limits of Hospitality is an honest, beautiful, powerful, and challenging book. A thickly theological ethic rooted in and informed by the experiences of Christian communities, this is a welcome, practical, and important contribution to the recent literature on Christian hospitality and Christian practices."

—M. Therese Lysaught, Ph.D.
Associate Professor of Theology
Marquette University

"Jessica Wrobleski is that rare kind of theologian who is a serious intellectual and a committed activist. This beautiful book is excellent both for its perceptive reflections on Christian hospitality and the personal narrative of someone who is hospitable. One should use the word *edifying* sparingly, but this book does indeed build up the mind and heart with its seamless blend of personal witness and its mastery of theological insights into hospitality."

—Lawrence S. Cunningham
John A. O'Brien Professor of Theology (Emeritus)

"Rooted in a deep desire to strengthen the practice of Christian hospitality, this book provides an insightful and incisive look at some of its limits and tensions. Jessica Wrobleski thoughtfully weaves together personal narrative, theoretical material, and practical wisdom in addressing the central challenges in offering welcome."

—Christine Pohl, PhD
Professor of Church in Society
Asbury Theological Seminary

The Limits of Hospitality

Jessica Wrobleski

A Michael Glazier Book

LITURGICAL PRESS
Collegeville, Minnesota

www.litpress.org

A Michael Glazier Book published by Liturgical Press

Cover design by David Manahan, OSB. Photo courtesy of Thinkstock/Ryan McVay.

1	2	3	4	5	6	7	8	9

Library of Congress Cataloging-in-Publication Data

Wrobleski, Jessica.
    The limits of hospitality / Jessica Wrobleski.
      p. cm.
    "A Michael Glazier book."
    Includes bibliographical references (p.   ) and index.
    ISBN 978-0-8146-5764-5 — ISBN 978-0-8146-5998-4 (e-book)
  1. Hospitality—Religious aspects—Catholic Church.   I. Title.
  BX2347.W76   2012
  241'.671—dc23   2011051742

Contents

Acknowledgments

As the following pages will attest, a spirit of gratitude must form the heart—as well as the limits—of hospitality, and I accordingly owe great thanks to many for their part in the completion of this book. Although I could recognize countless people for their insight and support, a few individuals and communities—some of whom will appear elsewhere in this book—ought to receive special acknowledgement. To begin, Hans Christoffersen, Eric Christensen, and others at Liturgical Press deserve significant thanks for their contributions to the production of this book.

The various communities of which I have been a part over the past several years have provided me with support, guidance, and inspiration for this project, and without them it simply would not exist. I am incredibly grateful for each of the people who contributed to making the community at 192 Mansfield Street a home for me during the time that I lived there. Among them, Scott Dolff has been a particularly essential companion and interlocutor, and I am more grateful for his role in my life and in this book than I am able to say. Conversations with many other teachers, colleagues, and friends at Yale University also helped to inform my doctoral dissertation, which was in fact the first version of this book. I consider it one of the great gifts of my life to have benefitted from Margaret Farley's wise and compassionate guidance as my dissertation director, and I am also thankful for the comments and advice of Shannon Craigo-Snell, Tom Ogletree, Gene Outka, Fred Simmons, Mike Wassenaar, Natalia Marandiuc, Linn Tonstad, Katie and Eric Bugyis, Jon and Jean Bonk, Sonali Chakravarti, Asia Sazonov, Ben Moser, Mark and Kristin Totten, Christiana Peppard, Khurram Hussain, Lani Rowe, Maureen McGuire, and others.

I am also deeply grateful to the St. Peter Claver Catholic Worker and the community of people—staff, volunteers, and guests alike—who gather at Our Lady of the Road in South Bend, Indiana, and for the many ways that they have contributed to this book. In particular, I have been inspired by and benefitted from conversations with Margie Pfeil, Aimee

Shelide, Sheila McCarthy, Mara Trionfero, Daria Spezzano, Joel Schmidt, Sade Murphy, Elliott Magers, Carrie Lucas, Kathy Schuth, Michael Griffin, Katie Mansfield, Claire Hoipkemier, John Fyrqvist, and many others. I am especially grateful for the opportunity to address the community's Friday night meeting in May 2010 and for their willingness to let me share selections from the Weather Amnesty logbook, which can be found in chapter 1. Michael Baxter has been an important friend and colleague to me over the past several years, and I am thankful for his contributions to this book. I am also deeply grateful for Doug Finn, whose insightful, generous, and faithful friendship has been essential through the writing process, and life more generally. In addition to those people I have encountered through the Catholic Worker, I am thankful for my students and colleagues at Saint Mary's College—particularly Phyllis Kaminski, Anita Houck, Megan Halteman Zwart, Kevin McDonnell, and Terry Martin—for their hospitality and for the ways they have helped to refine my thoughts here. I am also thankful for the companionship, support, and inspiration of others along the way, particularly Kevin Dugan, Jonathan Pierce, St. Thomas More Chapel at Yale, St. Augustine Catholic Church (South Bend), the Morgantown Church of Christ, Liz Paulhus, and my friends and colleagues at Wheeling Jesuit University.

Finally, beyond modeling a life of hospitality both to God and to other human people, my parents, Greg and Catherine Wrobleski, have supported the creation of this book in both direct and indirect ways. My mother took time to read and talk about much of what is written here, and I am endlessly grateful for her and my father's material and emotional support during this time and throughout my life. It is to them that I dedicate this book, for their hospitality to me has made everything else possible.

An Introduction

"Can Ani stay here?" he asked me.
"Sure," I responded. "Who's Ani?"

And thus was I introduced to the limits of hospitality.

Perhaps there was some virtue—something true to the spirit of hospitality—in that willingness to extend unquestioning welcome to a stranger. But I soon realized that other virtues and conditions are necessary to sustain the practice of hospitality over time and in diverse circumstances. Both then and now, as a student and teacher of Christian ethics, I am interested in how practices and virtues contribute to living faithful lives as followers of Christ. In particular, I have been interested in the virtues and conditions that are necessary to create places of hospitality, whether such places are the possessions of families and households, churches and communities of charity, educational institutions, or nation-states.

For several years in graduate school, I lived in community with others in a three-story house in New Haven, CT. Things were off to a rough start in our community at the beginning of my second year living there, even before the situation with Ani[1] arose. The shifting and reconfiguration of belongings that came with summer subletters and new housemates were more than a little disorienting, and within a few weeks a significant personality conflict had begun to emerge between the two women who were sharing the first floor. For financial reasons, they agreed to take a third roommate (whom none of us had met before she moved into the house) into the small two-bedroom apartment, with the result that someone was sleeping in every room but the kitchen and bathroom. Within days, one of the women was so frustrated with the situation that she was planning to move out of the house, so the landlord—who slept on a bunk bed in a shared room on the third floor—offered to convert the third-floor kitchen

[1] I have changed the names of the people in this story.

into a makeshift bedroom for her. The five residents of the second and third floors would now share the small kitchen on the second floor, in addition to the rent and cost of gas and electricity.

About the same time, Jim, who lived on the third floor and was a student at Yale Divinity School, agreed to let John—a homeless man whom he had met through church—stay on the third-floor futon so that John could try to get off crack cocaine and find a job and a more permanent place to live. Over one particular weekend, five or six students who were in town for a faith-healing conference were also sleeping on the third floor, my mother and brother were in town for a visit, and a housemate broke her nose in a soccer game. And then came Ani.

Ani had been sitting on the floor in one of the hallways at the Div School with her belongings gathered around her when Jim found her there. A former student, she had just been released from Yale–New Haven Hospital's psychiatric ward and had nowhere to stay; her father had tried to come to pick her up, but she had refused to go with him. Jim recognized her from school and, prior to asking me or anyone else in the house, had offered to help her. Although there was no room for her at our house— even space on the floor was tight—a friend who lived nearby agreed to let her stay temporarily, and I said that she could use our kitchen and come and go as she liked. Unaware of her psychological issues or her life situation in general, Jim and I felt no threat and saw no harm in welcoming her into "our" space. Moreover, it seemed the hospitable thing—the Christian thing—to do.

Perhaps, in a way, it was. But we had little idea of the effect that this "last straw" would have on our already strained household. Though there was general but unspecified agreement that we were trying to live together intentionally as a Christian community—coming together for meals and prayer, for example, and perhaps sharing in other activities—we soon realized that members of the house had quite different visions of what this common life entailed. For some, particularly my new roommate Laura, the practice of widespread hospitality was definitely *not* what they had signed up for. Due in part to past experiences with a mentally ill roommate, Laura found Ani's presence around the house deeply unsettling, burdensome, and even unsafe. At a meeting of the members of the house, she tearfully read aloud a letter that she had written to express her concerns to the community. In it, she suggested that not only had Jim and I caused her stress and even trauma by our indiscriminate hospitality, but we were also potentially doing more harm than good for Ani by enabling her to avoid the professional, psychological attention she needed. By failing to recognize the real needs—and limits—of both our guests and other hosts within the community, we had created a situation that was unstable and unsustainable. Although the situation was eventually resolved in a way that was in the best interest of all (Ani went to stay with her mother for a time before returning to New Haven to attend law school), the ability of our household to offer hospitality was not only limited but crippled for some time due to the stress caused by this situation.

Yet on the whole, it was more of a lesson than a loss; in the wake of this crisis within my own community, I began to reflect on the ethical questions surrounding the practice of hospitality, particularly hospitality that is informed by Christian theological commitments and practices. In response to the situation with Ani and with Laura's complaints to the community, I initially sought to articulate clear guidelines that could serve as a rubric for knowing when limits were necessary and justifiable—that is, "If space gets so crowded or a guest is threatening in such and such a way or creates problems of such and such a nature and extent, close the door!" *For the sake of hospitality itself, there must be limits to hospitality*—and I intended to provide the rules for when and how to draw such boundaries.

As I explored many different sources for understanding the nature of hospitality and its place within the Christian moral life and spoke with people who were committed to its practice, however, it became increasingly clear that there could be no algorithm or rule that would determine limits a priori or distinguish between ethically "legitimate" and "illegitimate" boundaries. Not only the vast variety of circumstances in which hospitality is a relevant attitude or practice but also the nature of hospitality itself—graciously and even sacrificially going out of one's way for the other—make advocating firm and fixed boundaries problematic. How much more so for Christians, for whom the practice of hospitality should be a manifestation of *agape*, a participation in God's welcome extended to all people through Jesus Christ! Are limits to hospitality then merely a regrettable concession to humans' finite and fallen condition?

In fact, as I will argue throughout the following chapters, not only the *practice* but also the *concept* of hospitality itself has limits—here understood not solely negatively ("There's no more room," "I can't take this anymore") but rather as *thresholds of possibility*, limits and conditions that allow hospitality to be what it is. At its core, I take hospitality to refer to *a host's willing and gracious reception of a guest into a safe and friendly space*. The differentiation of hosts and guests (and of the spaces they occupy), as well as reasonable assurance that neither will greet the other with hostility, entails that certain limits or boundaries are implied by the very meaning of hospitality. As Felicity Heal notes in her study of hospitality in early modern England, the image that is of greatest significance for an understanding of hospitality "is not closure as opposed to openness, but *enclosure*."[2] The ideal image of hospitality is not total openness—which would deny the integrity of the household and therefore the safety and significance of the welcome—but rather a balance between a generous openness and the safety of boundaries.

Despite its claims regarding the necessity of limits, however, readers may notice that the title of this book is not *Limits to Hospitality*. The use of the genitive in the actual title—*The Limits of Hospitality*—is intended to carry a double meaning: not only is it the case that hospitality cannot exist without limits, but it is also essential that these limits be formed and informed by the spirit of hospitality that they intend to protect. When boundaries are formed by fear, prejudice, callousness, or anger, they easily become impenetrable walls of hostility rather than limits of hospitality. Even the "no" of limits must be in some way informed by a "yes"—a spirit of hospitality—that affirms the other and sets limits in a way that minimizes hostility and violence when and however possible.

The concept and practice of hospitality therefore may be understood as a dynamic tension between finitude and openness, between the possibilities and limitations of embodied nature and the loving freedom of spiritual life. The development of virtues, which allow for discernment and enactment of hospitable limits, is empowered by hospitality to the Spirit of God in and through spiritual disciplines, both as individuals and within communities. My primary goal in writing this book, which is based on the conviction that a spirit of hospitality is not only an important part of a Christian ethic but also essential to a humane and peaceful society, is to aid Christians and all people of good will in *liberating* a spirit of hospitality—not despite but precisely because of its attention to limits. I hope to show that what may be limits from one perspective—identities, needs and resources, security—also constitute the necessary thresholds where hospitality can truly begin to grow and flourish.

One image that I have found helpful in thinking about the relationship between the limits and spirit of hospitality is that of an inflated latex balloon: without the balloon itself (limits), there is only undifferentiated

---

[2] Felicity Heal, *Hospitality in Early Modern England* (New York: Oxford, 1990), 8; emphasis added.

air, and yet without the air that is breathed into it, a balloon is merely a flat and lifeless piece of rubber. Much like human men and women, if a balloon is too rapidly inflated, it will pop violently and unexpectedly (one might have only limited success filling balloons with an air compressor). And yet, also like humans, what appears to be a tiny piece of rubber has tremendous potential for expansion if it is gradually stretched and filled with spirit-breath. This does not mean that a balloon—or a human person or community—can expand infinitely (unless, perhaps, it "gives its life" for the sake of union with the spirit-air that transcends it), but it does mean that a disciplined "stretching" can lead to the gradual expansion of human limits of and capacity for hospitality.

The issues addressed here are not only of interest because of situations like my own experience recounted above. Questions concerning hospitality and its limits are pertinent to any situation in which an individual or community is faced with the challenge of welcoming those who are different into a space over which they have some claim.[3] As a way of personally reaching out to others with whom one may not share common interests, beliefs, or ways of life, the practice of hospitality is an important means of fostering human connections in a world often marked by social fragmentation and impersonal interaction. Hospitality—a word that translates the term philoxenia, "love of the stranger," from New Testament Greek—can help to mitigate a culture of suspicion, isolation, and possessive individualism by opening a space to those who are different or unfamiliar. The practice of hospitality creates spaces for listening and dialogue with such others, and it is an essential element in the formation and flourishing of communities.

Those who are engaged in social services as well as ministry continually face questions of how to welcome others and when it may be necessary to draw boundaries. Civic communities, social groups, and even educational institutions must also reckon with the limits of hospitality. Although I believe that many of its claims are relevant to other contexts, this book primarily addresses those individuals and communities who understand their identity, their place in the world, and therefore their practice of hospitality to be shaped by the story of God's loving revelation in Jesus Christ. I have also tried to make this book as hospitable as possible without

---

[3] Of course, this is the question of hospitality as it presents itself to those who are at home. Although there are fascinating and important ethical questions that pertain to the responsibilities of those who are strangers or guests within a given space, the present inquiry will focus on the issues that arise in the practice of hospitality from the perspective of those who occupy the place of host.

losing sight of the theological and theoretical background that informs it. Those who find abstract theory unfriendly should feel free to skim over those sections of the book that are more conceptual (and that I intend to signal as such) and focus on the book's narrative and practical moments.

Readers will also find an unusual gathering of "guests" in the pages of this book, diverse textual interlocutors who have helped to shape my own thought in important ways. Though I have not refrained from marking out limits of critical evaluation and judgment, I have always tried to be hospitable even to those with whom I differ. In the conversation that follows you will hear the very different voices of Jacques Derrida and Henri Nouwen, of Dorothy Day and the Catholic Worker Movement, as well as feminist theologian Letty Russell and psychologists Henry Cloud and John Townsend. Even when he does not speak openly, those familiar with the thought of Stanley Hauerwas will also recognize his unmistakable voice throughout this book. You will certainly hear about a number of my own experiences of hospitality and the voices of guests I have encountered in the years that have passed since the episode I recounted above. I have tried to attend to the words of the Hebrew Bible and the New Testament as I have been writing, and it is my deepest hope that somewhere in the pages that follow you will hear the voice of the Spirit of peace and hospitality weaving herself into my own grateful words.

The book's first chapter articulates the basic notion of hospitality as a tension between openness and boundaries, the spirit and limits of hospitality. It offers a brief account of the significance of hospitality within Christianity, drawing a framework for a theology of hospitality from biblical texts and the reflection of the tradition over time as well as from more recent work on this subject. The words of Jesus in passages like Matthew 25—"I was a stranger and you welcomed me"—and the example of unlimited self-giving in the incarnation and crucifixion establish hospitality as both important and radical within the life of discipleship. I observe how such a vision bears a number of similarities to the notion of "absolute hospitality" that has been discussed—and deconstructed—by Jacques Derrida, and I identify the ways in which *every* practice of hospitality entails limits and conditions. At the same time, I distinguish my understanding of the limits of hospitality from that of Hans Boersma, who argues in *Violence, Hospitality, and the Cross* that not only human but also divine hospitality requires violence in a fallen and finite world. While hospitality calls for the deconstructive questioning of limits, it is also necessary to reconstruct limits that are, in fact, limits of hospitality: limits that remain informed by a spirit that nonviolently seeks to reach out in love. For this task the theoretical perspective of deconstruction is insufficient.

Although there can be no theory or rule that is adequate for determining the limits of hospitality in particular circumstances, it is necessary to have some guidance—or rather formation—to aid in their discernment. In the second chapter, I turn to the relationship between the practice of welcoming others into a home or community and spiritual practices that make space and time to welcome the Spirit of God. Looking to the writing of Henri Nouwen, I argue that there is a close connection between the practice of hospitality and spiritual life and that the virtues necessary to interhuman hospitality must begin with hospitality to God through disciplines of gratitude and humility. In particular, I consider the disciplines of prayer, solitude, fellowship, fasting, celebration, service, rest, confession, and forgiveness. While this approach does not provide a fail-safe solution or guarantee a perfect decision in difficult cases, it does encourage a way of living that develops a hospitable character through disciplined spiritual practice over time—including welcoming others in concrete acts of service and hospitality.

Having described, in a certain sense, the spirit of hospitality in the first two chapters, in chapters 3 and 4 I examine in greater detail the factors that form limits of hospitality: identities, possessions, and the (physical and emotional) security of hosts and guests. In chapter 3, I describe the way in which, at a conceptual as much as practical level, hospitality requires the differentiation and identity of hosts and guests that correspond to the differentiation of inside and outside spaces. Respecting identities is therefore important to hospitality, even as identity must be informed by openness to difference and indeterminacy. For Christians, both their positive identity and their difference from the broader society must be shaped by their communities' "three-dimensional" hospitality—to God, to differences within the community, and to other people outside its boundaries—if such communities are to become places of hospitality. Chapter 4 addresses the need for hosts to "possess" a space, as well as the practical issues of limited resources and physical safety. While recognizing the insightful psychological contributions of Henry Cloud and John Townsend's phenomenally successful 1992 book *Boundaries*, I also offer a theological critique of their work that points to the need to look beyond the economics of scarcity and the idolatry of security when discerning limits of hospitality.

Chapter 5 presents what may seem to be, in certain respects, a challenge to the argument that hospitality requires limits—or at least it witnesses to practices of hospitality that challenge limits of comfort and complacency. Here, I look to the radical hospitality of the Catholic Worker as recorded through the writing of Dorothy Day and others involved in the movement. Because of their commitment to the works of mercy and the philosophy of personalism, Day, Peter Maurin, and many others helped to inaugurate a movement that strives to practice radical hospitality by erasing distinctions between "Workers" and "guests" and maintaining a community of voluntary poverty and nonviolence. While the Catholic Worker prophetically challenges complacent and comfortable limits, I argue that even here certain limits—namely, those I have identified in chapters 3 and 4—still apply. Furthermore, both in its origins and in many of its contemporary embodiments, the Catholic Worker's practice of hospitality is invigorated and empowered by spiritual practices.

Although there will always be a risk of imperfection and failure in the practice of hospitality—practice does not make perfect, for one of the virtues that such practice intends to develop is greater openness to ever-new strangers and guests—a commitment to discerning and challenging limits is essential to the creation of hospitable places. In her reflections on Benedictine hospitality, Kathleen Norris writes that "like most serious and rewarding human endeavors, . . . hospitality is a process, and it takes time for people to figure out how best to incarnate it."[4] The chapters that follow here will show some of the reasons why the practice of hospitality—and the *process* of becoming hospitable—is not only serious and rewarding but also challenging, sometimes threatening to turn to hostility in a moment when inescapable tensions turn to outright conflict. For all of these reasons, the practice of hospitality must be ongoing, always growing in both openness and discernment. If the moral life is not to be reduced to a series of thou-shalt-nots, it is necessary to attend not only to the *what* of Christian ethics but also to *how* individuals and communities are able to exercise discernment in accordance with a spirit of genuine love. True and lasting transformation of social relations toward justice and wholeness must be founded in human minds and hearts that are renewed and transformed by making space for the work of God's Spirit within them, calling them beyond their present limits.

---

[4] Kathleen Norris, *Amazing Grace: A Vocabulary of Faith* (New York: Riverhead Books, 1998), 265.

Chapter 1

Deconstructing Hospitality

Human lives are stories, not arguments and certainly not concepts. Because this book probably contains too many arguments and discussions of concepts for its own good, it seems best at least to begin with a story.

Our Lady of the Road, Pray for Us

JC is a big man.

He was one of the first people I distinctly remember meeting in the first few weeks of the two years I lived in South Bend, Indiana. On a hot August morning in the parking lot of Our Lady of the Road Café, a "drop-in center" operated by the local Catholic Worker, a very big man was looking at my car.

"That's a real nice car you've got there," he said to me in a voice as deep as the South conjured up by his long, lazy way of speaking. With my parents' help, I had just bought a slightly used and shiny, deep cherry-red Honda several months before, and I was in fact quite pleased with it myself. He asked how old my car was, how many miles were on it, and said, "Yeah boy, I'd sure like to go for a ride in that car sometime." I told him perhaps another day, I had somewhere I needed to go in a hurry—and I *had* actually kind of meant it, at least the first part. Having been studying Christian theology and practices of hospitality for several years, I was trying to resist the instinctive fear of strangers one is taught as a child in white, middle-class America. "Don't talk to strangers!" we are told from the time we are big enough to walk to the park or the swimming pool by ourselves. Even so, I wasn't quite ready to go for a joyride with a stranger twice my size whom I had just met in a parking lot.

It was soon clear, however, that JC was no stranger to Our Lady of the Road—though he did seem to keep at a distance from other guests and members of the community, often on a couch or a chair in the corner, wearing headphones or writing in books. JC is no less than six feet five

1

inches tall and bears a notable resemblance to the actor Will Smith. I have seldom seen him without a hat, and he often wears a heavy coat and ski goggles—perhaps some sort of Southern adaptation for the winters in northern Indiana. In fact, JC was not actually from the South but had rather spent most of his life in the Midwest—Ohio and Indiana. He said he never really knew his parents but had lived with an uncle and was what he described as "a ward of the state" for a time. He was thirty-five years old—about three years older than me—when I met him. He takes pills that help with "chemical imbalances" but make him want to sleep a lot during the day. Like quite a number of South Bend's homeless population, he often goes to the public library during the day, where he sleeps and works on his "words."

JC is fascinated with words. Like me, he fills line after line and page after page of notebooks with words that he carefully copies out of newspapers, magazines, and books of all sorts. He knew I was a teacher, so sometimes when I talked to him he would ask me to define the more exotic words—magnanimous, epidemiology, insouciance, perjury—and he would explain to me how carefully he guards his notebooks of words. With a hint of contempt for his fellow guests in his voice, he sometimes told me how he was sure that such notebooks would be very much coveted by "these people here" and were likely to be stolen if he didn't keep a careful watch over them. There was something almost childlike in this big man's simple desire to spend hours a day collecting and hoarding words—not stringing them together into sentences or arguments or even necessarily knowing their meanings—simply to keep them in his possession, his power. Sometimes he would sound philosophical, almost poetic in his spoken words, and every so often there was anger in his voice as he told of his frustration with the police who woke him from his sleep and made him move out of a parking lot or doorway the night before.

JC's last steady job was with the South Bend *Tribune*, loading and shipping newspapers for delivery. While he was working there he had a steady paycheck and schedule, an apartment and car. He lost his job just a few months before I met him; in one telling of the story he had made it sound like the paper simply let him go because of cutbacks in an increasingly digital yet slow economy, though another time he hinted that there had been some trouble with a coworker. Since he had been living paycheck to paycheck, soon after he lost his job he was unable to pay his rent and moved into his car, which is where he was sleeping when I first met him. Within a few months he had given up the car—put it into storage in the next town—

because gasoline was too expensive. He spent a lot of time at Our Lady of the Road—I saw him there virtually every time I went—though, as I said before, he kept to himself, usually sleeping or reading in a corner of the room.

Sometimes I made a point of talking to JC; other times it seemed like he made the point of talking to me, waiting near my car in the parking lot until I finished up inside. Several times he asked whether I might have a room in my house that I could rent to him. As you might imagine, at a certain level, I thought, *Are you kidding?*—though instead I told him (honestly) that I liked living alone, and besides, my lease required any additional tenants to submit an application (references, proof of employment, etc.—I had actually found it pretty intimidating myself). But I couldn't entirely ignore his question and his need, either. In my journal—a regular discipline of prayer for me—that fall, I wrote:

> 2009-09-28
>
> Friday morning went to OLR and it was good. I *do* feel like that's my "church" in a significant way, my community. One thing left me in a dilemma, though—JC, the big man who I talked to about my car one of the first weekends I was in SB, asked me about my place—how much I pay, etc.—then asks if I'd want a roommate. "I want to try to get off of these streets before the winter. . . ."
>
> Oh Lord, is this you?
>
> On one hand, I feel like it would be ridiculous at so many levels to let this guy stay at my house that it almost feels embarrassing to admit I'm seriously considering it. Not only inconvenient, uncomfortable, but potentially unsafe . . . he seems sweet, but he himself has spoken of "chemical imbalances," and if something happened and he got upset or something . . . he's a LOT bigger than me—and yet also one of "the least of these. . . ." It seems positively immoral for me to have a perfectly empty and unused extra room while another human being—human person—has no place to stay. God, please give me wisdom and discernment as well as compassion in this matter.

I continued to see JC when I visited Our Lady of the Road through the following months, and one day in November when I was talking with him at breakfast, he asked whether I could give him a ride to the storage unit where he kept his things. It was Sunday, so the city buses weren't running, and the place he described was a significant distance away—the better part of a day to walk there and back from downtown. The chill of winter was beginning to send a shiver through the nights and early mornings, and he needed to get another coat, a sleeping bag, gloves, and so on.

Since JC wasn't a *total* stranger at that point, I agreed. I remember how big he looked in the passenger seat of my car, which I had always considered quite spacious—his knees up against the dash, even with the seat pushed way back. I can't recall what we talked about—cars, probably, or the weather—as we drove to the complex of orange-roofed self-storage units. I do remember being somewhat surprised by how full the unit was when he took out a key and opened it. Not only was his very small car parked inside, but also what appeared to be boxes of books and clothes, lamps, furniture, and a bicycle. And *why* was I surprised? Because a homeless man had possessions? Because he had enough possessions to fill a self-storage unit but no place to sleep, to store and restore, *himself*? I don't know why, exactly.

When I dropped him off at the library that afternoon, he again asked if I could rent him a room. There were shelters for the homeless in town of course, but he didn't like to stay in "those places"—people drank (he didn't), and he didn't appreciate the come-ons of the women there, and it was noisy and he couldn't sleep. I thought about the "Christ room" of which Dorothy Day and Peter Maurin had often spoken, saying that if every Christian household could give shelter to even *one* person, there would be little need for the dehumanizing institutionalization of people that so often marks large-scale solutions to poverty. Part of what the Christian personalism of the Catholic Worker advocates is taking responsibility for social need rather than delegating to the state or saying that such people are someone else's problems when they come to us and ask us for our help.

So I told JC that I couldn't rent him a room, but—whether out of a sense of responsibility or compassion or guilt or hospitality or pure foolishness or all of the above, I'm not sure—I gave him my phone number and told him that if the weather was really bad, he could call in an emergency. I did have a room in the attic where he could stay, I told him, but not on a regular basis (because of the lease). He would have to leave first thing in the morning, so I could get ready and go to work. The attic room was finished but basically uninsulated—typically unbearably hot when it was warm and barely warmer than outdoors when it was cold, so I didn't use it for anything but storing extra books and clothes—but at least JC would find shelter from the elements without noisy drunks or harassment from police or propositions from women who were possibly even more desperate than he. Several nights later, when it was raining and the temperatures were in the midthirties, my phone rang. I hesitated when I saw the unfamiliar local number, and then I answered the call.

"Hey, uh, . . . this is JC. . . ."

After an awkward acknowledgment of why he was calling, I described how to get to my house from the library. He rode his bike and was at my front door less than an hour later.

Unsurprisingly, I felt strange and uncomfortable when he showed up at my house. I had been making myself dinner when he arrived, and it seemed only right that I should offer him some as well. So the two of us sat there at my kitchen table, eating vegetable soup out of wide blue bowls, without much to say. I noticed again how big he was, how small my hands and feet and knees looked in comparison with his, and wondered what I was supposed to do with him in the hours that remained before my usual bedtime. Fortunately, he seemed quite content to retire to his room upstairs soon after we'd finished our soup.

Also unsurprisingly, I didn't sleep well that night. It wasn't so much that I was worried about any kind of harm from him as I was dismayed by the choices before me. The awkward experience and uncomfortable feeling of being alone in the house with him—as with *any* man I barely knew, frankly—and the recognition that big people make a lot of noise in small, squeaky houses made me realize that such "emergencies" could not become regular occurrences if I was to continue functioning in my own life and work. But how could I let someone asking for help sleep in the cold when I had an unused extra room?

As promised, he left before seven the next morning, and I had plenty of time to shower and get ready for work after locking the door behind him. I began to feel a sense of relief over the next few days when I didn't hear from him, although I continued to wrestle with this decision. I was beginning to think that the fact that I didn't feel I could tell anyone—colleagues, friends I knew at the Catholic Worker, and *certainly* not my parents—what I was doing without them thinking me a crazy fool indicated that perhaps they were correct in that assessment. I was also thinking that the next time I saw JC at Our Lady of the Road I would let him know that this arrangement wasn't going to work out. I continued to deliberate about JC in my written reflections, and I went to daily Mass that week with a particular intention to pray for wisdom and guidance in this matter.

I don't recall anything in particular about the Mass that day except that it was early in Advent—violet red—and that afterward I ran into a good friend who also spent time at Our Lady of the Road. As we talked, I explained to him the situation I was facing, the dilemma I felt, and to my surprise he didn't think I was completely stupid or crazy. But he also reminded me of the fact that somehow JC has survived this long, and—though it is certainly wrong that some should be without a home—he would likely continue to do so even if I wasn't the one to provide for him. The conversation gave me a greater sense of peace with my decision to say no to JC, but when I started to talk to him about it the following weekend at the café it seemed that he had already come to a similar conclusion on his own.

Despite my earnest desire to help, JC was simply too big of a guest for me, by myself, alone in a small house. Besides, as we both knew, Our Lady was about to open a season of Weather Amnesty for JC and other men like him who were without a place to stay on a winter night. And sometimes, it seems, when there are many together there is more room for all.

Our Lady of the Road Laundromat Café is located at 744 S. Main Street in South Bend, Indiana, a few blocks from the bus station and the Center for the Homeless. Since December 2006, OLR has been operated by the local Catholic Worker community (which also has residential houses several blocks away on St. Joseph Street), offering laundry and shower facilities and a hot breakfast to people in need from 8:00–11:30 a.m. on Fridays, Saturdays, and Sundays. On any given morning, many people also drop in to get out of the cold (or heat) and have a cup of coffee or converse with others who have gathered there. Generally, two people from the Catholic Worker staff are on duty each day of operation, but Our Lady of the Road relies significantly on the work of volunteers (including those who come as guests) to provide these services. Some days all available hands are needed to cut bread or make coffee or wash dishes, but many other times there are large groups of student volunteers or church groups to do these things. On those days, I played my guitar and sang folk songs while people worked and ate—and one could hardly imagine a more appreciative audience. In addition to its weekend operations, during the winter months (between December and April) Our Lady offers shelter for ten men on a first-come-first-served basis.

The communal practice of hospitality through Weather Amnesty involves the weaving together of countless lives and stories into a tapestry of warmth—not only the stories of the nights of keeping vigil, of conversations and late-night knocks at the door, but also the personal stories that brought the many volunteers to Our Lady of the Road and the many different stories of the men who stayed there as guests—including JC, who was there quite regularly. Over the course of the season, hundreds of volunteers—many of them Notre Dame or other local college students, faculty, and staff and others from the community who want to contribute—sign up in pairs to serve as hosts to keep vigil while ten guests slept on cots in the laundry room at OLR. For many people, it is a profound experience of community, as relationships are built between hosts and guests, and as every person who serves not only sees their own lives in a different (and often more grateful) light but also comes to know that they are supported by a wider circle of people who are committed to the practice of hospitality to the poor. Participating as a Weather Amnesty host, even if it only meant serving once or twice a month, allowed me to contribute to the creation of a space that was large enough for JC and many others, despite the fact that I could not provide such space on my own.

Even though—and perhaps precisely *because*—the space created by Weather Amnesty was quite large, it also required boundaries and limits that were clearly defined (if nonetheless hospitable) in order to make sure that it remained a safe and welcoming place for all. Every evening there was a standard routine (though there could also be deviations from this on special occasions such as Christmas, New Year's, and Super Bowl Sunday): at 8:00 p.m. guests were welcomed inside and "breathalyzed" by a Catholic Worker staff member to ensure that they had not been drinking (Our Lady of the Road does not permit drinking on the premises under any circumstances) before they were signed in and given sheets, blanket, and a towel to take a shower. If guests left for any reason, they were not allowed to return that night. Lights out was at 10:00 p.m.; after that time, all men were expected to stay quietly in their beds until wake up at 6:30 a.m. the next morning. At least one host was expected to stay awake at all times to make sure there were no problems. Possession of drugs or weapons or the threat of violence were grounds for immediate dismissal. Although sometimes guests would try to push the rules—refusing to take a shower or getting up in the middle of the night to smoke or make coffee—for the most part they realized that the rules were in their own interest as much as anyone else's, and they were deeply appreciative of the hospitality.

But as many hosts observed in the nightly logbook, it often seemed that the men who regularly came for shelter were in fact the ones offering a kind of hospitality to the volunteers. Consistent with the personalism of the Catholic Worker (see chapter 5), hosts were encouraged to get to know the guests' names and stories—to meet people as well as needs—and it is clear from some of the entries in the logbook (which served as a place for written prayers and reflections as well as noteworthy events) that a deep and genuine fondness for some of the regular guests took root in those who served as their hosts.

I am grateful to the South Bend Catholic Worker community not only for allowing me to share in this practice but also for allowing me to share some of these voices of hospitality, hope, and prayer as recorded in the nightly log, which offers a truer sense of this practice of hospitality in community than my voice alone could give.

11/30/2009

Brothers and Sisters, dear and loved—the first night of Weather Amnesty.

Pray for the restoration of your life through brokenness, repentance, and submission. Pray for provision and restoration for these men—a hope for them. Pray for warmth (I hope you've dressed warmly!). After all, what is one night with less sleep? Our schedules, our desires, our physical needs—they are not ours to control. . . . Share your life. Be honest. Realize the depths of His love and accept it for yourself. In that way you can extend it outwards.

Time is our life—life-time. And so we give our life when we give our time. Multiply our time, Lord, as you multiply all good things—as you multiplied the loaves and the fishes, as you multiply the graces poured out on your people. Thank you for the gift of each other—may we recognize You always, and may peace be upon this house.

12/8/2009

Without cost you have received—without cost you are to give. . . .

Thanks Wayne and Jim for sharing . . . and for showing me how.

We prayed a rosary in the women's restroom—5 Hail Marys for each man.

Our Lady of the Road—pray for us.

4:33am, December 15

Snoring and coughing and farting—oh my!

Have been kind of amazed by the racket that is produced during sleep by a room of ten men—though it has actually quieted considerably since earlier tonight. . . .

I was also struck—earlier this evening, as men were getting their showers, eating and talking with one another, or just resting in their beds—by how different it feels here in the evening for Weather Amnesty than for the regular breakfast and laundry-café. There is a stillness, a slowness, a different sort of happy-to-be-off-the-street-for-now-ness. . . . "Different times of day bring about different dispositions of the soul" (Hegel).

Thank you, God, for this holy place, for the organizational and physical work of the staff that is necessary to this particular practice of hospitality. Thank you for the extended community of people who gather here—for the nourishment of the friendship of people who desire to live just and holy lives of peace and mercy, thank you Lord. Thank you also for the "community" of guests, and for the ways that my comfortable life is challenged and called into question by those who have suffered the world's injustice and violence and unholiness.

May this place always be a place of warmth and rest and nourishment and holy peace, by the presence of your Spirit here. . . . May this Christmas season truly bring new birth and a greater awareness of your kingdom, for which we wait in joyful hope.

12/19/09

Saw flashing lights and went to the door to investigate. Saw the feet of a man sleeping by the door—what to do? It's snowing and cold but it's after 10—surely can't be a good idea to let him in—but to pretend that I just didn't see him? What is our purpose if not to help in any way we are able—within the framework of what OLR has established as rules. Important not to set a precedent. The man could be angry out there—should I be afraid to approach him? Discussed with Sheila and other volunteers—decided to encourage him to go to [another shelter]—offer a cookie and tea perhaps—give him a blanket if he insists on staying—but he was gone when I went out, so I left the blanket and returned to the recliner to pray for him—that he will be inside tomorrow and that he finds shelter tonight. That was 2 hours ago and I can't shake the guilt and concern—what of the others outside?

Dec 22–23

It's striking to realize that this is the best option for all these guys, while for me, I can look forward to a room of my own, a real bed to sleep in tonight, or maybe even later today. These guys will wander the streets, stopping inside for a meal here or there, maybe a place to warm up, and then to come back here to wait outside for a couple of hours to get back in here. How long, O Lord? You who were homeless . . . make a home here with us.

12/29

To note: Scott/Wayne is here tonight. He blew an 0.0 but I told him he can't come to OLR Fri–Sun AM because he drank outside the door (and inside) last weekend. He was upset, thinking he was "barred" but I insisted he is still welcome for WA (if he's not drinking) but just can't come to b'fast this weekend. He may need to be reminded of this. Be prepared for another (resistant) conversation.

January 6 – Epiphany

One of the "men" here tonight is only 20 years old and has been staying in the shelters around SB for the past year. I didn't catch all his story, but apparently he was given a bus ticket here (from Arizona) to find an uncle in the area, who he never did find. He seems like just a boy—I can hardly imagine . . . thinking about him in comparison with the ND students who volunteer here—what different worlds they inhabit!—is thought provoking. . . .

1/7/2010

Another quiet night. Seymour welcomed me with a big smile. It's enough to make me feel more welcome here than in my own neighborhood.

Full house tonight, mostly familiar faces. Had to turn away 3, including Chris, the 20 yr old. He stayed until he had to leave. John found him another shelter for tonight and made sure he got there OK. I'm appreciative for the gentle and helpful spirit of John, and our guests.

Reflecting on my own comfortable, if simple, life. Mostly, I keep my complaints about shoveling snow and lugging firewood to myself. Now I count my blessings, having assurance of a warm, comfortable bed at night and shelter all day. Coming here keeps me humble.

I count it all joy to give up one night of comfort for the safety of others. Sometimes it's even fun.

January 18, 2010

John told me that he doesn't want to live anymore. . . .
       But he also explained that all he needs is love. . . .
       I think he does want to live,
       and I pray he does.
Ernest, age 71, cried . . . and before turning over to sleep, he called out to us, "Hey—thanks for being good listeners." Thanks for sharing, Ernest.
       Mel's thickness that broke into laughter for a moment, James' honesty, Moe's kind eyes, and Cedric's sad eyes, Jim's kindness, and Paul's singing. . . .
       Each man, each person, each heart is a letter in God's great story.

1/22/10, almost 2am

This is my first night at Our Lady of the Road. It has been peaceful and smooth—I can sense the easy familiarity of routine, and I feel welcomed by the guests.

There are only 8 guests tonight, all of them regulars if I can judge by the speed at which the cots come out and conversation reached a comfortable flow.

I will remember the conversations I had with these men tonight for a long time. It is a powerful thing to remember what they mean. With our stories and varied backgrounds and different presents and unknown futures we share what transcends these circumstances— just a connection from human being to human being that allows us to move outside ourselves, a little bit closer to understanding how to love.

1/23

Amazing the difference a few degrees can make. Apparently if the temperature is above 32 a person doesn't need shelter? I know that's the policy over at the Center, but it's still cold and icky out there. God bless the Worker for opening their doors while the others take the night off!!

Men were banging on the door looking for shelter after realizing that there was no Amnesty at other places—finally had to put up a sign to say that there was no more room at this inn—heartbreaking to think of where they're spending this night—prayer and blessings to them out there.

11:08pm, January 30

Lord, teach us to see. Teach us to see not only the extravagance of Yourself, reflected in the lights of the trees, but also in the faces and lives of those we serve. May we wonder at the laughter and tenacity of these men in spite of the brokenness they've experienced. May we learn to be vulnerable to seeing, learn to cast aside our assumptions and protective pride and distance and learn to love. May your Spirit bridge between us in ways that we wouldn't imagine, healing both of our wounds and overcoming ourselves. May your Eucharistic vision strike us so deeply that we are left ringing, burning with hope.

Feb. 3

Played Uno with Chris and Ray. Chris is the same age as Jen and I. Why did God decide I got two loving parents and all the support in the world to end up at Notre Dame while Chris ended up on the street?

February 9

Mel offered me a hand warmer and showed me his new "collectors' item" pin.

JC let us look at his words.

John seems to be struggling—kept his head phones on all night, wouldn't talk. I'm worried about him. Does he yet know that he is loved?

Jim made dinner for the whole bunch of us tonight! So unexpected, so thoughtful. Got to learn more about him finally—just a regular guy, kind hearted. . . .

And dear, dear Cedric—I was afraid he'd never open up . . . but tonight he's the one who brought Daniel and me two full plates of food, wearing a shy smile—he was so glad, so grateful to share.

I praise the Lord for these men—all so complex, so real, so trying, clinging to HOPE.

February 26

Bless us, your children, however foolish we may be; help us to live in hope, with energy to give our small gifts in faith that you might transform them for the good of the world. Bless the men who stay here, the staff who make this place, this community, possible. May your Spirit of peace ever dwell with us here.

3/20

Welcome back! After many warmer nights (above 32) and sunny days it's nice to be here with the men—welcoming old friends, delineating what is an increasingly less clear line between volunteer and guest. Most of the time they know better what is going on than we do! As the season winds down the difference between 30 and 34 must not feel that stark for the men—yet there is an arbitrary line drawn about when we offer shelter and when we do not. So many lines to think about—artificial boundaries. JC is especially restless tonight and was especially talkative, perhaps sillier. . . . Some of the regulars back in a routine of whatever, the OLR WAM routine broken by the sunshine. . . . I pray for their safety and wish they were here with us and finding the peace many claim to see only here. God, protect them from the elements, from their self-destructive habits and patterns, from the violence of that life.

The Spirit of peace does seem to dwell among the community of people who gather at Our Lady of the Road—even when things do not run smoothly or when conflict and injury arise. I am sure that the staff and those who actually live at the Catholic Worker on St. Joseph Street could share many additional stories of both the challenges and the joys of life in a community of hospitality.

Yet I hope that these brief episodes I have shared have helped to show that in addition to its positive core meaning of offering welcome and love to strangers, hospitality is shaped by the need to discern limits in the tensions between giving and receiving, safety and risk, solitude and community, comfort and need. Although hospitality cannot persist as absolute openness—a surrender of one's home or self, the erasure of distinctions between outside and inside—neither can a place be hospitable if it does not retain a spirit of openness and gift-like generosity. That is, while total openness and surrender eliminate a host's ability to designate and dispose of a given space in a hospitable way, at the same time, if this tension is definitively resolved in favor of total control over a space or violent enforcement of its boundaries, the gracious welcome at the heart of hospitality is lost. And ultimately, for Christians, "the wideness of God's mercy and the generosity of God's welcome must frame our thinking about limits and boundaries."[1]

In her insightful study of Christian hospitality, Christine Pohl discusses some of the concrete ways that "communities struggle with boundaries and . . . without them"[2] in the context of practicing hospitality. Yet such boundaries are not only a regrettable practical concession to our finite and flawed human condition; they also in a certain way contribute to why hospitality is such a valuable human and Christian practice—and why it is more than simply a synonym for love or kindness. In their moments of asymmetry as well as of mutuality, our human experiences in the roles of host and guest offer important and profound insights into the ways that human lives are shaped by both displacement and belonging, by scarcity and abundance, vulnerability and security, being in control and awaiting the unforeseeable. Authentic humanity is not found in escaping one or the other of these polarities but rather in embracing each and living within a dynamic tension that affirms life in all its messiness and limitation while recognizing such experiences are not the ultimate reality of human life.

As Augustine recognized, we best practice hospitality to strangers when we see that we too are on pilgrimage, guests on our way to God's great eternal

---

[1] Christine Pohl, *Making Room: Recovering Hospitality as a Christian Tradition* (Grand Rapids, MI: Eerdmans, 1999), 129.

[2] Ibid.

banquet of love. He pointed toward this paradox when he encouraged his listeners to acknowledge the duty of hospitality in a homily on the Gospel of Luke: "You take in some stranger, whose companion in the way you yourself also are, for we are all strangers," he wrote. "That person is a Christian who, even in his own house and his own country, acknowledges himself to be a stranger. For our country is above, where we shall not be strangers. . . . Remember Christ is the keeper, so why do you fear you might lose what you spend on the poor?"[3]

Why, indeed? Most contemporary people—whose hospitality falls far short of that commended by Augustine and other early Christian writers— could offer a hundred reasons, a thousand different fears, that prevent them from offering their homes and possessions to those in need. Many of these are no more than excuses for the isolation of wealth from poverty and for the violent and possessive individualism of contemporary Western culture, the unbelief of believers. And yet there may be some legitimate concern buried beneath the fears and excuses. How is hospitality possible if, as Paul describes in the thirteenth chapter of his letter to the Corinthians, I give away my life and all of my possessions—so that all that remains is love?

"For mortals it is impossible, but not for God," Jesus told his disciples. "For God all things are possible" (Mark 10:27).

Perhaps with God, Paul or Augustine or the gospel writers might tell us, love is enough.

Christian Hospitality

From the tradition's beginning in the ministry of Jesus and the prac- tices of the earliest Christian churches through medieval monasteries and contemporary ministries of social justice, hospitality has been an important ideal in Christian life. One could make a case, however, that the importance of welcoming strangers in the ancient church was simply a reflection of the culture from which it emerged; in both the ancient and modern Near East, hospitality is a cardinal social virtue, a quality that distinguishes civilized peoples from barbarians and "one of the pillars of morality upon which the universe stands."[4] Or perhaps, apart from any

---

[3] Augustine of Hippo, Sermon 61, in Amy Oden, *And You Welcomed Me: A Sourcebook on Hospitality in Early Christianity* (Nashville: Abingdon, 2001), 45.

[4] John Koenig, *New Testament Hospitality: Partnership with Strangers as Promise and Mission* (Eugene, OR: Wipf and Stock, 2001), 2. Additional discussion of the significance of hospitality within the cultural context of ancient Christianity can be found in John Bell Mathews, "Hospitality

cultural or religious impetus, the practice of hospitality is, as Raimon Panikkar has written, "essential to anyone who harbors feelings that are fully human; feelings, I might go so far as to say, that are indicative of a good state of health."[5] Even those who have recently argued for the notion of a "hospitable God" as the core of Christian faith also state that it would be "deeply inhospitable, not to say just plain wrong, to suggest that hospitality is a prerogative of Christian faith alone."[6] Nonetheless, although Christians have certainly not been the only, nor the best, practitioners of hospitality, when looking at the life of Jesus it is difficult to argue against the claim that hospitality bears a particular connection to the heart of Christian mission and identity. This connection will be a focus of chapter 3; however, it also seems worth asking whether there is, in fact, something distinctive about Christian hospitality.

The Greek word in the New Testament that is translated "hospitality" (which actually does not appear often in the gospels, though its presence in the narratives of Jesus' life is surely felt)—φιλοξενία (philoxenia), meaning literally "love for strangers"—indicates that for the New Testament writers hospitality was not simply a matter of entertaining friends and relatives but rather extended to unknown persons, whether potential friends or enemies. But this was really no different from other practices of the time or even from many cultures today; indeed, throughout much of the developing world, hospitality toward strangers remains an almost absolute obligation. Within the ancient Near East, it was common to extend an unquestioning welcome to anyone in need; only after a stranger's basic needs had been addressed would he be expected to share his identity or stories of his travels.[7] Such indiscriminate welcome was not only due to a concern for the vulnerability of a stranger in a society where kinship-based community was essential to survival but also, ironically, from fear of that same stranger, who might be not only a powerful ally but also a potential

---

and the New Testament Church: An Historical and Exegetical Study" (ThD diss., Princeton Theological Seminary, 1964); Ladislaus Bolchazy, *Hospitality in Early Rome: Livy's Conception of Its Humanizing Force* (Chicago: Area Publishers, 1977); and Andrew Arturbury, *Entertaining Angels: Early Christian Hospitality in its Mediterranean Setting* (Sheffield, UK: Sheffield Phoenix, 2005).

[5] Raimon Panikkar, foreword to Pierre-François de Bethune, *Interreligious Hospitality: The Fulfillment of Dialogue* (Collegeville, MN: Liturgical Press, 2010), xi.

[6] George Newlands and Allen Smith, *Hospitable God: The Transformative Dream* (Burlington, VT: Ashgate, 2010), 4.

[7] Mathews points to the *Odyssey* as an example of this custom; see "Hospitality and the New Testament Church," 33.

enemy or a divine emissary. Through his hospitality, the host could hope
to ingratiate himself to allies, enemies, and gods and thereby guarantee
the good fortune of his household.[8] Not only in paradigmatic stories
such as Abraham's welcoming the strangers at Mamre (Gen 18:1-15) or
Rahab's hospitality to the spies at Jericho (Josh 2) but throughout the
Torah and the testimony of the prophets, the Hebrew Scriptures identify
the practice of hospitality to the vulnerable as an important moral duty,
which in turn shaped the thought and practice of Jesus, Paul, and the early
Christian communities.[9]

Although historical sources tend to differ on the extent to which early
Christian hospitality was distinct from that practiced by the surrounding
Judaic and Hellenic culture, nearly all agree that Christians understood—and
in some measure, continue to understand—what they were doing in a
distinctive way: that is, as a way of *participating* in the activity of God in
Christ through welcoming those who are most powerless and undesirable
or who seem to have the least to offer in return. In passages such as Luke
14:13-14, Jesus instructs his listeners: "When you give a banquet, invite the
poor, the crippled, the lame, and the blind. And you will be blessed, because
they cannot repay you, for you will be repaid at the resurrection of the
righteous." In his actions as well, Jesus extends welcome and fellowship to
powerless social outsiders, such as those suffering from illness or disability
(e.g., Mark 2:1-12; Luke 17:11-19; John 9:1-12), "sinful" women (Luke
7:36-50; John 4:1-29), and others who were outcasts or seemed to have
little to offer in return for his attention (Matt 19:13-15; Mark 5:1-20; Luke
19:1-10; 23:43). If the heart of Jesus' mission on earth was proclaiming
the kingdom of God through challenging exclusionism and reaching out
to those on the margins, as New Testament scholar John Koenig and others have contended,[10] it is only fitting that Christians should do likewise.

---

[8] In discussions of ancient custom such as this, I use masculine pronouns because of
the likelihood that in such cases the "agent" of hospitality—the one who opens the door
as "master" of the household—was male. This is not to deny the importance of women
or male servants to the actual carrying out of such hospitality. For further discussion of
this topic, see "Love and Limits" in chapter 4.

[9] In certain places in the Hebrew Scriptures, the near-absolute duty to guests is taken
to extremes that should be unequivocally condemned—such as Lot's offer of his virgin
daughters in place of his guests to appease the men of Sodom in Gen 19:8 or the story of
the rape and murder of the Levite's concubine at Gibeah in Judges 19:22-30—and that I
believe offer a strong argument for the ethical necessity of limits to hospitality.

[10] Koenig, *New Testament Hospitality*, 86. Cf. Brendan Byrne, *The Hospitality of God: A Reading of
Luke's Gospel* (Collegeville, MN: Liturgical Press, 2000); Daniel Groody, *Globalization, Spirituality,*

Many have in fact noted the remarkable inclusiveness and egalitarianism of the earliest Christian communities, who spoke and wrote of hospitality "to the sick and the injured, to the widow and the orphan, to the sojourner and stranger, to the aged, to the slave and imprisoned, to the poor and hungry. At times," writes Amy Oden, "it seems there is no class of people not included within the scope of hospitality."[11] In a homily on the Letter of Paul to the Romans, John Chrysostom comments:

> If you are always so scrupulous about the character of your guests, many a time you will pass by a person of esteem, and lose your reward. Yet whoever receives someone not of high status has no fault found with him, but is even rewarded. . . . So don't busy yourself with people's lives and doings. For this is the very extreme of stinginess, to nitpick about a person's entire life to avoid giving them one loaf of bread. For if this person is a murderer, if a robber, or whatnot, does he therefore seem to you not to deserve a loaf and a few coins? And yet your Master causes even the sun to rise on him![12]

Such advice indicates that Chrysostom and other early Christians saw themselves as coparticipants with Christ in extending God's gracious welcome to all people, regardless of whether they are worthy of such beneficence. Indeed, not only indiscriminate love of strangers but even of enemies (Matt 5:44; Luke 6:27-30, 35; etc.) is commended and practiced by Jesus—perhaps most dramatically in his extension of table fellowship to his betrayer (Mark 14:18-20)—and his disciples as a sign of the kingdom of God.

At the same time as Jesus acts as host by proclaiming God's kingdom, however, he also deepens the significance of hospitality through his identification with the guest. Throughout his ministry, Jesus was dependent on the hospitality of other people, a prophet with "nowhere to lay his head" (Luke 9:58), who also extends welcome to those who receive him. Based on his words in the Gospel of Matthew, Christians believe that by offering food, shelter, and companionship to a stranger in need, they offer it to Jesus Christ himself:

> Then the king will say to those at his right hand, "Come, you that are blessed by my Father, inherit the kingdom prepared for you from

---

and Justice (Maryknoll, NY: Orbis, 2009), 49–50, 225; Pierre-François de Bethune, *Interreligious Hospitality*, especially chapter 5.

[11] Amy Oden, *And You Welcomed Me*, 20.

[12] Ibid., 63.

the foundation of the world; for I was hungry and you gave me food, I was thirsty and you gave me something to drink, I was a stranger and you welcomed me, I was naked and you gave me clothing, I was sick and you took care of me, I was in prison and you visited me." Then the righteous will answer him, "Lord, when was it that we saw you hungry and gave you food, or thirsty and gave you something to drink? And when was it that we saw you a stranger and welcomed you, or naked and gave you clothing? And when was it that we saw you sick or in prison and visited you?" And the king will answer them, "Truly I tell you, just as you did to one of the least of these who are members of my family, you did it to me." (Matt 25:34-40; cf. Matt 10:40-42)

Though other cultures and religions embrace the idea that a stranger (ξένος) may be a representative of the gods, in Christianity "the link between the ξένος and the divine Lord is . . . the most direct and personal conceivable."[13] That is, hospitality is not only significant as a form of evangelical proclamation but also as a direct expression of love for God—particularly when it is granted to those who seem least to conform to expectations or to offer a promise of return in kind.

A significant number of recent books have reaffirmed this perspective by stating that the distinctive nature of Christian hospitality is due to its being founded in the community's true worship of and partnership with God. These range from those who liberally interpret the Christian God as unconditional, inclusive love ("For God, to be is to act hospitably," write George Newlands and Allen Smith[14]) to those who state that true hospitality can only be known in and through the triune God as revealed in Christian orthodoxy and tradition. For these authors, as for the earliest Christians, God is ultimately host, guest, and home, and human practices and reflection on hospitality must begin from an understanding—or better, an experience—of God's hospitality. Many of these authors have done a fine job of articulating this theological ground of Christian hospitality, and in the following pages I not only concur with but also draw upon many of their insights. The hospitality of God will never be far from view. But the focus of the questions here will be somewhat different; namely, what facets of hospitality cause us to find it useful as a metaphor for God's

---

[13] Gustav Stählin, "ξένος," in *Theological Dictionary of the New Testament*, ed. Gerald Kittel and George Friedrich, trans. Geoffrey W. Bromiley (Grand Rapids, MI: Eerdmans, 1964), 5:16. Cf. Mathews, "Hospitality and the New Testament Church," 283–84.

[14] Newlands and Smith, *Hospitable God*, 98.

love as well as for human relationships? How can we best practice such hospitality given the limits and vulnerabilities of human existence?

For, one might ask, if God's eschatological welcome serves as the paradigm for Christian hospitality and every guest is to be received as Christ, can there be any real justification of limits to Christian hospitality? If Christ's self-giving *even to the point of death* is the model of Christian love, is not every effort at self-preservation falling short of this ideal? Questions such as these are perennial as Christians reckon with the implications of the Gospel in light of the finitude, tragedy, and weakness that mark the human condition; nonetheless, it is clear from biblical and ancient sources that early Christian communities were aware of the necessity of limits. While the hospitality of these communities to traveling apostles and teachers (such as Paul and his companions) was essential to the growth of Christianity, the practice of unconditional hospitality could be abused. The author of the *Didache*, an instructional text of the early church (ca. 100 CE), addresses these issues directly by advising that persons who offer "renegade" teachings ought not be welcomed and by explaining how to discern the authenticity of a preacher or prophet (chap. 11). Additionally, chapter 12 of this document recognizes a tension between generosity toward outsiders and the needs of the community:

> Everyone who comes to you in the name of the Lord must be welcomed. Afterward, when you have tested him, you will find out about him, for you have insight into right and wrong. If it is a traveler who arrives, help him all you can. But he must not stay with you more than two days or, if necessary, three. If he wants to settle with you and is an artisan, he must work for his living. If, however, he has no trade, use your judgment in taking steps for him to live with you as a Christian without being idle. If he refuses to do this, he is trading on Christ. You must be on your guard against such people.[15]

Other sources, both ancient and contemporary, attest to the tension between helping a traveler "all you can" and asking that he contribute concretely to the community or observe its rule, making judgments that safeguard the well-being of all without allowing hospitality to become unduly conditional.

---

[15] *Didache* 12:2-5, in *The New Testament and Other Early Christian Writings: A Reader*, ed. Bart Ehrman (New York: Oxford, 1998), 116.

The practice of hospitality within monastic—particularly Benedictine—communities underscores the necessity of balancing hospitality with distance, openness with boundaries. The Rule of Benedict contains detailed instructions for the reception of guests, directing that "all guests who arrive be received as Christ" and met "with every mark of love," while advocating discernment and keeping guests somewhat separate from the life of the community: "No one is to speak or associate with guests unless he is bidden; however, if a brother meets or sees a guest, he is to greet him humbly, as we have said. He asks for a blessing and continues on his way, explaining that he is not allowed to speak with a guest" (RB 53.23–24).[16] While to some readers this may not seem the most hospitable way to greet guests, those who are familiar with the Benedictine way of life say that there is something profoundly hospitable in the space that is offered to guests at a monastery—the "physical, psychological, and spiritual space, solitude, and stillness to hear the voice of God"[17]—which also allows for the community's commitment to other parts of its mission and which the following chapter will argue is necessary for sustaining the practice of hospitality and negotiating its limits.

Other examples of Christian communities that deliberately try to make hospitality a central part of their way of life may not have exactly the same guidelines for receiving guests, but it is inevitable that some sort of limits and guidelines will emerge, if not in principle then at least in practice. Certainly, the force of the Gospel message challenges any arbitrary limits to hospitality—and perhaps even those which are legitimate—and encourages Christians to adopt a posture of openness, a spirit of hospitality that recognizes that one is both a guest of and cohost with God in Christ and that also seeks to welcome Christ in every needy stranger. At the same time, however—as I have stated already and will continue to argue throughout this book—the distinctive nature of hospitality makes certain limits essential. In such a view, limits are not only a negative restriction on the practice of hospitality but are also thresholds or conditions of its possibility. Indeed, just as the literal threshold—the doorway or gate—is the physical location of hospitality, so too it is at these limits that a spirit of hospitality becomes incarnate. In the sections that follow, I intend both

---

[16] *Rule of Saint Benedict 1980*, ed. Timothy Fry (Collegeville, MN: Liturgical Press, 1981).

[17] Laura Swan, *Engaging Benedict: What the Rule Can Teach Us Today* (Notre Dame, IN: Ave Maria, 2005), 133. Cf. Kathleen Norris, *Amazing Grace: A Vocabulary of Faith* (New York: Riverhead Books, 1998), 262–67; Daniel Holman and Lonni Collins Pratt, *Radical Hospitality: Benedict's Way of Love* (Brewster, MA: Paraclete Press, 2002).

to show the necessity of limits and to advocate that such limits be formed nonviolently if they are in fact to remain limits of hospitality.

Violence and Absolute Hospitality

Although the pull of radical, unconditional openness may have a particular force for Christians, similar tensions—between generous openness and protective boundaries or, in other words, between absolute and conditional hospitality—are present in any and every practice of hospitality because they are present in the concept of hospitality itself. In this section and the following, I draw from the work of philosopher Jacques Derrida, who is known for his articulation of the theoretical perspective known as deconstruction. Deconstruction may be understood as a way of looking at concepts, texts, and practices from multiple angles or examining the tensions and contradictions internal to them—so that the very idea of definitive or stable meaning is called into question. As I understand it, deconstruction is not nihilistic (as some contend) but is rather a call to epistemic humility, a persistent caution against assuming that we have attained perfect justice or truth or a final ethical solution. It may nevertheless seem odd to turn to the deconstructive work of Jacques Derrida to aid in articulating a practical approach to hospitality and limits—and as I will argue toward the end of this chapter, his work can only take us so far in this respect—but in fact his deconstruction of the idea of absolute hospitality is helpful to show the tensions inherent in every actual instance of hospitality.

In this section I also consider theologian Hans Boersma's critique of Derrida in his book *Violence, Hospitality, and the Cross: Reappropriating the Atonement Tradition.*[18] (Those readers who have minimal interest in the abstract and technical details of these arguments may want to focus their reading on this section's introductory and concluding paragraphs.) In addition to his critique of Derrida (which I find unwarranted), my attention to Boersma is due to the fact that while one of his fundamental claims in his book is quite correct—namely, that hospitality by its very nature entails certain limits and boundaries—many of his other claims (e.g., that not only human but also divine hospitality requires violence and that violence "is not necessarily and universally a negative thing"[19]) misunderstand the

[18] Hans Boersma, *Violence, Hospitality, and the Cross: Reappropriating the Atonement Tradition* (Grand Rapids, MI: Baker Academic, 2004).
[19] Ibid., 144.

limits of hospitality and are therefore unhelpful in practice. It is simply not the case that every boundary, restraint, or limit entails harm. An ideal hospitality is not hospitality without boundaries or limits but rather hospitality that enacts such limits while minimizing violence or harm to those who may be excluded.

Derrida begins his consideration of hospitality—which was a prominent theme in his later work—by looking at what he refers to as "pure" or "absolute" hospitality, which welcomes whomever or whatever arrives, without calculation or limit, without concern for self-protection. Such hospitality holds nothing in reserve but rather entails the surrender of one's home, one's identity, even one's life. Like the "pure gift" of which Derrida has written elsewhere, such hospitality must be entirely free from circles of exchange and reciprocity; even the exchange of gratitude or feelings of enjoyment in the other's company would diminish the gift character of absolute hospitality. Such pure hospitality gives fully not only without expectation of return but also with a gratuitousness that makes any return in kind impossible, when I "give of my very substance to the other,"[20] offering even my own self or "life-space" to my guest. Here, Derrida's indebtedness to philosopher Emmanuel Lévinas's understanding of hospitality is evident. For Lévinas, hospitality is so radical that a person must be willing to become not only host but "hostage" of the other: "In being a host, in owning a home, . . . I must always tremble before the thought that I have, through ownership and possession, evicted the neighbor and made of her a refugee."[21] In Lévinas's thought, my responsibility to the other person is so profound "that I ought to be willing to surrender my home unconditionally to whoever comes."[22] Although without such a "home" I have no space into and from which to welcome others, a truly unconditional hospitality requires that I relinquish even the conditions that make hospitality possible.

Absolute hospitality also involves the paradox that the host "welcomes what she does not welcome," that she is "ready to not be ready" for her unexpected visitor.[23] On this point, Derrida distinguishes hospitality of

[20] John Caputo, The Prayers and Tears of Jacques Derrida: Religion without Religion (Bloomington, IN: Indiana University Press, 1997), 176.

[21] Ibid.

[22] Mark Dooley, "The Politics of Exodus: Derrida, Kierkegaard, and Levinas on 'Hospitality,'" in Works of Love, vol. 16 of International Kierkegaard Commentary, ed. Robert Perkins (Macon, GA: Mercer University Press, 1999), 174–75.

[23] Jacques Derrida, "Hostipitality," in Acts of Religion, ed. Gil Anidjar (New York and London: Routledge, 2002), 362.

invitation—a conditional welcome that is acquainted with and prepared for the guest—and hospitality of visitation, which entails a willingness to welcome what is unknown, unexpected, and even disturbing. He identifies pure or absolute hospitality with the latter, which bears significant similarities to the "indeterminate messianism" of which Derrida has written elsewhere: the messianic for Derrida represents the possibility of perfect justice, in light of which every existing system may be deconstructed.[24] As Derrida sees it, any concrete attempt to instantiate justice will inevitably result in some people being silenced or injured by the structures produced by such an attempt, so that the messianic must always remain indeterminate and "to-come" and cannot be identified with a particular people or cause. Absolute hospitality or openness to messianic justice therefore requires radical vulnerability and risk, for there would be no way in principle to eliminate every possibility of harm while remaining open to "the good Messiah."[25] Indeed, pure hospitality "may be terrible because the newcomer may be a good person or may be the devil; but if you exclude the possibility that the newcomer is coming to destroy your house—if you want to control this and exclude in advance this possibility—there is no hospitality."[26]

Such statements are undoubtedly troubling, and this vision of unconditional hospitality has been subject to criticism from those who quite rightly fear that it is likely to lead to the growth of violence and injustice rather than of mutual welcome. Though he in fact addresses Lévinas more directly than Derrida, Thomas Ogletree offers a helpful critique and modification of the idea of absolute hospitality in his book *Hospitality to the Stranger*. While he is, on the whole, highly appreciative of Lévinas and the "decentering of perspective" effected by his thought, Ogletree also insists upon the necessity of limits to the claims that the "other" can make upon a moral actor.[27] His criticism is not so much that Lévinas finds the

[24] For a discussion of Derrida's "indeterminate messianism," see John Caputo, *The Prayers and Tears of Jacques Derrida*.

[25] Jacques Derrida, "Perhaps or Maybe," *The Warwick Journal of Philosophy: Responsibilities of Deconstruction* (1997): 6. Cf. John Caputo, *What Would Jesus Deconstruct?* (Grand Rapids, MI: Baker Academic, 2007), 76–77.

[26] Jacques Derrida, "Hospitality, Justice, and Responsibility," in *Questioning Ethics: Contemporary Debates in Continental Philosophy*, ed. Richard Kearney and Mark Dooley (London: Routledge, 1998), 70.

[27] Thomas Ogletree, *Hospitality to the Stranger: Dimensions of Moral Understanding* (Louisville, KY: Westminster John Knox, 2003), 56.

origin of moral obligation in the encounter between persons as it is that "he seems to resolve the moral issues raised in the encounter wholly in favor of the other."[28] In contrast, Ogletree affirms the self or moral actor as also being a center of value and of intrinsic worth. Although the self's egoistic enjoyment must be criticized in light of the needs and enjoyment of others, such enjoyment may be justified to the extent that it is *necessary* for the development of a moral orientation to the needs and desires of those same others. Ogletree is concerned that, on Lévinas's terms, the oppressed would have no legitimate grounds for asserting their rights against their oppressors, nor does Lévinas provide an adequate foundation for a moral community based on mutual respect and care.[29] I find Ogletree's work persuasive in this regard, and I believe that my own conclusions about hospitality are compatible with the critique he offers.

As mentioned above, another critique of absolute hospitality comes from Hans Boersma in his book *Violence, Hospitality, and the Cross: Reappropriating the Atonement Tradition.* Like Ogletree, Boersma is also wary of a pure hospitality that refuses to challenge evil, and he argues that, in a finite and fallen world, even divine hospitality—demonstrated most paradigmatically on the cross—requires violence. The primary goal of Boersma's argument here is to vindicate the divine violence of traditional theories of atonement and election against those who want to minimize God's involvement in the violence of the crucifixion.[30] Using hospitality as a metaphor for divine love, he argues that "God's hospitality requires violence, just as his love necessitates wrath. . . . Divine violence, in other words, is a way in which God strives toward an eschatological situation of pure hospitality."[31] Boersma's discussion of the violence of divine hospitality in the atonement is ambiguous, however, as it is not clear whether he is referring primarily to God's involvement in the actual violence of the crucifixion (including the injustice of an innocent death) or to the "violence" that excludes those who rebelliously reject God. His criticism of Derridean absolute hospitality

[28] Ibid., 55.

[29] One can find places in Lévinas's work that seem to temper one's obligation to the "other" in light of one's responsibility to additional people: "In any given society, my responsibility for all may even manifest itself in limiting itself. . . . The me can be brought, in the name of unlimited responsibility, to be concerned with itself." Lévinas, *God, Death, and Time,* trans. Bettina Bergo (Stanford, CA: Stanford University Press, 2000), 182. On the whole, however, his philosophy appears to call for unlimited, unconditional hospitality.

[30] Hans Boersma, *Violence, Hospitality, and the Cross,* 40–41.

[31] Ibid., 49.

is essentially that "the lack of a transcendent warrant for human hospitality (i.e., the God of the cross and resurrection) creates a utopian impatience in Derrida that insists we introduce pure hospitality here and now."[32] Boersma sees this as both tragic—because such unconditional hospitality is impossible given the limitations of the created order—and dangerous because "the result would be more violence rather than less: one might end up welcoming devils rather than saints."[33]

Violence, Hospitality, and the Cross is undoubtedly an impressive work of scholarship, and Boersma's insistence that even divine hospitality is circumscribed in a fallen and finite world is helpful to a consideration of human hospitality. Attention to the cross as a point of orientation at the center of Christian life is also essential to any adequate understanding of that life. Other elements of Boersma's argument, however, are quite problematic. First, Boersma presents a dismissive and oversimplified reading of Derrida's work on hospitality, which serves to provide a postmodern straw man as a foil to his own arguments defending the violence of traditional Christian doctrines of atonement and election. Contrary to his claim that Derrida "impatiently" rejects the violence of a conditional hospitality in favor of a pure hospitality, a more careful reading of Derrida's work shows that he is fully attuned to the necessity of conditions and criteria that limit hospitality in practice. Boersma writes that Derrida's recognition of the need for limits is an "incidental concession," and he objects to Derrida's reference to acts of limited hospitality as "hospitable narcissism."[34] While I don't have a particular stake in valorizing Derrida on these points, it simply seems disingenuous to ignore his frequent references to the necessity of conditional hospitality, even to the point that he identifies an "indissociability" of absolute hospitality and a conditional ethics. That is, according to Derrida, between unconditional and conditional hospitality, "one calls forth, involves, or prescribes the other."[35] This dynamic—the mutual necessity of absolute and conditional hospitality—will in fact be a topic of the following section.

---

[32] Ibid., 36.

[33] Ibid., 35.

[34] Boersma, *Violence, Hospitality, and the Cross*, 31–32, 37, esp. n47.

[35] Jacques Derrida, *Of Hospitality: Anne Dufourmantelle Invites Jacques Derrida to Respond*, trans., Rachel Bowlsby (Stanford, CA: Stanford University Press, 2001), 147.

Far more troublesome than his mischaracterization of Derrida, however, is Boersma's repeated assertion that both divine and human hospitality *necessarily* involve violence and that the pervasiveness of violence in human life "is not necessarily and universally a negative thing."[36] Throughout the book, he goes to significant lengths to affirm that violence—whether divine or human—may not only be a tragic necessity but a positive good, a *requirement* of hospitality. He claims to appeal to an "Augustinian understanding of violence as any use of coercion that causes injury, whether that coercion is positive or negative," and he argues that an insistence on nonviolence often involves an arbitrary understanding of violence as something physical, while discounting other (verbal, emotional, structural) forms of harm or injury that may be more subtle if no less damaging.[37] While he seems to want to distance himself from the "postmodern philosophers" (such as Lévinas and Derrida) for whom "violence is inscribed in the very nature of things and cannot be avoided,"[38] he also states that "violence is *an integral part* of what it means to be human"[39]—including in the human life of Jesus. Boersma argues that Jesus' life can only be understood as nonviolent if one takes a "narrow view of violence as the use of physical harm" and states that Jesus' actions were "offensive to many and often encroached on people's personal space and well-being."[40]

Yet it seems to me that Boersma conflates a number of important distinctions in his defense of redemptive or hospitable "violence." While I certainly agree that every concrete instance of hospitality entails limitations, I do not agree that every limit is necessarily coercive or violent, nor that every infringement on the liberty or comfort of others (as in the examples of disciplining a child, restraining a person who would otherwise be in danger, or Jesus' "encroachments" on the comfort of the religious authorities) entails injury or harm.[41] But it seems to me that Boersma's position here attributes violence to finite existence as such: "Hospitality can only be hospitality in our world when it is accompanied by the violence

---

[36] Boersma, *Violence, Hopsitality, and the Cross,* 144.

[37] Ibid., 17, 44.

[38] Ibid., 35.

[39] Ibid., 144; italics added.

[40] Ibid., 92.

[41] Cf. Miroslav Volf's distinction between "differentiation," "exclusion," and "judgment" in *Exclusion and Embrace: A Theological Exploration of Identity and Otherness* (Nashville: Abingdon, 1996), 64–68.

of certain boundaries, including those of time and space," he writes.[42] Such a view either casts the meaning of "violence" so broadly as to render it virtually meaningless or denies the goodness of creation.[43] While one might certainly argue that the structures of sin into which we are born make some amount of violence (tragically) unavoidable, this claim is significantly different from saying that violence is integral to what it means to be human. It would be better to say that violence—that is, the harm that we inevitably do to ourselves and others—is a *deviation* from what it means to be human in any normative sense. Christians understand the truth of our human life to be revealed most clearly in Jesus' life of compassion, communion, and *noncoercive* power, as well as his prophetic challenge to those who are corrupt or complacent—a challenge that, because of its truth, is ultimately healing, not harmful, even for those who find it offensive.

In contrast to Boersma's approach, one might look to the arguments of Thomas Merton, Stanley Hauerwas, and others who emphasize the relationship between the Gospel and nonviolence.[44] It seems more true to the narrative of Jesus' life and the witness of early Christians to see the power of Jesus' life and death in its *noncoercive* character—that is, in Jesus' cross "we see decisively the one who, being all-powerful, becomes vulnerable even to being a victim of our refusal to accept his Lordship"[45]—and the power

---

[42] Boersma, *Violence, Hospitality, and the Cross,* 53.

[43] That Boersma goes to such lengths to argue for the pervasiveness of violence in human life is perplexing in light of his sustained critique of René Girard (chap. 6: "Atonement and Mimetic Violence"). Boersma claims that Girard's nonviolent theory of the atonement carries the unacceptable cost of denying the goodness of creation because of the latter's assertion that violence is embedded in the origins of human culture. Yet it seems to me that Girard's theory of human culture and mimetic violence—which could certainly be extrapolated as an effect of the fall (cf. Marjorie Hewitt Suchocki, *The Fall into Violence: Original Sin in Relational Theology* [New York: Continuum, 1994])—has far more potential for affirming a good creation than does Boersma's assertion of the "beneficial role of violence in connection with redemption and a politics of hospitality" (*Violence, Hospitality, and the Cross,* 151).

[44] In particular, I have in mind Merton's brief essay "Blessed are the Meek," in *Faith and Violence: Christian Teaching and Christian Practice* (Notre Dame, IN: University of Notre Dame Press, 1968), and Hauerwas' *The Peaceable Kingdom* (Notre Dame, IN: University of Notre Dame Press, 1977), although the whole of each man's work attests to the nonviolent nature of the kingdom proclaimed by Jesus. One can find similar themes in the thought of many others, from Martin Luther King Jr. to Mohandas Gandhi to John Howard Yoder to Dorothy Day.

[45] Stanley Hauerwas, "Jesus and the Social Embodiment of the Peaceable Kingdom," in *The Hauerwas Reader,* ed. John Berkman and Michael Cartwright (Durham, NC: Duke University Press, 2001), 127. Cf. Merton, *Faith and Violence,* 10; Newlands and Smith, *Hospitable God,* 103.

of his disciples' lives in their ability to follow him in this regard. Although Jesus calls and invites people to see the world differently, he does not force this upon them—nor does he encourage his disciples to do so (e.g., Matt 10:11-23). "True justice"—or hospitality—"never comes through violence, nor can it be based on violence," writes Stanley Hauerwas. Rather, "it can only be based on truth, which has no need to resort to violence to secure its own existence."[46]

It is also truer to the nature of hospitality to recognize a *qualitative* difference—and not merely a different degree of violence—between boundaries that are erected from hatred, prejudice, and possessiveness and those that exclude due to the limitations of human finitude. While the violence or nonviolence of an action cannot be determined solely by an agent's motive or intent, neither are these irrelevant to it. Boersma essentially whitewashes over the moral quality of all human action by his claims that there can only be degrees of violence rather than anything pacific in human life—and that violence as such is not necessarily bad. It is at this point—that is, the ethical implications of Boersma's defense of not only divine but also human violence—that his contentions are most problematic.

Despite his stated belief that theology originates in and is accountable to the church[47] and despite his final chapters discussing the church as the "public face" of God's hospitality in the sacraments and proclamation of the Gospel, it is not clear how Boersma's defense of the necessity of violence ("coercion that causes injury") to hospitality is applicable to Christian practice. Given his arguments that violence is not only necessary but in many instances beneficial, on what basis does Boersma elsewhere state that violence "should be avoided and countered as much as possible"?[48] How exactly are humans to determine whether "violence is limited to that which is justifiable in the interest of the absolute hospitality of the eschatological future"?[49] Why should Christians not in fact *maximize* their "redemptive" violence in the service of eschatological hospitality? My suspicion is that at some level Boersma recognizes that violence cannot be normative—even when its consequences may be good—and that it cannot ever in fact move us closer to the hospitality of God's kingdom.

---

[46] Stanley Hauerwas, "The Servant Community," in *The Hauerwas Reader*, 391.

[47] Boersma, *Violence, Hospitality, and the Cross*, 205.

[48] Ibid., 48.

[49] Ibid., 145.

The Limits of Hospitality

When thinking about conditional—as opposed to absolute—hospitality, it is worth keeping in mind two different ways in which conditions function. On one hand, a condition may refer to something required or demanded as an essential part of an agreement between two parties. In the case of hospitality, conditions of this sort are stipulations that limit hospitality on the basis of the identity or behavior or some other feature of the guest; for example, I may decide to welcome others on the condition that they speak my language or share my political views or are able to reciprocate my hospitality. A significant degree of variation is possible in conditions of this sort, as they are based on the more or less arbitrary and voluntary discretion of hosts and guests. If guests cannot or will not meet such conditions, the welcome is withdrawn. Such conditions may be quite minimal—for example, the willingness to welcome others provided that they do not have malevolent intent—or extensive to the point of being downright inhospitable. The "hospitality" of luxury hotels may be a paradigmatic example of conditional hospitality of this sort: guests are treated to a lavish welcome, but on the condition that they pay a correspondingly high price, observe social protocol, make reservations ahead of time, and so forth. (It is for this reason that I do not think the "hospitality industry" generally merits the name.[50])

On the other hand, "conditions" may entail those features of a situation that are necessary for the possibility of a certain result, apart from any decision or volition of those involved—such as when we speak of oxygen, sunlight, and water as the necessary conditions for plant growth. In the case of hospitality, the conditions of its possibility consist of the separate identities of host and guest, as well as a host's sufficient "possession" of a space for her to offer it to her guests with assurance that it is a place of relative safety. While "conditions" in this latter sense may inform the restrictions placed on hospitality in the former, hosts or guests cannot change or do away with them at will and still be involved in a relationship of hospitality. Both types of conditions serve to place limits on hospitality, but the latter are also inescapable requisites of its practice. These limiting conditions, which must also always be inspired and shaped (or perhaps troubled and

---

[50] Cf. Elizabeth Newman, *Untamed Hospitality: Welcoming God and Other Strangers* (Grand Rapids, MI: Brazos Press), 28–29.

deconstructed) by the pull of absolute, unconditional hospitality, will be the focus of the third and fourth chapters of this book.

As I mentioned in the previous section, Derrida's work on hospitality not only discusses the idea of absolute hospitality, which he sometimes refers to as "the Law of hospitality,"[51] but also the conditions that are necessary to hospitality in practice (Derrida's discussion of conditions, unsurprisingly, equivocates between the two meanings noted above). Acknowledging that hospitality would become "perverse" if it were to "simply open the door to anyone," he states that it is necessary "to produce laws and rules in order to select, in the best possible way, the ones we host, we welcome."[52] Such criteria and conditions for welcome he designates "the laws of hospitality." In truth, however, these two form an inseparable "double law": while the unconditional Law of Hospitality "would be in danger of remaining a pious and irresponsible desire, without form or potency, and of even being perverted at any moment" without the conditions that render it concretely effective,[53] so too would these conditions "cease to be laws *of hospitality* if they were not guided, given inspiration, given aspiration . . . by the law of unconditional hospitality."[54] Commenting on Derrida's "double law," Mark Dooley writes, "While I know it is impossible to be unconditionally hospitable, I am nevertheless invited to challenge the dominant meaning of this word so to enlarge its range and scope. Hoping for unconditional hospitality is a way of ensuring that conditional hospitality does not become *too* conditional."[55]

Elsewhere Derrida has described hospitality as involving a sort of "self-limitation"; that is, even as I "give" my space over to my guest—perhaps saying "make yourself at home" and truly wishing her to feel so—by the offer itself I reaffirm my possession of the home I offer to her. Hospitality requires both mastery and surrender, possession and gift, identity and openness.

This "double law" has led Derrida also to write of "hostipitality," a playful combination of "hospitality" and "hostility" that calls attention to the

---

[51] See, for example, Jacques Derrida, *Of Cosmopolitanism and Forgiveness*, trans. Mark Dooley and Michael Hughes (London and New York: Routledge, 1997), 22; *Of Hospitality: Anne Dufourmantelle Invites Jacques Derrida to Respond*, 79.

[52] Derrida, "Perhaps or Maybe," 9.

[53] Jacques Derrida, *On Cosmopolitanism and Forgiveness*, 22–23.

[54] Derrida, *Of Hospitality*, 79. Cf. "Principle of Hospitality," *Parallax* 11.1 (2005): 6.

[55] Dooley, "The Politics of Exodus," 169.

relationship between them.[56] Indeed, the Latin term that may mean either "host" or "guest" (*hospes*), from which the English "hospitality" originates, is etymologically connected to the word for "enemy" (*hostis*), from which we get the term "hostility." A common theory explaining this connection points to the ambiguity of strangers—who, as noted above, could be *hostis* as well as *hospes*—in the ancient world. But, as Seyla Benhabib has noted, there remains a similar ambiguity at the "threshold" of any instance of hospitality, "a moment of anxiety, generated by the undecidability of the other's (the host's) response: Will I be greeted with hospitality or rejected with hostility? Will you admit me beyond the threshold or will you keep me waiting at the door or even chase me away?"[57] Even beyond this (as most of us can attest from spending holidays with family or attending a social gathering where the conversation suddenly becomes uncomfortably adversarial), once guests have been welcomed in, there is often only a thin margin between the hospitality that welcomes the distinctiveness of hosts and guests and the hostility for which this is precisely the source of conflict. Unfortunately, mere good will is not always sufficient to make enemies and strangers into friends. In fact, it seems that the closer one gets to absolute, unconditional hospitality—by tirelessly welcoming those who are unknown, unpleasant, ungrateful, or dangerous—the greater the potential for hostility becomes. To say that hospitality inescapably contains the potential for hostility and can easily degenerate into its opposite is not, however, to say that it will inevitably do so; in many cases, the most seemingly challenging practice of hospitality may prove to be most rewarding and transformative for both guest and host alike.

To put this in other words, we might envision hospitality as being constituted by a tension between the desire to offer an unconditional welcome—which I will generally refer to as the "spirit of hospitality" from this point forward—and the limiting conditions that make a particular welcome possible: Hospitality seeks to make the guest feel she "belongs" or is "at home," and it acknowledges the fluidity of "host" and "guest" roles—*and* it recognizes her separateness and irreducibly independent identity. Hospitality appreciates the needs *and* the gifts—the vulnerabilities

---

[56] Derrida writes that hospitality is "a Latin word which allows itself to be parasitized by its opposite, 'hostility,' the undesirable guest which it harbors as the self-contradiction in its own body." "Hostipitality," *Journal of the Theoretical Humanities*, 5.3 (2000): 3. Cf. Derrida, "Hostipitality," in *Acts of Religion*, ed. Gil Anidjar (New York: Routledge, 2002).

[57] Seyla Benhabib, "Hospitality, Sovereignty, and Democratic Iterations," in *Another Cosmopolitanism*, ed. Robert Post (Oxford: Oxford University Press, 2006), 156.

and the strengths—that both host *and* guest bring to their relationship. In each of the polarities that I will argue constitute the limits of hospitality in the following chapters—namely, identity/indeterminacy, possession/gift, and security/risk—each extreme must maintain an influence or "pull" on the other if hospitality is to maintain its integrity as such. The most adequate way of describing the ongoing influence of the spirit of hospitality is to say that such a spirit strives to form boundaries *nonviolently*. Though hospitality may always be haunted by the possibility of overt hostility on the part of hosts or guests—especially as a person or community moves closer to (and thereby, in many cases, expands) its limits—the limits of hospitality must never betray the spirit of welcome they intend to protect.

What exactly do I mean by "nonviolent" limits? At the most obvious and basic level, limits of hospitality should not physically threaten or harm any persons involved. If maintaining "identity" or "security" is accomplished through physical violence on the part of guests or hosts—whether fists or guns or militarized borders or ethnic cleansing—hospitality is lost. While I fully acknowledge the insidiousness of other forms of violence, from verbal abuse to structural injustice, at the same time I do not believe it is merely arbitrary to identify physical harm as a paradigmatic form of violence insofar as our physical embodiment is the condition of our experience of any other form of violence or hospitality. One of the reasons I believe hospitality is such a powerful moral concept is because it accounts for our essential embodiment as humans[58] in a way that more abstract notions of love or justice do not necessarily. As chapters 3 and 4 will explain in greater detail, even when hospitality functions metaphorically, it relies upon some notion of bounded and "safe" spaces: welcome is meaningful when I can welcome another into a place where they experience a sense of home, not harm. Limits—including physical limits of walls or bodies—are necessary to this but must always stop short of violence if hospitality is not to cross the threshold of hostility.

The violence of words or thoughts may be more subtle but no less problematic in the practice of hospitality. Not only words that assault or insult (including "behind the back" of another) but also those that manipulate or deceive—including, perhaps, the well-meaning deception

---

[58] Though there are many such arguments regarding human embodiment and personhood available, I am particularly appreciative of Margaret Farley's discussion of humans as "embodied spirits" or "inspirited bodies" in *Just Love: A Framework for Christian Sexual Ethics* (London: Continuum, 2006), 120ff.

that reduces hospitality to politeness or entertainment—undermine if not destroy hospitality.[59] While hospitality requires truth telling and even a certain amount of confrontation, it is also receptive to the truth of the other. Henri Nouwen explains:

> Confrontation does not mean putting conditions on the guest, but it means being articulately present to the guest, offering yourself as a point of orientation or frame of reference. . . . Receptivity and confrontation are the two inseparable sides of Christian witness. Receptivity without confrontation leads to a bland neutrality that serves nobody. Confrontation without receptivity leads to an oppressive aggression which hurts everybody.[60]

Here, Nouwen articulates another way of understanding the poles of the tension that constitutes hospitality (receptivity and confrontation) and how maintaining the influence of each allows for the enactment of non-violent boundaries. Additionally, we may harbor violence in the thoughts and intentions that lie behind our outward expressions of hospitality and boundaries—harmful stereotypes, prejudices, resentment, and hatred—although I am not ready to say that such violence of thought should necessarily constrain our practice of hospitality; most people can identify times in their lives when "acting better than you feel" has succeeded in genuinely changing how they feel, or when getting to know another person despite one's reservations has resulted in a surprising transformation of perspective. If hospitality becomes an extended exercise of hypocrisy or stockpiling of resentment, however, it may be that a limit has been crossed.

Perhaps the most troublesome (if most elusive) form of violence that threatens to turn hospitality to its opposite, however, is the "structural violence" of exploitative economic and social systems that allow some to live with power and abundance and others to be dispossessed of both. I am not arguing that white skin or the English language or private property *per se* are violent—though I am not unsympathetic to those who do argue this, and it may be on these points more than others that our limits must be subject to deconstruction (see chap. 4). Those who are born into positions of privilege can no more help this than those who are born

---

[59] See Newman, *Untamed Hospitality*, 23–30.

[60] Henri Nouwen, "Hospitality," in *On Hospitality and Other Matters*, Monastic Studies 10 (Pine City, NY: Mount Savior Monastery, 1974), 26ff. Cf. Reinhart Hütter, "Hospitality and Truth: The Disclosure of Practices in Worship and Doctrine," in *Practicing Theology: Beliefs and Practices in Christian Life* (Grand Rapids, MI: Eerdmans, 2001).

into situations of poverty and oppression, yet the former have opportunities (and therefore, I would argue, responsibilities) to challenge the perpetuation of violence that the latter may not. It may be impossible to extricate oneself entirely from the social structures of sin that mark the human condition—here, perhaps, I accede to Boersma the inevitability of violence—but it is possible to use the resources that such structures afford to challenge and transform them through building relationships of hospitality in ways that strive to affirm rather than violate other people.

To be sure, the host is the one who is "at home," who not only has resources to offer but also enjoys a feeling of familiarity in the space he or she inhabits; the guest, on the other hand, is the one who is "out of place," who may be not only vulnerable and in need of assistance but also possibly ill at ease in her or his current location. At the same time, although hospitality may involve disparities of power, possession, and belonging, if such inequalities were the only or the central feature of hospitality, it might serve to legitimate problematic disparities and reinforce unjust and patronizing relationships. Such "deformation" of hospitality is a primary concern of Letty Russell, who cautions that hospitality is distorted "when it is practiced as a way of caring for so-called 'inferior people' by those who are more advantaged and able to prove their superiority by being 'generous,' rather than using a model of partnership."[61] Though I greatly appreciate Russell's emphasis on partnership throughout her work, I nonetheless think that partnership—and the expectation of equality that it implies—remains but one pole of yet another constitutive tension in hospitality, namely, the tension between partnership and service. It would be inhospitable (perhaps even violent) to preclude a guest's ability or desire to contribute in a meaningful way, especially because of his or her alleged "inferiority." At the same time, however, there would be something strange (if not violent) about "hospitality" that *assumes* guests are responsible "partners" in the household chores.[62]

---

[61] Letty Russell, *Just Hospitality: God's Welcome in a World of Difference*, ed. J. Shannon Clarkson and Kate Ott (Louisville, KY: Westminster John Knox, 2009), 80. Cf. de Bethune, *Interreligious Hospitality*, 115–16: "Excessive generosity results in endangering the relationship for lack of balance. The images of the lavishly laid table . . . do not properly convey the idea of hospitality. . . . In order for everyone to experience the welcome, it is necessary to ensure that all are treated as being fundamentally equal"; and Koenig, *New Testament Hospitality*.

[62] Christine Pohl has similar reservations about reducing hospitality to a "partnership between strangers." She writes that "when we describe everyone as a stranger, we wash out some of the crucial distinctions between socially situated persons and persons who are

The dynamics of these tensions—and the necessary challenge of avoiding violence at the limits of hospitality—will be the subject of the following chapters, particularly chapters 3 and 4. In concluding this section, however, I want to make clear that by arguing that boundaries must be formed and influenced by a spirit of unconditional openness, I am not saying that they should be vague or ambiguous. On the contrary, it is often precisely when limits and expectations are made completely clear that they are most hospitable, where hosts and guests alike are most able to feel free to enjoy the spaces they share. Inexplicit or nebulous "boundaries"—esoteric protocols, veiled opinions, erratic inconsistencies—are often experienced as a passive aggression that invites uneasiness and hostility. For this reason, it is necessary to be able to *decide* and to *define*—as well as to deconstruct—the limits of hospitality.

Decisions and Tensions: The Limits of Deconstruction

With respect to actually putting the concept of hospitality into practice, however, deconstruction will only take us so far. Derrida has explained,

> You have to make a decision not simply to open your house, that's not the decision, you open your house to anyone, this is pure hospitality, it requires no decision. It's impossible but requires no decision. Now, if you close the border and the house, no decision either, no hospitality. The decision occurs when you want to reach an agreement between your desire for pure, unconditional hospitality and the necessity of discrimination. . . . For this decision I have no criteria.[63]

By this statement Derrida points to the notion of "undecidability"—a situation in which there is an overabundance of necessitating reasons due to the fact that justice makes a demand from both sides. Such was the dilemma I felt with JC: on one hand, I felt responsible for my own safety and my ability to function in my work, but I also felt it would be wrong to

---

truly disconnected from social relations. If we see ourselves only as strangers, and reject the responsibility associated with being hosts, then we will squander opportunities to create hospitable environments and situations." *Making Room*, 90. Pohl nuances this perspective in "Hospitality from the Edge: The Significance of Marginality in the Practice of Welcome," *Annual of the Society of Christian Ethics* (1995).

[63] Jacques Derrida, with Richard Kearney and John Caputo, "Desire of God," in *God, the Gift, and Postmodernism*, ed. John Caputo and Michael Scanlon (Bloomington, IN: Indiana University Press, 1999), 134.

deny his request for help when I had an extra room. Paradoxically, Derrida claims that such undecidability is the condition of a truly responsible decision—"otherwise," writes John Caputo on this theme, "we can beg off and say we were just following the law."[64] An "undecidable" situation requires an actor to rely ultimately on his own judgment, rather than simply applying criteria for decision in a mechanical way, and thereby to accept responsibility for the choice and its consequences. (Of course, even in ordinary circumstances, when a person is "merely" applying rules or principles, she must make a decision whether or not to follow them; the human process of decision making is hardly one of mechanistic un-folding.) Attempting to define the limits of hospitality often entails just such a situation, leading Derrida frequently to characterize hospitality as *aporia*—meaning literally, "no way out," "something that does not allow passage," and which therefore requires a sort of arbitrary or blind leap to who knows where.

So how, then, are Christians and other practitioners of hospitality to act in light of this situation? Is there a way to construct a practice of hospitality that neither resolves the deconstructive challenge of absolute hospitality nor gives in to its dangers? Or is it simply a blundering series of more or less violent choices?

It is in part Derrida's inability to offer guidance for decisions that leads me to characterize hospitality as a tension rather than using his language of paradox or *aporia*. The image of a tension in which it is necessary to respect and negotiate competing demands—as if one were mediating the interests of diplomats and politicians or trying to resolve a dispute between "labor" and "management"—allows for give and take at either pole as long as the other also maintains its "pull." Though individuals and com-munities must decide and define, it is also important to inhabit a generous posture that remains willing to adjust, to make just a little more room for indeterminacy, generosity, and risk. The process of discerning limits is not, then, a matter of fanciful escape from an undecidable situation but rather requires the ongoing development of virtues that allow for the skillful enactment of hospitable boundaries. While offering no fail-safe solution to the challenge of hospitality, in the following chapter I intend to show that the Christian tradition has resources that can aid in the development of a spirit of hospitality and the discernment of nonviolent limits. Not only through engaging in the communal practice of hospitality but also

---

[64] Caputo, *What Would Jesus Deconstruct?*, 67.

through classical spiritual disciplines such as prayer, fasting, confession, celebration, and service, Christians can become *hospitable people*, gracefully able to incarnate—and therefore delimit—the spirit of hospitality.

Chapter 2

The Spirit of Hospitality

She who reconciles the ill-matched threads
of her life, and weaves them gratefully
into a single cloth—
it's she who drives the loudmouths from the hall
and clears it for a different celebration

where the one guest is you.
In the softness of evening
it's you she receives.

You are the partner of her loneliness,
the unspeaking center of her monologues.
With each disclosure you encompass more
and she stretches beyond what limits her,
to hold you.

—R. M. Rilke[1]

Having recognized the dynamic limits of hospitality in the previous
chapter as well as the wide variety of circumstances in which it is practiced,
the only way to proceed is with humility—and gratitude.

In this chapter, perhaps more than any other in this book, I write with
a profound sense of humility, as I am not only attempting a description
of spiritual life—a mystery both ancient and ever new, which far wiser
people than I have sought for centuries to understand—but also making
claims about the relevance of Christian spiritual disciplines to an ethic of

[1] R. M. Rilke, "Wer seines Lebens viele Widersinne," in *Rilke's Book of Hours: Love Poems to God* (New York: Riverhead Books, 1996), 64.

hospitality. Drawing upon the work of Henri Nouwen and others, I hope
to show that through regular spiritual practices (such as prayer, solitude,
fasting, celebration, and service) a person places herself in a posture of
openness to a God who may surprise and challenge as well as comfort and
strengthen her. "God persistently challenges conventional truth and the
world's way of looking at things," writes Parker Palmer. "God is a stranger
to us, and it is at the risk of missing God's truth that we domesticate God,
reduce God to the role of a familiar friend."[2] When writing about God
or the work of God's Spirit, then, it seems one should always be humbly
aware of one's own limitations and biases and the ways in which it will
always be a temptation to make God into one's own image. Furthermore,
in addition to my humility before the Christian theological and spiritual
tradition, I also make the following argument with deep humility before
the spiritual practices of other religions; my discussion of the relationship
of traditional Christian spiritual disciplines to the formation of a hospitable
and discerning character is not meant to say either that such practices are
unique to Christianity or that the distinctive practices of other religious
and spiritual traditions do not also lead to deep and challenging practices
of hospitality.[3]

It is not only in writing about hospitality and spiritual life that the
virtue of humility is important, however. In practice, as well, humility is
crucial; recognizing appropriate limits requires admitting that we cannot
do everything and do not know everything, understanding that our hospitality and our spiritual lives will always be limited and imperfect, and
yet being willing to try—and try again—anyway. Letting go of pride and
learning to resist those cultural attitudes that say we always need more
and must "have it all together"—perfect furniture, perfect food, perfect
family—before letting others in can be as challenging as learning to be
open to those with whom we disagree or otherwise find difficult. Each
of these, however, is essential to the practice of hospitality. By humbly allowing hospitality to God to form the spiritual and moral foundation of

[2] Parker Palmer, The Company of Strangers: Christians and the Renewal of America's Public Life (New York: Crossroad, 1981), 59.

[3] See, for example, Pierre-François de Bethune's discussion of Buddhist practices of tea drinking, meditation, and monastic life in Interreligious Hospitality: The Fulfillment of Dialogue (Collegeville, MN: Liturgical Press, 2010), and Louis Massignon's account of Islamic hospitality in L'hospitalité sacrée (Paris: Nouvelle Cité, 1987). As mentioned at the beginning of the previous chapter, the practice of hospitality to strangers is of utmost importance in many tribal cultures.

hospitality to other humans and by weaving disciplines of gratitude into all of life, a person is empowered in the virtues that both recognize and reach beyond current limits.

Hospitality as a Movement of the Spiritual Life

In an age when twenty percent of Americans describe themselves as "spiritual but not religious,"[4] the terms "spiritual life" (or "spirituality") and "spiritual practice" require some clarification. Often spirituality designates something deeply private and subjective, in contrast to the external and communal forms of religion. Despite the radical individualism of many contemporary notions of spirituality, however, I would argue that any true spirituality—that is, a spirituality that is oriented toward *genuine value*—involves values, meanings, and practices that are intelligible to others. As something based in lived experience, spirituality is also sometimes contrasted with the intellectual or dogmatic dimensions of religion or philosophy; that is, spiritual life must be *lived and practiced*, not simply a set of ideas. The very idea of a practice suggests some socially meaningful standard of excellence (or virtue) toward which one's practice aims; that is, it would make little sense to speak of "practicing" basketball if one never learned to dribble, pass, or shoot the ball or of "practicing" piano if one never made music.[5] Without a doubt, the "standards of excellence" of spiritual practices are of a significantly different nature than those of other activities, but this does not mean that they are absent altogether. While spiritual life necessarily involves reflection and growth at an individual level, it is also possible (and perhaps even necessary) to speak of the spiritual life of a community insofar as its members share in common practices and values.

Perhaps most importantly, spirituality or spiritual life suggests an orientation to an ultimate reality, something that transcends but also embraces

---

[4] Robert C. Fuller, "Spiritual, But Not Religious," accessed 6/29/2011, http://www
.beliefnet.com/Entertainment/Books/2002/07/Spiritual-But-Not-Religious.aspx. Cf.
www.sbnr.org.

[5] See Alasdair MacIntyre, "The Nature of the Virtues," in *Virtue Ethics*, ed. Roger Crisp and Michael Slote (New York: Oxford University Press, 1997), 123–24; Dorothy Bass and Craig Dykstra, "A Theological Understanding of Christian Practices," in *Practicing Theology: Beliefs and Practices in Everyday Life*, ed. Dorothy Bass and Miroslav Volf (Grand Rapids, MI: Eerdmans, 2001), 20–21; Elizabeth Liebert, "Practice," in *The Blackwell Companion to Christian Spirituality*, ed. Arthur Holder (Oxford: Blackwell, 2005), 503.

the mundane and superficial aspects of life. It involves and engages the human spirit, which might be understood as the deepest center of the person that also serves to connect her to a source of truth and meaning that is beyond her. Spiritual life is directed toward personal growth and transformation so as to live in greater harmony with and truer apprehension of this reality; it can be defined as "the experience of consciously striving to integrate one's life not in terms of isolation and self-absorption but of self-transcendence toward the ultimate value one perceives."[6] In somewhat simpler terms, Daniel Groody writes that "while spirituality in general deals with living out what people most value, Christian spirituality involves living out what Jesus most valued. In other words, Christian spirituality is about following Jesus, living out the values of the Kingdom of God, and generating a community transformed by the love of God and others."[7]

One of the central claims of this book is that spiritual practices that cultivate receptivity to the Spirit of God are necessary to a full and flourishing practice of hospitality. This claim will be elaborated through a discussion of specific and concrete practices in the following section, but first it will be helpful to look to the work of Henri J. M. Nouwen, who describes how hospitality names an important dimension of spiritual life. Nouwen, whose writings incorporate knowledge of psychology as well as theology and spirituality, often characterizes spiritual life as a series of "movements," indicating its transformative and dynamic character. Furthermore, for Nouwen spirituality is not only dynamic but also fundamentally relational, requiring attention to a person's self-relation, her relationships with other people, and her relationship to God.[8] It is important to note, however,

---

[6] Sandra Schneiders, "Theology and Spirituality: Strangers, Rivals, or Partners?" *Horizons* 13.2 (1986): 266. Because of its attention to lived experience and personal growth, it seems that spiritual life should bear an obvious relation to morality and ethics (one might even find it challenging to distinguish Groody's definition of spirituality from morality/ethics). Nonetheless, this has not always been understood to be the case. Particularly in the modern period, morality has generally been presented as a series of decisions made in accordance with rational (i.e., universally intelligible) principles or in order to achieve the best outcome. Philosophers—and many theologians—sought to de-emphasize "superstitious" or "irrational" aspects of religious practice (i.e., those not scientifically verifiable or demonstrating obvious utility) as superfluous to moral life. Even in many virtue-based approaches to ethics, there may be little attention paid to the ways in which spiritual practices such as prayer or communal worship are significant in the acquisition of virtue.

[7] Daniel G. Groody, *Globalization, Spirituality, and Justice: Negotiating the Path to Peace* (Maryknoll, NY: Orbis, 2007), 240–41.

[8] Henri Nouwen, *Reaching Out: The Three Movements of the Spiritual Life* (New York: Doubleday/ Image Books, 1975).

that each of these relationships is inextricably bound up with the others. For Nouwen, the ultimate truth about human persons (which is revealed through the Gospel of Jesus Christ) is their fundamental identity as God's "beloved": that is, as a son or daughter who is unconditionally chosen, accepted, and loved by God. By recognizing this truth, men and women can find the peace of solitude in place of the experience of loneliness and feelings of hospitality in place of hostility and competition in their relationships with others.

This relational emphasis that seeks wholeness and healing through communion with God must be distinguished from other approaches to spirituality that emphasize striving for moral or spiritual "perfection."[9] Rather, Nouwen states that "it is of great importance that we leave the world of measurements behind when we speak about the life of the Spirit"[10]—that is, it would be the antithesis of spiritual development to see it as simply another form of "achievement" or to remain caught up in a mind-set that evaluates and values people based on their accomplishments. He seldom fails to call attention to human woundedness and brokenness or to the always-incomplete nature of the spiritual journey. In fact, in ways that are suggestive for this project, he sometimes writes not of "movement" but rather of "poles between which our lives vacillate and are held in tension."[11] As several biographies and many autobiographical works attest, Nouwen often wrote from his own experiences of loneliness, depression, woundedness, and frustration, which he saw as an inevitable part of the human condition. Despite his attention to human brokenness, however, Nouwen's work is persistently hopeful for the healing made possible through the love of God revealed in Jesus Christ, the paradigm of the "wounded healer."

Again, for Nouwen the core truth of human existence—and therefore the foundation of genuine spiritual life—is that humans are intimately known and unconditionally loved by God, so that he writes that self-rejection (which can take a great variety of forms) is the greatest enemy of the spiritual life.[12] He expresses the difficulty of grasping this reality in a world full of voices that call such belovedness into question and lead

[9] See Michael Christensen, foreword to Wil Hernandez, *Henri Nouwen: A Spirituality of Imperfection* (New York: Paulist Press, 2006).

[10] Nouwen, *Reaching Out*, 17.

[11] Ibid., 18.

[12] Henri Nouwen, *Life of the Beloved: Spiritual Living in a Secular World* (New York: Crossroad, 1992), 33.

people to seek ultimate fulfillment in accomplishments, possessions, and human relationships. Yet the pursuit of such things apart from God serves only to bring deeper anxiety and loneliness. Rather than trying to avoid these feelings by staying constantly busy, filling one's every minute with sounds and distractions, Nouwen commends making time in silence and solitude to listen to one's own heart and to the voice of God that says, "You are my Beloved." To this end, he recognizes the need for times of actual withdrawal from other people and activities, but for Nouwen the real goal is to develop "solitude of heart," an inner quality of peace and rest that does not depend on actual physical isolation.[13] Echoing Nouwen, Richard Foster explains that Jesus calls us from loneliness to solitude: "Loneliness is inner emptiness. Solitude is inner fulfillment. Solitude is more a state of mind than it is a place. . . . Crowds, or lack of them, have little to do with this inward attentiveness. . . . Whether alone or among people, we always carry with us a portable sanctuary of the heart."[14] This "portable sanctuary" is built by reaching out to one's innermost self through "a reaching to a center where a new encounter could take place, where we could reach beyond ourselves to him who speaks in our solitude."[15]

Finding solitude in oneself and the experience of the love of God in one's solitude allows a person to reach out freely to others from genuine compassion and curiosity rather than from the desperate hope that they will be the solution to loneliness or from the fear that they will harm or outshine her. Without solitude of heart, human relationships are easily deformed, becoming needy and greedy, sentimental, exploitative, idolatrous, and even violent, as "our own and other people's lives" are seen as "properties to be defended or conquered and not as gifts to be received."[16] Relationships become violent—in thoughts, words, and sometimes actions—when a person's unfulfilled needs lead her to have unrealistic expectations of other people, or her "illusion of immortality" leads her to view them with suspicion in order to defend her life and possessions at all costs. To reach a "nonviolent intimacy," Nouwen writes, humans have to "unmask the illusion of immortality"—that is, to recognize the limitations of all human life—and to "reach out beyond the limits of our

[13] Nouwen, Reaching Out, 37–38.

[14] Richard Foster, Celebration of Discipline: The Path to Spiritual Growth (San Francisco: HarperSanFrancisco, 1998), 96–97.

[15] Nouwen, Reaching Out, 122.

[16] Ibid., 119.

existence to God out of whose intimacy we are born."[17] Nouwen thus offers the paradoxical conclusion that solitude is the basis of hospitality and community—or in other words, hospitality "requires first of all that the host feel at home in his own house."[18]

Nouwen characterizes spiritual development in a person's relationships with others as a movement from hostility to hospitality, in which her attitude toward others—particularly strangers—moves away from perceiving them as threatening and hostile, and she is able instead to see them as potential friends. He writes that the most important movement of our lives "is not a movement from weakness to power, but a movement in which we can become less and less fearful and more and more open to the other and his world. This movement, allowing us to receive instead of to conquer, is the movement from hostility to hospitality."[19] He often characterizes hospitality as the creation of free or empty space that enables guests "to dance their own dance, sing their own song and speak their own language without fear."[20] The hospitable host—one who has come to terms with her own loneliness rather than trying to use her guests as a means for its relief—offers guests a friendly space "where they may feel free to come and go, to be close and distant, to rest and to play, to talk and be silent, to eat and to fast."[21] A hospitable space is a "free" space both in the sense of being gift-like (that is, there is no ulterior or instrumental purpose in offering welcome) and in the sense of being receptive to the stories, gifts, and needs of others. Challenging the connotation of hospitality as "tea parties, bland conversations and a general atmosphere of coziness," Nouwen explains that the task of creating a truly welcoming space amid the preoccupation, competition, and suspicion of contemporary society is more like "the task of a policeman trying to create space in the middle of a mob of panic-stricken people."[22] The desire and ability to create such spaces is relevant to a wide variety of contexts, from family and education to healing professions, social service, and liturgical celebration.[23]

[17] Ibid., 31, 120.
[18] Henri Nouwen, *The Wounded Healer: Ministry in Contemporary Society* (New York: Doubleday/ Image Books, 1979), 89.
[19] Nouwen, "Hospitality," in *On Hospitality and Other Matters*, Monastic Studies 10 (Pine City, NY: Mount Savior Monastery, 1974), 3.
[20] Nouwen, *The Wounded Healer*, 91–92.
[21] Ibid., 92.
[22] Nouwen, "Hospitality," 8–9.
[23] See Nouwen, *Reaching Out*, 83ff.

Nouwen's discussion of hospitality frequently makes reference to several paradoxes, or tensions, involving (1) receptivity and confrontation, (2) emptiness and articulate presence, and (3) poverty and plentitude. As mentioned in the previous chapter, Nouwen maintains that while hospitality requires receptivity to the guest "on his or her terms, not ours," it also asks for confrontation "because space can only be a welcoming space when there are clear boundaries, and boundaries are limits between which we define our own position. Flexible limits, but limits nonetheless."[24] Confrontation in this sense does not refer to aggression but rather to the way in which a host is really present to her guest, offering herself—her values, opinions, gifts, and vulnerabilities—as a point of orientation or frame of reference. As receptivity, hospitality places no demands or conditions on the guest; as confrontation, it tells the guest where (and with whom) he is.

Closely related to this is the tension between emptiness and articulate presence. Nouwen writes that the "paradox" of hospitality is that it wants to create a "friendly emptiness" where there is room for strangers to laugh, dance, cry, and feel free to be themselves, even as they are greeted by the "articulate presence" of the host. Like an empty house without food or chairs or pictures or curtains, a host's blank neutrality is not in fact a welcome. On the contrary, "we can enter into communication with the other only when our own life choices, attitudes and viewpoints offer the boundaries that challenge strangers to become aware of their own position and explore it critically."[25] In the context of Christian hospitality, Nouwen explains that this dynamic involves a person's witness to the ways that her life has been formed by the Gospel of Jesus without making hospitality into a means of proselytizing. The purpose of hospitality, he writes, "is not to change people, but to offer a free and friendly space where change can take place."[26]

The tension between poverty and plentitude is also important to Nouwen's understanding of hospitality. He writes of the paradox that poverty—by which he means humility about one's knowledge and experience—makes a good host. Whereas a person who is full of opinions and believes she has everything figured out is not inclined to be particularly receptive to the insights and ideas of others, poverty of mind entails the

[24] Ibid., 98.
[25] Ibid., 99.
[26] Nouwen, "Hospitality," 8.

humble willingness to recognize the incomprehensibility of the mystery of life. By the persistent refusal to assume that he or she can figure out this mystery, poverty of mind allows a person "to listen to the voice of God in the words of the people, in the events of the day and in the books containing the life experience of men and women from other places and other times."[27] Similarly, poverty of heart is the attitude that the experiences, emotions, histories, and abilities of others—however different from one's own—have value. It is through such poverty that a person opens herself to true abundance as she welcomes the gifts as well as the needs that her guests bring. Hospitality involves a willingness to receive from the guest as well as to serve him, an experience that "tells us that we can only love because we are born out of love, that we can only give because our life is a gift, and we can only make others free because we are set free by Him whose heart is greater than ours."[28]

Indeed, even as the experiences of solitude and hospitality are rooted in the realities of everyday life and relationships—including experiences of loneliness, anxiety, and brokenness—they also look beyond these to the experience of prayer: "All that has been said about solitude and hospitality points to someone higher than our thoughts can reach, someone deeper than our hearts can feel and wider than our arms can embrace, someone under whose wings we can find refuge (Psalm 90), and in whose love we can rest, someone we call our God."[29] Nouwen describes the movement from illusion to prayer as the "first and final" movement of the spiritual life, in which human illusions of control and misguided pursuits of meaning are transformed into reliance on God and recognition that life is a gift to be received with gratitude and given to others. Far from being something "of secondary importance if not a complete waste of time and evasion of reality,"[30] prayer is the basic receptive attitude out of which all of life receives its vitality. Prayer, which refers to moments of passive contemplation as well as active intercession or expressions of thanksgiving, is the way that humans make space for the transforming presence of the Spirit of God. It is "living with God, here and now" through putting into practice Jesus' words to his followers: "Make your home in me, as I make mine in you" (John 15:4).[31] Prayer can therefore, in a certain sense, be

[27] Ibid., 104–5.
[28] Nouwen, *The Wounded Healer*, 91.
[29] Nouwen, *Reaching Out*, 122.
[30] Henri Nouwen, *Peacework: Prayer, Resistance, Community* (Maryknoll, NY: Orbis, 2005), 38.
[31] Ibid., 33.

understood as a human practice of hospitality to God, which expands and empowers hospitality toward other people. Because God is the guest whom no human home or heart can contain, welcoming God involves risk as well as consolation, humility as well as hope, affirmation as well as transformation of human lives, limits, and dreams.

Disciplines of Gratitude

Given the breadth of the understanding of spiritual life articulated above, it seems as if it might be difficult to separate out certain actions or habits as specifically spiritual practices—and indeed, an authentic spirituality should inform the whole of one's life in an integrated manner. At the same time, in certain practices the relationship to an ultimate value or meaning (in the case of Christian spirituality, loving fellowship with God as made known through Jesus Christ by the Holy Spirit) is more explicit and immediate, such that we tend to refer to prayer or meditation as spiritual practices in a way that doing the dishes or grocery shopping generally are not. Earlier in this chapter, I wrote that "standards of excellence" in Christian spiritual practices are different in nature than in other practices, in that spiritual growth does not depend exclusively, or even primarily, on human effort. It may be that excellence—if we would want to use such a term—in spiritual life is much more a matter of *attentiveness* than of achievement. The length and breadth of the Christian spiritual tradition, from the apostle Paul to John Paul II, affirms the way in which spiritual growth is ultimately a gracious gift of God. Responding to philosopher Alasdair MacIntyre, theologian Sarah Coakley expresses criticism of a sole emphasis on human powers to achieve excellence in spiritual life, and to counter this she turns to "the apparently passive practice of contemplation, in which an ostensibly time-wasting attentiveness is claimed to be the unimpeded receptacle of divine grace."[32] Much like the practice of hospitality at a literal level, in which a host's active preparation and effort are only one part of a "successful" practice, contemplative prayer requires the recognition that the Spirit of God is beyond human control; the house may be in order, food on the table, but if no guest arrives—or if the host is too busy to actually attend to her guest—this is a limited hospitality indeed. As Richard Foster explains in his classic *Celebration of Discipline*, "by

---

[32] Sarah Coakley, "Deepening Practices: Perspectives from Ascetical and Mystical Theology," in *Practicing Theology*, ed. Dorothy Bass and Miroslav Volf, 80.

themselves the spiritual disciplines can do nothing; they can only get us to the place where something can be done."[33]

But this coming to the place "where something can be done" is no small matter, either, and saying that spiritual growth is a gift does not mean that one ought simply to wait for it passively. For this reason, it is fitting to speak of *disciplines* rather than simply *practices* of the spiritual life. That is, while a person may engage in a recognizable practice (such as worship, confession, or hospitality) only sporadically or when "moved" to do so, a discipline indicates a regular and committed practice. William Spohn explains the significance of this distinction:

> Praying only when we feel like it is unlikely to produce a disposition of reverence, and writing the occasional check for the homeless will not instill Christian hospitality as part of our characters. . . . Not every act of worship or hospitality to the poor will be moving, any more than every conversation in a long marriage will be a deep experience of intimacy. What keeps marriage vital is showing up, being attentive and available to the spouse. Practices like regular worship and service to the poor . . . are places where the community over time has learned that Christians need to show up, to be available to the work and healing that God will do in and through them.[34]

Nouwen also writes that disciplines are necessary to spiritual life as a way of creating space for God in busy and worry-filled human lives: "Through a spiritual discipline we prevent the world from filling our lives to such an extent that there is no place left to listen."[35] God speaks constantly, but humans are often too busy or preoccupied to hear. Though a person may initially feel like a particular discipline—intentionally taking time in solitude or communal worship or meditating on Scripture—is uncomfortable or a waste of time, faithfulness to a discipline (meaning both regularity and duration) gradually transforms it into something joyful and life sustaining.

---

[33] Richard Foster, *Celebration of Discipline: The Path to Spiritual Growth* (New York: HarperCollins, 1988), 7. Readers will see below that my discussion of the disciplines relies significantly on Foster, who provides a profound and erudite yet remarkably accessible account of spiritual disciplines in this book.

[34] William Spohn, "Spiritual Theology and Christian Ethics," in *The Blackwell Companion to Christian Spirituality*, ed. Arthur Holder, 276–77.

[35] Henri Nouwen, *Making All Things New: An Invitation to the Spiritual Life* (San Francisco: Harper & Row, 1981), 68.

In part for this reason, I have chosen to designate the practices that I discuss in this chapter "disciplines of gratitude"—a phrase that may initially sound contradictory to some. How can one make a *discipline* of gratitude—or be grateful for a discipline? Is not gratitude something spontaneous and joyful, whereas discipline (derived from the Latin term *disciplina*, which refers to training or instruction) is willful and unpleasant or even punitive? Quite to the contrary, most worthwhile pursuits in life—those things that bring us the most meaningful joy and pleasure—often involve not only persistence in "training" in order to excel but also greater ease and delight over time as disciplines form and transform habits of body, mind, and heart.

An example from personal experience may help to illustrate this. About six years ago, I decided that I was going to learn to play guitar after seeing a girl with hands about the same size as mine playing quite well. (This was significant because I had tried to learn several times previously, and after each unsuccessful attempt I concluded that my hands were simply too small to form the chords and make the strings sound properly.) When I saw this particular young woman playing, I thought perhaps there was hope for me. In the beginning it's not particularly pleasant; as anyone who plays guitar knows, the initial processes of building callouses on fingertips, of training hands to make many strange shapes and move seamlessly between them, of strengthening hand and forearm muscles and coordinating strumming patterns with chord changes, aren't much fun. Yet I was persistent—and did have enough background in music that some elements of this initial discipline came relatively easily—so within a month or so I was able to play a few simple songs. It seems that my hands were not too small at all but rather needed proper training. My guitar-playing discipline continued, but from that point on, it certainly felt different; rather than painfully working to ingrain new habits in muscles and mind, I was making music, learning new songs, and playing the ones I knew better than I had before—and I couldn't get enough of it. When I broke my left arm in a car accident several years after I started playing, getting back to guitar was probably the primary motivation for my commitment to the disciplines of physical therapy. Singing and playing guitar hardly feel like a discipline anymore but rather a regular (and possibly indispensible) part of my life that enriches the whole. Most people who have had success in a sport or musical instrument or learning another language or other skills could share similar experiences of the gratitude and joy that are born of discipline. This is equally so with more directly spiritual disciplines.

Furthermore, as the title of Foster's book indicates, the purpose of the spiritual disciplines is *liberation* from slavery to fear and self-centeredness: "When the inner spirit is liberated from all that weighs it down," he writes, "it can hardly be described as dull drudgery." He explains that celebratory actions like singing and dancing characterize the disciplines of spiritual life as expressions of gratitude for this experience of freedom.[36] It is entirely appropriate, moreover, to speak of *cultivating* gratitude as a way of life, developing intentional practices that attend to the pervasiveness of grace even in the "ill-matched threads"—the struggles and suffering and shortcomings and wounds—of one's life. In some ways, this is not altogether different from Christian attitudes about love: although love is a "commandment," the *works* of love are meant to move a person beyond simply dutifully meeting obligations. Brother David Steindl-Rast further explains the link between love and gratitude:

> We grow in love when we grow in gratefulness. And we grow in gratefulness when we grow in love. Here is the link between the two: thanksgiving depends on our willingness to go beyond our independence and accept the give-and-take between giver and thanks-giver. But the very "yes" which acknowledges our interdependence is the very "yes" to belonging, the "yes" of love. Every time we say a simple "thank you" and mean it, we practice that inner gesture of "yes." And the more we practice it, the easier it becomes. The more difficult it is to say a grateful "yes," the more we grow by learning to say it gracefully. This sheds light on suffering and other difficult gifts. The hardest gifts are, in a sense, the best, because they make us grow the most.[37]

Practices that encourage mindfulness and thankfulness in all circumstances are particularly relevant to the limits of hospitality, as they allow individuals and communities to live more fully in the spirit of affirmation that Steindl-Rast describes above. The statement that hospitable boundaries must in some way affirm even what they limit or exclude—never denying the humanity of those who wish us harm or whose needs we cannot meet, nor despairing due to our own weaknesses and failures, nor growing resentful in the face of suffering—is put into practice through making gratefulness an attitude that pervades all of life. Spiritual disciplines are

---

[36] Foster, *Celebration of Discipline*, 2.
[37] David Steindl-Rast, *Gratefulness, the Heart of Prayer: An Approach to Life in Fullness* (New York: Paulist Press, 1984), 176.

"disciplines of gratitude" in that they involve both the cultivation and the expression of gratitude—in other words, they are both the seeds and the fruit of wholeness and hospitality.

As I stated in the last section, concrete disciplines of gratitude can in fact be understood as practices of hospitality to God that, when regularly carried out, help to form a person in such a way that he or she is able to navigate the tensions described in the previous chapter. But how, exactly?

Although this question will in a certain sense form the backdrop of the rest of this book, I want to identify a few important general ways in which spiritual disciplines are relevant to forming limits of hospitality. First, as I have already suggested by describing spiritual practices as "making space" for God, there is a kind of structural analogy between the act and attitude of welcoming other human people and the acts and attitudes that welcome God. Just as encounters with other humans may be surprising, challenging, and transformative, and in much the same way that welcoming them demands moments of both activity and passivity, so too with God. Like humans—though to an infinitely greater degree—God transcends what is possible to know or to control. Moreover, although welcoming God in spiritual practices is free of the dangers of evil and violence that are possibilities when welcoming other humans, this does not mean that it will be "safe"—on the contrary, it may introduce new forms of suffering or insights and possibilities that radically challenge one's comfort. "Genuine spirituality is not cozy, and seldom makes you comfortable," write David Homan and Lonni Collins Pratt in their book on the radical hospitality of the Benedictine way. Rather, "it challenges, disturbs, and leaves you feeling like someone is at the center of your existence on a major remodeling mission. While affirming how wonderful you are, better than you really know, spirituality is meant to change you."[38] The challenge involved in welcoming God therefore helps to develop the virtue of courage, also a necessary part of extending welcome to other humans.

At this point, I should make clear that I am in complete agreement with the argument that hospitality is not, in the first instance, a human virtue but rather a divine virtue. Hospitality finds its fullest and truest expression in the mutually giving and receiving life of the persons of the Trinity and in God's creative and sustaining relationship to the world. By arguing that human individuals and communities should practice hospitality to God as

---

[38] David Homan and Lonni Collins Pratt, *Radical Hospitality: Benedict's Way of Love* (Brewster, MA: Paraclete Press, 2002), 35.

the foundation of their practices of hospitality to other humans, I am in no way suggesting that this would be possible without God's prior welcome and affirmation or that humans do not also become the *guests* of God through these practices. Even the best human efforts at hospitality are of course dramatically limited in comparison with the incomprehensible hospitality and transcendence of God—and precisely for this reason, I believe that human hospitality *in its difference from* God's unlimited hospitality raises enough issues to merit consideration in its own right. Also for this reason, however—and out of the biblical conviction that humans, in some mysterious way, are bearers of God's image—it is appropriate to say that humans can and do have the capacity and even the vocation to practice hospitality to God.

Other important virtues—including but not limited to generosity, prudence, patience, and inventiveness—also may be acquired through these practices. One trait that is particularly significant to the practice of hospitality that may be developed through such disciplines is the ability to be attentive to one's guests—even when it may feel like this is a waste of time. I would venture to say that everyone has had the experience of having a conversation with another person and finding their thoughts wander to other things to the point that they are scarcely aware of what the other is saying. Sometimes when we feel we are unable to solve a person's problems or heal their wounds, we are most tempted to remain busy to avoid being confronted with our own powerlessness. Most people have also been on the other side of this dynamic, when it is clear that the person they are talking to is distracted or impatient to move on to another activity. In an age when we are taught to believe that time is money—the universal standard of value—and that the optimal use of one's time involves virtually infinite networking and multitasking, it can be extremely challenging and countercultural (though perhaps all the more important for this reason) to simply *be present where and with whom we are.* By setting aside time to "practice the presence of God," people can also learn to be patient and attentive with other humans, regardless of the instrumental value of that time. "In our utilitarian culture, in which we suffer from a collective compulsion to do something helpful, practical, or useful," Nouwen writes, "contemplative prayer is a form of radical criticism. It is not practical or useful but a way of wasting time for God. It cuts a hole in our busyness and reminds us that it is God and not we who creates and sustains the world."[39] Even in disciplines that are more "active" than contemplation,

---

[39] Henri Nouwen, *Clowning in Rome: Reflections on Solitude, Celibacy, Prayer, and Contemplation* (Westminster, MD: Christian Classics, 1979), 53.

however—service, study, or confession, for example—people can learn to recognize their own limits with neither condemnation nor complacency.

A final way that practices of hospitality to God are vital to hospitality to other humans is by aiding in the discernment of true limits—that is, limits that are not merely manifestations or justifications of fear or pride or materialism. Jesus told his disciples that he would send the Spirit to guide them to all truth (John 16:13), where "Truth does not mean an idea, a concept, or doctrine, but the true relationship. To be led into truth is to be led into the same relationship that Jesus has with the Father."[40] Through finding a truer source of identity and security in God, the false sources of identity and security that lead to violence can be recognized as the idols and illusions that they are. This is not, as the following chapters will show, to deny the reality or necessity of these limits but rather to find a deeper sense of identity and security than that offered by nation or denomination—one that is not threatened but rather enriched by those who are different—as well as a greater ability to separate real needs from markers of social status and the unquenchable desires of consumer culture. Self-deception about our motivations will always be a danger, for as long as we are human we are prone to excessive self-regard and the desire to conceal our sin even from ourselves. A full and flourishing—if nonetheless human—practice of hospitality flows from the ability to see ourselves and others honestly, humbly, and with gratitude for what lies beyond as well as within our lives' present limits in accordance with Jesus' words: "The Spirit will take from what is mine and make it known to you" (John 16:15).

✦ ✦ ✦ ✦

I focus here on five pairs of spiritual disciplines that are relevant to hospitality, namely (1) *prayer of word and prayer of silence*, (2) *solitude and fellowship*, (3) *fasting and celebration*, (4) *service and rest*, and (5) *confession and forgiveness*. There are certainly other equally illuminating ways of grouping or categorizing these and other disciplines, though pairing them in this way helpfully indicates or even replicates some of the dynamics that are present in the practice of hospitality, which itself can certainly be called a spiritual discipline. Though it would be a mistake to understand these as pairings of active and passive practices—there are both active and passive dimensions of each practice described here—they do suggest the dynamic polarity or dialectic between extension and withdrawal, which can be seen even in the life and ministry of Jesus. In some ways, it might

---

[40] Nouwen, *Making All Things New*, 54.

be said that the significance of each partner of these pairings is necessary to fully appreciate the significance of the other. This is by no means an exhaustive treatment of (or even sufficient practical guidance for) these disciplines but rather intends to indicate how the tensions of hospitality are mirrored in other dimensions of spiritual life. Developing a sensitivity to the appropriate balance of each partner in a pair—or pole of a tension or moment of a dialectic—can also shape a person to be better able to discern limits of hospitality.

Prayer of Word and Prayer of Silence

One of the most significant ways that Christians make space to welcome God is through prayer, which is often understood as communication or communion with God. "All the great saints in history and all the spiritual directors worth their salt say that we have to learn to pray, since prayer is our first obligation as well as our highest calling," writes Nouwen. He explains that "the paradox of prayer is that it asks for a serious effort while it can only be received as a gift. We cannot plan, organize, or manipulate God; but without a careful discipline, we cannot receive him either."[41] It is clear from the writings of Paul that the discipline of prayer is a discipline of gratitude: learning to "pray without ceasing" involves learning to "give thanks in all circumstances; for this is the will of God in Christ Jesus for you" (1 Thess 5:17-18).

As communication, prayer obviously may take the form of word—that is, expressions of thanksgiving, intention, or intercession—which is probably what is most often meant when people think or speak of prayer. Such prayers may be extemporaneous or formal, made by individuals or corporately, spoken aloud, sung, or simply uttered in one's heart. Whatever its form, however, prayer is always intended to engage the hearts as well as minds and voices of those who participate. As I have already mentioned, I regularly make a practice of writing prayers in a journal and have found that the prayer of word (in this or any form) can be of significant value in developing a greater awareness of what is going on. That is, why exactly am I thankful or angry or anxious? How do I describe this? The discipline of taking time to make hopes and worries and reasons for gratitude explicit in written words—as if in a letter to God—not only serves as a helpful step in self-critique as I am faced with my own selfish motivations and petty

---

[41] Nouwen, *Reaching Out*, 123, 126.

fears but also provides grounds for encouragement and further thanks as I reread and reflect on how struggles, pain, and even my own sins have been woven into a larger story by hands more skillful than mine.

In the prayer of silence, sometimes called contemplation, a person does not necessarily *do* anything but rather seeks primarily to make herself available and attentive to God "with empty hands, naked, vulnerable, useless, without much to show, prove, or defend."[42] Although Scripture or a sacred word may facilitate the prayer of silence, in many ways its intention is to allow the self and its thoughts to step aside to make room for the inspiration and direction of God's Spirit. Though silent contemplation is a part of many spiritual traditions, the practice of intentional silence in communal worship and prayer is particularly significant to Quaker spirituality. As Roger Vanden Busch explains,

> As a community soaked in silence, a greater awareness and responsibility toward one another begins to emerge. We begin to experience a deeper sense of community, identity, and solidarity. This silent togetherness may give us a greater sensitivity and concern for the poor. If we truly share from our own surplus, there will be enough to go around. This quiet time may allow us to critique our own consumer mentality where we collect, accumulate, and buy but never seem to be satisfied. . . . In a world that seems to be so void of silence, we need to create periodic worlds of silence where we can be in touch with the cosmic dimensions of our lives.[43]

Perhaps it is no wonder that the Quakers historically have been among the Christian denominations most hospitable to women and people of color and to the needs of the poor. Learning to step away from occupations and preoccupations, from the noise that fills our lives to the point of drowning out the voice of God and even of our own heart, is not easy. "We often use the outer distractions to shield ourselves from the interior voices" of worry or pain.[44] Yet, as a part of coming to live in a "true address"—the place where we can be addressed by God[45]—prayer of silence is necessary to building hospitable and discerning lives and communities.

---

[42] Nouwen, *Making All Things New*, 76.

[43] Roger Vanden Busch, "The Value of Silence in Quaker Spirituality," *Spirituality Today* 37 (1985): 326, 335.

[44] Nouwen, *Making All Things New*, 70.

[45] Ibid., 37.

Practicing prayer of silence is also an important way of developing listening practices with other humans, of really hearing others' opinions and concerns in all their complexity rather than asking for sound-bite synopses that we can quickly digest and incorporate into our own narrative. Resisting this sort of violence in the context of hospitality therefore requires commitment to listening to the stories of other people and recognizing the limits of our conceptions of them.[46] In addition to the context of offering hospitality to strangers, the ability to step aside, to stop talking and make room for the voices of others, is essential to intimate relationships of marriage, family, and friendship as well as to the broader world of policy making and diplomacy. Silence may also often be necessary to hear our own hearts telling us when and how to extend or draw limits to hospitality.

Solitude and Fellowship

Disciplines of solitude and fellowship also help to shape a person in such a way that she is better able to practice hospitality. Depending on personal temperament, it is likely that one or the other of these comes quite naturally, whereas the other may be less enjoyable and require greater discipline. Becoming more aware of God's presence in time alone as well as time with other people can help a person to know when it is God (rather than her own fears or frustrations) calling her to one or the other. Like the practice of silent prayer, in the discipline of solitude it may be challenging at first not to feel lonely or to seek out distractions from one's own inner noise. With time, however, a person experiences that he is not alone with his loneliness—that God is present in his solitude—and he is therefore able to develop the solitude of heart that allows for genuine fellowship.

I use the term "fellowship" to indicate a being-with-others that is broader than what is often meant by the term "community." As the fol-

---

[46] It is worth noting here that (in contrast to Boersma's interpretation in which finite existence as such is violent) even for Emmanuel Lévinas, it is not so much finite existence and conceptual thought per se as it is the attempt to contain the infinite (human persons and their stories) in conceptual thought in the way I have just described that entails violence. "Violence," writes Lévinas, "does not consist so much in injuring and annihilating persons as in . . . making them play roles in which they no longer recognize themselves." Within "totalizing" modes of thought and relationship, "individuals are reduced to being bearers of forces that command them unbeknownst to themselves," as they are categorized and conceptualized by others. Emmanuel Lévinas, *Totality and Infinity: An Essay on Exteriority*, trans. Alphonso Ligis (Pittsburgh: Duquesne University Press, 1969), 21.

lowing chapter will explore in greater detail, "community" implies some degree of shared identity or purpose among its members, whereas I take "fellowship" to refer to *any* coming together with others—family dinners, "girls' nights out," book clubs, golf outings, car pools, youth soccer tournaments, and birthday or holiday parties all can be occasions for fellowship, even if it would be a stretch to call the persons involved a community in any meaningful sense. Fellowship becomes a spiritual discipline when it is sought out regularly and with the intention of finding the presence of God in experiences of human togetherness. This admittedly will be more difficult in some circumstances than in others—it may perhaps be easier to experience the presence of God at a prayer group than at a football tailgate party—but this is due to our own distraction rather than to the absence of God.[47] The practice of true hospitality requires not only that we ourselves become "like quiet cells where God can dwell"[48] in our solitude but also that we learn to find Christ in every stranger and his Spirit in every gathering of strangers or friends.

Fasting and Celebration

One very important pairing of spiritual disciplines involves the partners of fasting and celebration. While the discipline of fasting has been taken to ascetic extremes in the effort to cultivate total detachment from bodily existence, and while excessive celebration can become gluttonous and degenerate, each of these also plays an important part in spiritual life.

Traditionally, the discipline of fasting has involved periodic abstention from food (and sometimes also from liquids), although "fasting" from a cell phone or automobile or alcoholic beverages or television (or even a

[47] I do want to make two qualifications of this statement. First, it is an important and long-standing part of the Christian mystical tradition to speak of the experience of the *absence* of God in the "dark night of the soul." Without denying the profundity of such experiences or the idea that God may at times "withdraw" to the point that a person may be truly unable to detect even a trace of God's presence, as long as a person draws breath, it is metaphorical to say that God is "absent." God's ongoing and sustaining presence in creation is necessary for humans even to be able to experience God's "absence." The second qualification pertains to situations where "fellowship" is truly evil and an affront to God (one might imagine instances of gang rape or organized crime groups or even the interaction promoted by certain bars and clubs). Here, too, I would say, God is not absent; God is present and suffers with those whose dignity is violated even if the violent perversion and destruction of true fellowship is so overwhelming that these are all we can perceive as humans.

[48] Nouwen, *Making All Things New*, 79.

Facebook account) can also be an effective means of developing a truer sense of one's needs and of calling awareness to the ways that we grow dependent on nonessentials. Depending on what exactly a person is giving up, this can also open up time for other activities—including, perhaps, the practice of hospitality. "Fasts" of this sort might be seen as steps on the way to what has been described as the discipline of simplicity, in which all of life is arranged around a few consistent purposes, deliberately excluding what is not necessary for human well-being. Richard Foster describes the discipline of simplicity as an inward spirit of trust that involves "a joyful unconcern for possessions."[49]

The great difference between a "fast" of this nature and a traditional fast from food, however, is that in the latter a person voluntarily forgoes not only a comfort but a true human need. Like many other disciplines, fasting is ultimately connected to prayer. Many accounts of fasting describe how this practice not only made room for prayer in a busy schedule but also deepened a person's ability to trust and rely on God. The developments in an individual who made a commitment to fast once a week for two years indicate how faithfulness to a discipline is necessary to the realization of its true significance:

- I felt it a great accomplishment to go a whole day without food. Congratulated myself on the fact that I found it so easy. . . .
- Began to see that the above was hardly the goal of fasting. Was helped in this by beginning to feel hunger. . . .
- Began to relate the food fast to other area of my life where I was more compulsive. . . . I did not have to have a seat on the bus to be contented, or to be cool in the summer and warm when it was cold. . . .
- Reflected more on Christ's suffering and that of those who are hungry and have hungry babies.
- Six months after beginning this fast discipline, I began to see why a two-year period has been suggested. The experience changes along the way. . . . For the first time I was using the day to find God's will for my life. Began to think about what it meant to *surrender* one's life.
- I now know that prayer and fasting must be intricately bound together. There is no other way.[50]

[49] Foster, *Celebration of Discipline*, 87. Cf. Dallas Willard, *The Spirit of the Disciplines: Understanding How God Changes Lives* (San Francisco: HarperSanFrancisco, 1988), 170ff.

[50] Elizabeth O'Connor, *Search for Silence* (Waco, TX: Word Books, 1971), 103–4; quoted in Foster, *Celebration of Discipline*, 58.

In addition to deepening one's experience of prayer, the willingness to forgo one's desires or needs (whether in a prayerful fast or simply for the sake of meeting another's immediate needs) not only may serve to make room for someone else but also may foster compassion and solidarity with those who go without basic necessities on a regular basis. Fasting may also be an expression of sorrow or repentance (e.g., John 3:5) or as part of a person or community's spiritual preparation for a significant event, as the church's Lenten fast is intended to prepare its members for the celebration of Easter.

Indeed, celebrating the spiritual seasons of the liturgical calendar—its vigils and Ordinary Time as well as its days and seasons of feasting—is an important discipline in itself, one that can help communities and their members recognize the ebbing and flowing rhythms of human life. Of course, the seasons of human life do not always correspond to the church's calendar—not every Christmas season is joyful, nor is every August "ordinary"—but by faithfully observing the spiritual significance of the passage of time, people can better appreciate the truth that "for everything there is a season, and a time for every matter under heaven" (Eccl 3:1). It is not incidental that hospitality takes place not only in space but also in time. Developing sensitivity to when it is an appropriate time to weep or to laugh, to mourn or to dance, is an important part of extending and discerning hospitality.

Not all hospitality is celebratory, of course, any more than every fast is sorrowful, but if rejoicing and celebration were ever entirely absent from one's practice of hospitality, it would be limited indeed. Even Derrida recognizes that "if I say to the other, . . . 'Come in,' without smiling, without sharing some sign of joy, it is not hospitality. . . . The welcome must be laughing or smiling, happy or joyous."[51] It may seem strange to think of celebration as a discipline, and it is true that it may do more harm than good at times to try to force or fake a spirit of joy and celebration. But the serendipity of joy does not preclude being intentional about its cultivation and expression through humor, games, music and dance, festive food and drink, or decorations. While one should never feel that hospitality *requires* elaborate food or special table linens or the like, such things can be a way of honoring and celebrating the presence of a guest, of offering an uncalculating welcome to strangers. Furthermore, because

[51] Derrida, "Hostipitality," in *Acts of Religion*, ed. Gil Anidjar (New York: Routledge, 2002), 358–59.

celebratory ritual often accompanies important milestones in the life of a community, it can also be an important means of nonviolently forming identities; that is, rather than defining itself *against* some other, a community is able to welcome others into a celebration of identity, as is often the case with holidays and festivals of special significance to specific ethnic groups.

The identity-forming nature of celebration should be nowhere more apparent than in the church's worship, its liturgy. One of the central convictions of Elizabeth Newman's book *Untamed Hospitality* is that the church's hospitality is founded in its worship, which is to claim that "neither of these is only a human venture. . . . Our worship of God rests on the fact that in the beginning there is always gift, the overflow of God's eternal triune communion. In worship, as we enter this communion, we learn to be God's guests and hosts."[52] Newman very helpfully identifies liturgy as an occasion of celebration and hospitality that makes a community into "a whole greater than the sum of its parts."[53] The celebration of faith in liturgy both grounds and is an expression of the church's hospitality, as many writers have thoughtfully described.

As a discipline of gratitude, it is of no small importance that the center of Christian celebration, Christian worship, Christian identity, and Christian hospitality is thanksgiving—Eucharist. In her memoir, *One Thousand Gifts*, Ann Voskamp meditates on the significance of this:

> "And he took bread, gave thanks and broke it, and gave it to them . . ." (Luke 22:19 NIV). . . .
>
> I thumb, run my finger across the pages of the heavy and thick books bound. I read it slowly. In the original language, "he gave thanks" reads "*eucharisteo*." . . .
>
> The root word of *eucharisteo* is *charis*, meaning "grace." Jesus took bread and saw it as *grace* and gave thanks. He took the bread and knew it to be *gift* and gave thanks.
>
> But there is more, and I read it. *Eucharisteo*, thanksgiving, envelopes the Greek word for grace, *charis*. But it also holds its derivative, the Greek word *chara*, meaning "joy." Joy. Ah. . . .
>
> Deep *chara* joy is found only at the table of the *euCHARisteo*—the table of thanksgiving. I sit there long . . . wondering . . . is it that simple?
>
> Is the height of my *chara* joy dependent on the depths of my *eucharisteo* thanks?

---

[52] Elizabeth Newman, *Untamed Hospitality: Welcoming God and Other Strangers* (Grand Rapids, MI: Brazos Press, 2007), 45.

[53] Ibid., 49.

So then as long as thanks is possible . . . I think this through. As long
as thanks is possible, then joy is always possible. *Joy is always possible.*
Whenever, meaning—now; *wherever*, meaning—here. The holy grail
of joy is not in some exotic location or some emotional mountain
peak experience. The joy wonder could be here! Here, in the messy,
piercing ache of now, joy might be—unbelievably—possible! The
only place we need see before we die is this place of seeing God,
here and now.[54]

As the title of her book suggests, from this epiphany Voskamp begins to
make a list of one thousand things for which she is grateful—mundane,
ordinary things that are also full of beauty and wonder,[55] as well as experiences of suffering—in an effort to transform *all* of life into Eucharist.
The joy of Christian hospitality—whether in the celebration of the liturgy
or in the trials of daily life and human limits—must always rest on this
foundation.

Service and Rest

The discipline of service to others is probably the practice most obviously connected to hospitality. Of course, making a regular practice of
actively doing good for others can help to form a more humble and hospitable character, but acts of service in and of themselves do not necessarily
guarantee this. As Foster explains, grand acts of service can often conceal
pride and self-righteousness or be motivated by a misplaced desire for
human acclaim and recognition. Service can also be done with resentment or out of fear. Yet true service, as he calls it, is content with small
and even hidden acts of service; it involves not only performing discrete
acts of service but *becoming a servant.* Foster particularly recommends hidden
service as "a rebuke to the flesh and . . . a fatal blow to pride" that can
also mysteriously send "ripples of joy and celebration through any community of people."[56] Service in hiddenness and service in small, seemingly
insignificant things may in fact have a greater effect on the development
of character than large and impressive acts of service: "In the realm of the
spirit," he writes, "we soon find that the real issues are found in the tiny,
insignificant corners of life. Our infatuation with the 'big deal' has blinded

[54] Ann Voskamp, *One Thousand Gifts* (Grand Rapids, MI: Zondervan, 2010), 32–33.
[55] For example, "364. Sound of spruce cones thumping buckets with spring / 365.
Cackle of crows high in the limbs, iridescence on wings" (ibid., 71).
[56] Foster, *Celebration of Discipline*, 134.

us to this fact." But "it is not elevation of spirit to feel contempt for small things."[57] By learning to find joy in service that goes unacknowledged or that seems insignificant, a host also grows in her capacity to perform the humble and menial tasks necessary to hospitality as well as to serve even ungrateful guests without resentment and hostility.

Beyond learning to serve in small and unacknowledged ways, the *discipline* of service also means maintaining a commitment to serving even if one does not really feel like it and there is no pressing need—a discipline of "showing up" in the event that God's blessing should appear. One of my most memorable experiences of this came on a miserably cold and rainy February day in New Haven, when I decidedly did *not* feel like keeping the commitment I had made to serve at the soup kitchen at church. In part because of my work on hospitality and spiritual disciplines, the previous fall I had decided to make a commitment to help at the church's Wednesday soup kitchen every week, to show up even on those weeks when I was busy or tired or not in the mood to serve, to regard this service with the same seriousness that I would a class or other obligation. Work at the soup kitchen—which had been in operation for almost twenty-five years, through some difficult and violent days in that city—was, for the most part, one of the great joys of my time in graduate school. I got to know not only a multigenerational group of fellow volunteers—from college students to retirees—but also a colorful and beautiful collection of people who came there as guests (we served lunch to somewhere between two and three hundred guests each Wednesday throughout the school year). Although I would serve soup or distribute diapers when such help was needed, I found that the most distinctive and valuable service I could offer was to play my guitar and sing during the lunch hour. I became known as the "guitar lady" to both volunteers and guests, and since there were usually plenty of people to help with other tasks, most days I would simply play music and visit with guests, who expressed their appreciation for the ways that this soup kitchen was different from others in town.

On this particular morning, however, in addition to the inhospitable weather, I had not slept well at all the night before and was feeling under pressure to do my own work. Back and forth I went, trying to decide whether to keep the commitment I had made or just skip it and stay in that day. As the usual time for me to go to the kitchen approached, I was still wearing the T-shirt I had slept in and I had not washed my hair for

[57] Ibid., 135–36.

days. At about the last possible minute, I decided to put on a headband and a pair of jeans, pack up my guitar, and go to the soup kitchen. And I found that the joy with which I was greeted when I arrived outshone even a cold and rainy dreary winter Connecticut day.

"Hey!" exclaimed Sandra Rodriguez[58] when she saw me. "Rock 'n' roll! You look like a hippie today!" she told me, with obvious approval. Sandra, an outgoing Hispanic woman in her fifties or sixties who was a regular at the kitchen and often shared pictures of her babies and grandbabies with me, who had lost most of her teeth, who kept a motherly eye out for the other guests, seemed to think that today was an improvement over my usual appearance: "You got your hair all back and your shirt is all wrinkly!" she observed. I had to laugh—and to say, "Thank you." Somehow the rest of the morning seemed to be marked by similar exuberance and appreciation for my songs and my presence, and I was able to find delight and refreshment in my coworkers and guests. However bedraggled and tired I felt, I was not immune to the joy that is kindled by disciplined and grateful service.

But the other side of the discipline of service is that of rest, meaning not only taking a step back from one's labors but also learning to be a graceful recipient of the service of others. It may seem strange to speak of "learning to rest," but it can in fact be remarkably difficult not to allow one's work and obligations to creep into every moment of every day, especially when these are good things, "productive" not only in terms of concrete accomplishments but also in that they produce a sense of meaning and even identity for many people. "It is very hard not to be busy," Nouwen writes. "Being busy has become a status symbol. People expect us to be busy and have many things on our minds." He acknowledges how we have even come to see being busy as synonymous with being important![59] A discipline of rest, such as Sabbath keeping or even an afternoon tea, may not only encourage awareness of limits and a sense of humility about one's own importance—the world will not, in most cases, fall apart if we take time to rest—but also will likely invigorate, energize, and inspire further service.

For many people, however, learning to *receive* the service of others may be an even more challenging and humbling part of the discipline of rest. When, at almost thirty years old, I broke my arm and my mother had to

---

[58] This name has been changed.
[59] Nouwen, *Making All Things New*, 24.

help me bathe for the first several days, it was one of the more humbling experiences of my life—sitting naked in a bathtub as she washed me, just as she had done when I was a child. Yet it called my attention to the ways that I am prideful even in my desire not to be a burden to others. Self-sufficiency and independence are such esteemed values of American culture that even if they do not always say so explicitly (though often enough they do), many Americans see it as a sign of weakness and even moral failing to rely on others for help. As I have already stated in a number of ways, however, the limits of hospitality expand not only when communities share in its practice but also when guests are invited to serve and to contribute in meaningful ways.

Confession and Forgiveness

The final set of disciplines that I will consider in this section is the pair of confession and forgiveness. Without diminishing the importance of the sacramental practice of reconciliation (confession to and absolution by a priest, usually accompanied by some form of penance), I want to interpret each of these more broadly as they relate to hospitality. Particularly at its tension-filled limits, hospitality requires that its practitioners are willing to admit mistakes, to confess sins, faults, and failings, and even simply to ask for the advice of others when dealing with a difficult situation—that is, to "confess" what's going on and seek the wisdom of other people. Christine Pohl explains, "If the practice of hospitality by its very nature led practitioners to the practice of Sabbath-keeping, both together lead practitioners to the practice of discernment, as they make difficult decisions about when and how to 'close the door.' Tensions related to these difficult decisions can erupt in anger; practitioners learn the need for practices of confession and forgiveness as they continue to live in their common life."[60]

Indeed, all significant and enduring relationships—marriages and families, friendships, even professional colleagues and partners—will require both admission of wrongdoing and ongoing forgiveness for it when selfishness, cowardice, or simply shortsightedness lead people to hurt one another. Forgiveness itself might be seen as a practice of hospitality, of welcoming one who has made him- or herself "strange" and distant through his or her sin. Encouraging forgiveness does not mean

---

[60] Christine Pohl, "A Community's Practice of Hospitality: The Interdependence of Practices and of Communities," in *Practicing Theology*, ed. Dorothy Bass and Miroslav Volf, 134.

that those who have sinned do not face judgment and consequences for their actions, but it does mean that the relationship is affirmed even as limits are drawn. For Christian communities in particular, the willingness to confess sins and failings before God, one another, and the world, and to extend forgiveness for these things, must shape its practices of hospitality. "What makes a Christian community," writes Nouwen, "is a life of mutual confession and mutual forgiveness in the name of Jesus. Christian community is a faithful fellowship of the weak in which, through a repeated confession and forgiveness of sins, the strength of Jesus Christ is revealed and celebrated."[61] As Christians take part in this discipline and in the regular examination of conscience that ought to accompany it, they may not only come to see how their hospitality has been limited in violent ways but may also find forgiveness for this—and therefore greater freedom to continue the practice, imperfect though it may be—with gratitude for what lies within as well as beyond the limits of hospitality.

The Limits of Virtue

In response to the question of whether human charity (love) can increase indefinitely, Thomas Aquinas stated that "it is not possible to fix any limits to the increase in charity in this life," not only because human charity is "a participation in the infinite charity which is the Holy Ghost" but also because "whenever charity increases, there is a corresponding ability to receive a further increase."[62] That is, humans ought never to rest complacently with the limits of their love, but they ought rather to seek deeper and fuller participation in and communion with the Spirit of infinite charity. As a person grows in her ability to dwell with God—to be a dwelling place, a home, for God—the love of God that she experiences *becomes her own in some real manner.* Precisely for this reason, however, such love necessarily "incurs a limitation, while at the same time retaining its infinity."[63] So too, God's Spirit of infinite welcome and absolute joy can inspire and inhabit even the limits of human hospitality. I have tried in this chapter to show some specific ways that human individuals and communities can grow in both their capacity to welcome others and their

---

[61] Nouwen, *Peacework*, 102.

[62] Thomas Aquinas, *Summa Theologica*, trans. Fathers of the English Dominican Province (Notre Dame, IN: Ave Maria Press, 1948), II-II, q. 24, a. 7.

[63] Gérard Gilleman, *The Primacy of Charity in Moral Theology*, trans. William Ryan and André Vachon (Westminster, MD: Newman Press, 1959), 157.

awareness of limits through disciplines that are, in a sense, hospitality to God. In concluding this chapter, however, I want to make a few remarks concerning the limits of virtue—that is, concerning the problems related to evil, discernment, and imperfection. However, with Aquinas, I do not think it is possible to "fix" limits to human love or hospitality—the lives of the saints provide many examples of extravagantly selfless love and courage—but this does not mean that there are not limitations all the same.

The first point I want to make is to recognize the existence of deep and horrifying evil in human life—acts that involve such violence, cruelty, depravity, and malice that they seem to be of a different magnitude or category than the harms caused by fear, brokenness, or even self-centeredness. Sadly, it is all too easy to cite examples of this, although the crimes that have come to be known as "home invasions" are often particularly horrific and violent distortions of hospitality.[64] There can be no explanation or justification of such evil, and it is absolutely not my intention to say that, with just a little more practice in virtue, we can or ought to welcome those who commit such acts—nor will it always be an option to draw nonviolent limits when another person is intent on harming our families or others for whom we are responsible. Perhaps physical restraint or debilitation without serious injury is possible, and if so, this should always be preferred to lethal force. At the end of the day, I would not deny a parent's right to defend his or her children in whatever way necessary—but it should be entirely clear that at this point *we are no longer talking about hospitality*. One could argue that in such a case my hospitality to my *children* requires my violence toward the intruder, but here too, the hospitable relationship between myself and my children already seems to be so compromised by the presence of violence that such situations should not be made normative. Perhaps the most profound hospitality that can be offered to perpetrators of evil is to try to understand and to forgive, to continue to affirm the image of God—however distorted or fragmented—in such people.

The second point I want to make in relation to the limits of virtue relates back to the fact that in many situations, the best choice is far from clear. It is for this reason that I frequently use the language of "discernment," in which a decision has a strong subjective component; it is as much the perceptive ability of the discerner as the presence of objectively

---

[64] See, for example, Cathleen Kaveny, "A Horrific Crime: But Is Execution the Answer?" *Commonweal* (December 17, 2010), at commonwealmagazine.org/horrific-crime, accessed 7/08/11.

right and wrong choices that is decisive. I am not necessarily referring to formal processes of discernment such as those prescribed by Ignatius of Loyola's *Spiritual Exercises*—in the context of hospitality, a person or community seldom has such a protracted period in which to make a decision—although familiarity with such practices of discernment is likely to contribute to the ability to make good decisions more generally. Precisely because hospitality often requires a decision "in the moment," it is all the more important that a person is able to spontaneously make a decision that honors both the limits and spirit of hospitality. Yet this does not make it easy, nor does it guarantee a good decision. In an interesting and relevant passage on "the limits of submission," Foster writes:

> Often the limits of submission are extremely hard to define. What about the marriage partner who feels stifled and kept from personal fulfillment because of the spouse's professional career? Is this a legitimate form of self-denial or is it destructive? . . . These are extremely complicated questions simply because human relationships are complicated. They are questions that do not yield simplistic answers. There is no such thing as a law of submission that will cover every situation. We must become highly skeptical of all laws that purport to handle every circumstance. Casuistic ethics always fail. It is not an evasion of the issue to say that in defining the limits of submission we are catapulted into a deep dependence upon the Holy Spirit. The Spirit is an accurate discerner . . . [who] will be to us a present Teacher and Prophet, instructing us what to do in every situation.[65]

Be as it may that the Spirit speaks truth to us in every situation, there are some choices that will be incredibly difficult all the same. While helpful and necessary to the practice of hospitality, the gifts and virtues developed through spiritual disciplines will not always be sufficient to provide a concrete decision that is perfectly free from error and violence. As I said at the end of the last chapter, virtue is not a fail-safe solution to the challenges raised by the practice of hospitality. Nonetheless, better and better practices come from those who have the humility to admit error as well as the fortitude to persist despite their failings.

For as long as we have human blood flowing through our veins, our spiritual lives, our loves, and our hospitality will remain imperfect. One of the reasons why Nouwen's perspective on spirituality is so profound is

---

[65] Foster, *Celebration of Discipline*, 121.

because of his recognition that spiritual growth is seldom a linear march toward complete wholeness and perfection. Rather, our fears and hostilities and illusions and wounds remain with us, surfacing every so often, even as they are transformed by gratitude to grace:

> To live this short time in the Spirit of Jesus Christ means to reach out from the midst of pains and to let them be turned into joy by the love of him who came within our reach. We do not have to deny or avoid our loneliness, our hostilities and illusions. To the contrary: when we have the courage to let these realities come to our full attention, understand them and confess them, then they can slowly be converted into solitude, hospitality, and prayer. This does not imply that a mature spiritual life is one in which our old lonely hostile self with all its illusions simply disappears and we live in complete serenity with a peaceful mind and a pure heart. . . . Transformed in love, however, these painful signs become signs of hope, as the wounds of Jesus did for the doubting Thomas. Once God has touched us in the midst of our struggles and has created in us the burning desire to be forever united with him, we will find the courage and the confidence to prepare his way and to invite all who share our life to wait with us during this short time for the day of complete joy.[66]

Amen. Thanks be to God.

---

[66] Nouwen, *Reaching Out*, 161–62.

Chapter 3

The Limits of Identity

Like JC, Lanay[1] was one of the first people I remember meeting when I moved to South Bend. She had been living at the Catholic Worker on St. Joseph Street for several months when I came there for dinner the first time, and my sense was that she occupied that liminal yet wide and common dwelling place in a House of Hospitality, the space between "Worker" and "guest." Though the nature of this distinction—or lack thereof—will become clearer in chapter 5, one very crude rule for marking this difference designates as "guests" those who come to a house because they need a place to stay, while "Workers" are those who come out of personal commitment or curiosity and who take responsibility for the practice of hospitality. Yet it is often the case that those who come out of need become some of the most committed and responsible members of a community, and those who initially come for ideological reasons soon realize that they need the house and its guests even more than they are needed there.

On that first evening that I came to dinner in the backyard of the Women's House (dinner is held nightly at 6:30 p.m. and open to all), Lanay was working to coordinate an open-mic café night at Our Lady of the Road and was looking for performers to share a song or poem, so I volunteered to sing and play guitar. Lanay herself is a talented poet, and at the café night she shared some of her work, which I found beautiful and moving. Though she and I didn't really speak much or spend a lot of time together, I regularly saw her at dinner or other events around the Worker over the months that followed the café night, and I learned that she had been a student at Notre Dame for several years before withdrawing because of some sort of emotional breakdown. Originally from Houston, Texas—though with no trace of a southern accent—Lanay apparently had always found the winters in South Bend challenging, and indeed there were numerous times when I saw her through that first year that she

[1] This name has been changed.

seemed moody and depressed. Though I didn't really know the whole story, I had gathered that beyond the harshness of Michiana winters, Lanay had a number of other challenges to face on a daily basis as a survivor of childhood sexual abuse and a difficult family background.

That was really the extent of my contact with Lanay for most of the first year that I knew her, but at the end of the following August, she called me to say that while she had been out of town that month, her room at the Worker had been given away and she was without a place to live. This seemed strange to me, so I called a friend on the staff and asked her what was going on. Apparently, there had been a conflict between Lanay and members of the staff over whether she should go on a retreat at an abbey several hours away. Staff members thought that she should stay closer to South Bend, but Lanay insisted on going. My friend indicated that Lanay's departure from the house "was not graceful" and that I should not feel obligated to put her up at my house (in addition to the attic room, I had a small second bedroom for guests). I had significant reservations: even apart from the stipulations in my lease, I really didn't *want* a roommate long term, and especially not a roommate whom I barely knew with emotional problems and no job. But we agreed that she would find somewhere else after two weeks, and so she came to stay at my house.

For those first two weeks that Lanay stayed with me, she got up around the same time as I did, and I dropped her off on campus at Notre Dame or sometimes at her therapist or St. Margaret's House, a day center for women that offers a variety of programs and support services. I soon realized that she is quite the social butterfly, as well as thoughtful, artistic, and articulate. Like me, she keeps a regular journal (we have almost identical handwriting!), and in addition to making beautiful silk painting and photography, she is a culinary artist. At the beginning of the second week, we went grocery shopping so that she could buy ingredients to make dinner for the two of us and one of our mutual friends. I recall being delighted and humbled by the fact that she bought artisan lettuce, organic radishes, cilantro, bean sprouts, and other delicacies with food stamps in order to prepare a beautiful meal for us—it seemed the guest had become the host!

I found myself genuinely appreciating her company and increasingly admiring her spirit and resilience as I realized what completely different worlds we came from and what tremendous challenges she had overcome. She grew up in a broken and chaotic family background—she had never met her father and had moved with her mother and half brother around some rough areas of Houston, sometimes staying in shelters and moving more than once a year. She had been repeatedly sexually abused by her stepfather from age eleven to thirteen, and she left home at seventeen to live at Covenant House, a shelter for homeless teens. A quiet and thoughtful child, she says she always felt out of place in the world in which she grew up and would escape from the chaos through reading. She did well in school and applied to top colleges, earning scholarships everywhere she applied—including Harvard and the University of Notre Dame.

Due to pressures from her family to enter a lucrative profession, she enrolled at Notre Dame as a premedicine major but soon realized that this was not for her. Despite making many friends and taking on a number of leadership roles, a variety of academic and social pressures and the cold and dark winter days got to be too much for her. In March of 2009, she attempted to commit suicide by overdosing on lithium, which she regularly took to treat bipolar disorder. Though a sensitive friend had suspected that she was in trouble and she was able to receive the medical attention necessary to save her life, she was forced to take a medical leave of absence from the university and subsequently went to live at the Catholic Worker. I met her several months later. When she moved on from my house to stay with other friends at the end of the two weeks, I was actually kind of sad to see Lanay go, but I found great joy in experiencing firsthand the way that hospitality can build bridges between different social worlds, turning strangers into friends.

Sadly, the months that she was without a permanent place to stay in the fall were only the beginning of another string of challenges for Lanay. She eventually found a place to live and received wonderful news that she had been awarded an artist's fellowship to work on her poetry at the Vermont Studio Center for the following summer. Things seemed to be looking up, but no sooner had she begun to settle into that house than she was raped by an unknown man who had broken in while she was in the shower. Other friends and I came together to support her through that time, and once again I was amazed by her strength and resilience. In January she moved out of that house and took a job as a live-in nanny for a family with three small children on the other side of town. When I first talked to her about her new job, it sounded like she was making the best of a chaotic and frustrating situation—erratic hours with a tantrum-prone four-year-old and his baby brother—but by the end of February it was clear that the situation was even worse than it had seemed. Not only was she being paid criminally low wages to be "on call" with the kids practically 24/7 (even to the point that she was forced to miss appointments with her therapist), but she also had to deal with the parents' tantrums and messes as well as those of the children. One weekend at the end of February, after the mother—who was expecting a fourth child within weeks—yelled at her, I told Lanay she should move in with me for the rest of the spring. Never mind the lease, I thought; I was moving in a few months anyway.

Unlike the fall when I had been nervous and somewhat reluctant to make space for Lanay as a long-term guest, this time I actually cleared out the spare room so she could settle in—and she did it so beautifully that it was a gift in itself. She brought her art—including a framed set of sepia-toned photos that she had taken on a service trip in Appalachia and a high café table that she had decoupaged with thoughtful and clever quotes clipped from magazines—as well as her poetry and thoughtfulness. Soon after Lanay moved in, friends gathered at "our" house for evenings of music and poetry and fellowship. That spring she applied and was accepted for readmission to the university to complete her degree, and her personal statement was an inspiring testament to the graces of gratitude and community.

Although I occasionally found myself missing the space that I had to myself (Lanay is a big woman), or getting annoyed when she used my computer, or feeling resentful that she seemed to be just "hanging out" while I was working, I was aware that in general these had more to do with the selfish limits of my own hospitality than anything she did or failed to do. For the most part, it was great to have her as a guest, and even though I always remained, in a certain way, host in that particular situation, there were also times when she made me feel like a special guest in my own home. She allowed me to experience the way in which both the distinctive identities and the delightful fluidity in the relationship between hosts and guests shape the experience of hospitality. In early May, Lanay left for Houston, where she visited with friends and family before embarking on an artistic-poetic summer adventure in New England. She hopes to complete her degree in studio art from the University of Notre Dame in 2012.

Hospitality as the Relationship of Host and Guest[2]

The rest of this chapter and the following consider in greater detail the conditions that make hospitality possible and practical—conditions

[2] Although the following sections are important to the conceptual argument about the nature of hospitality that I am presenting in this book, readers with less taste for abstract discourse may want to skim this and proceed to the section on "Hospitality and Christian Identity."

that must be held in tension with a spirit of unconditional hospitality if they are not to become so fixed as to rule out hospitality altogether. If a person or community were to try to get rid of such limits entirely, however, hospitality would cease to be, instead developing into a violation of the relationship between host and guest (when the identity of one or the other is destroyed or deemed inferior) or dissolving into an entirely different sort of relationship. In a sense, these limits *define* hospitality—they mark out its boundaries, they identify what it is—but at the same time, as a relationship between "strangers," hospitality is also very much about *crossing* boundaries and eluding attempts to define it once and for all.

I actually mean to indicate two separate tensions when I refer to the "limits of identity" (or a tension between identity and indeterminacy) in this chapter. First, hospitality requires the identities of host and guest *as such*. In this sense, the *difference between* host and guest (and the roles that they play) is more significant than any positive identifying features of either; the important thing is that a distinction between host and guest is preserved. That is, without host and guest, without a home (bounded space) that is somehow distinguishable from its surroundings, it does not make much sense to speak of hospitality. At the same time, however, as is indicated by the definition of hospitality as "partnership with strangers" or many biblical or anecdotal accounts of hospitality, there is also indeterminacy and fluidity in these roles; the best experiences of hospitality are often those in which guests also take on some of the roles of hosts and hosts also experience the presence of their guests as refreshment and gift. In such cases, the distinction between host and guest is maintained in some sense, but who is who is not always entirely clear: the identities of host and guest are in tension with indeterminacy and openness.

Second, the identities of hosts and guests are important to hospitality in the sense of the positive features of a person or community that make it who or what it is (qualities such as religious or professional background, nationality, gender, race, ethnicity, and the stories and practices that pertain to each of these). Just as a house must be inhabited in some way to be hospitable, the distinctive personal and communal identities of hosts and guests are part of what makes hospitality meaningful. On the other hand, when people and communities seek to avoid indeterminacy and change through violent means, this can give rise to some of the worst forms of hostility. In both of these ways, then—with respect to difference and to identity—limits of hospitality must also be open to indeterminacy in light of the deconstructive but necessary pull of absolute hospitality.

These dynamics are present in any practice of hospitality, yet they take on distinctive significance in relation to Christian identity and hospitality, which will be the focus of the second part of this chapter.

While hospitality may be understood as a certain set of actions (e.g., offering a friendly greeting, providing food and drink and a place to rest, engaging in conversation) or a disposition of openness, at the most essential level hospitality entails a *relationship between hosts and guests in a specific place and time*. In terms of the concept of hospitality and as well as in its practice, hospitality requires both differentiation and identity—but each must also remain in tension with a spirit of openness if limits of identity are to remain hospitable.

Hospitality and Difference

The well-known optical illusion that may be seen as either two dark faces silhouetted against a white backdrop or as a white vase contrasted with a black background (sometimes called Rubin's vase) is probably familiar to most readers. It is significant here because it represents how difference (black/white, figure/background) is fundamental to identity (face/vase) but also because it shows the way in which identity may be shifting and indeterminate. An object—or a community, or a person, or a space—is identifiable as what it *is* in part because it can be differentiated from what it *is not*. Not only in optical illusions such as this but in human experience more generally, perceptions of difference are often crucial to perceptions of identity: "this" is distinct from "that," "inside" is distinguishable from "outside," "we" are different from "them." Just as a teacher would not be a teacher without the existence of a student and a mother or father must have a child in order to be a parent, host and guest rely upon each other for their identities as such. Without this differentiation it would make little sense to speak of hospitality.

At the same time, however, it is not uncommon for guests and hosts to experience a certain role reversal in which the stranger is the one who provides refreshment and a sense of orientation or bestows some gift or honor upon his hosts. In fact, sometimes it is *only* with the presence of guests—the opportunity to be hospitable—that one really comes to feel at home at all, as food is shared and memories are formed. As noted in the first chapter's description of Weather Amnesty, it often seemed that many of those deemed "guests" because they had nowhere else to stay were in fact more at home at Our Lady of the Road than their "hosts" on a given night; in cases such as this, one wonders, "Who is *really* a guest?" This fluid-ity or indeterminacy in the distinction between host and guest is nowhere more clearly seen than in the life of Jesus, who welcomed people into the kingdom of God even as he broke bread in the homes of others. Amos Yong points out that from his conception in Mary's womb to his burial in the tomb of Joseph of Arimathea and throughout his ministry, Jesus is "the exemplary recipient of hospitality," and yet "those who welcome Jesus into their homes become, in turn, guests of the redemptive hospitality of God."[3]

Again, it is important here to emphasize that the most basic distinction between hosts and guests is not because of intrinsic and fixed differences between them but is rather a function of their relationship to a particular space. It is interesting to note, in fact, that in a number of languages—for example, Greek, Latin, and French—the same word is used for both "host" and "guest" so that their meanings are entirely dependent on the *context* in which they occur. I am not intrinsically a host or a guest, nor is my neigh-bor—rather, when she comes to visit me, I am a host and she is a guest. When I come to her house, these roles are reversed. That is, in addition to the presence of a guest, a host is a host because she is "at home" in a given space—a neighborhood or office or church, for example—which is distinguishable from other spaces. Likewise, a guest is a guest because he is in some way foreign to that space and because (leaving aside the ques-tion of unwelcome guests for the moment) he is willingly received by a host. To state this differently, we might say that the verb "to welcome" is not only transitive ("I welcome *you*") but also locative ("I welcome you *into my home*"). Even if the space that a guest is being welcomed into is metaphorical—in the sense of welcoming another person into one's life or social group—we might still say that welcome implies welcome *into* somewhere that is distinct from other spaces. Thus, the roles of host and guest are dependent on the differentiation of spaces established by the walls of a house, the borders of a territory, or criteria for membership in a particular community. While such boundaries and roles are essential to hospitality, there is also a sense in which hospitality itself serves to de-construct them: hospitality requires not only the enclosure of walls that separates the home from the street but also the permeability of doorways that allows admission and passage from one to the other. Hospitality aims

---

[3] Amos Yong, *Hospitality and the Other: Pentecost, Christian Practices, and the Neighbor* (Maryknoll, NY: Orbis, 2008), 101–2.

to make the guest feel that he is at home, that he has a place, even if he is away from home and out of place.

For this reason, one might say that there are temporal as well as spatial limits to hospitality, not only in the sense that indefinite or long-term guests may arouse the resentment of their hosts by burdening the resources of the household, but also because as a person comes to find a place or settle into his new surroundings over time, he should come to feel and act less and less like a guest. As Harry Murray explains in his study of the Catholic Worker, hospitality is distinguished by its "intermediate" time frame: "At the lower end of the time frame, one must speak of gift-giving rather than hospitality. However, at some indeterminate point of duration, in most cultures one would no longer speak of hospitality. A guest who stays for weeks, months, or years usually must be adopted into the group."[4] That is, on the one hand, even when a guest has no intention of settling permanently, after a certain amount of time (traditionally—among monastic communities, for example—two or three days), it is reasonable to expect him or her to contribute to the work of the household or community in some way. In other cases—such as welcoming a new family to a neighborhood, or new members to a church, or immigrants to a nation—one could say that hospitality must point beyond itself, from the relationship of host and guest to the reception of guests as full members of a community. Paradoxically, it would be a sign that a community or place was somewhat inhospitable if newcomers were permanently regarded as guests rather than recognized as full members who also identify with and are responsible for it. This inhospitable characterization of some as hosts and others as permanent guests and outsiders is not an uncommon pattern in the context of the relationship between immigrants and citizens.[5] Because indeterminacy has been replaced by an impermeable boundary and fixed roles, the tension between openness and limits—and therefore hospitality itself—has been lost.

In the case of literal, physical boundaries, it is not difficult to imagine a hospitable boundary in contrast to a hostile or inhospitable one: screen doors and sheer curtains, unlocked gates and unmarked property

[4] Harry Murray, Do Not Neglect Hospitality: The Catholic Worker and the Homeless (Philadelphia: Temple University Press, 1990), 19.

[5] Cf. Michael Waltzer, Spheres of Justice: A Defense of Pluralism and Equality (New York: Basic Books, 1983), 316–18; William Barbieri, The Ethics of Citizenship (Durham, NC: Duke University Press, 1998); Ali Behdad, A Forgetful Nation: On Immigration and Cultural Identity in the United States (Durham, NC, and London: Duke University Press, 2005).

lines contrasted with high, thick walls, alarm systems, electric fences, and barbed wire. In many cases, however, the contrast between hospitable and inhospitable boundaries is not quite so obvious. Especially with respect to communities of people, the quality of their boundaries is influenced by a number of often invisible factors, one of the most important being members' understanding of their difference from those outside the community. Are others seen as inferior, possible "contaminants" to the purity of the group? Or are those who are different regarded with curiosity or even honor? Hospitable limits of identity must involve a relationship to others that does not try to annul or annihilate differences but rather strives to welcome others precisely in and through the ways that they are different.

In *Just Hospitality: God's Welcome in a World of Difference*, Letty Russell characterizes hospitality as "reaching out across difference to participate in God's actions bringing justice and healing" in place of the fear of "others."[6] Difference is crucial to Russell's definition of hospitality; at the same time, hospitality is also a movement to *reach across* the limits and boundaries that difference creates. Here and throughout her work, Russell is committed to challenging views that essentialize otherness in ways that deny or demean the humanity of those who differ from a dominant identity. Human history—with its legacies of tribalism, slavery, colonization, misogyny, and coerced orthodoxy—is replete with examples of how difference has been used to justify domination. Rather than pluralism being an indication of deviation from God's will, Russell argues that God's intention for creation is to make "a world of riotous difference."[7] In light of this, she claims that "there are no others, for all are created by God and no one is an *other*,"[8] and that differences—of gender, race, language, religion, and sexuality, for example—are not something to be feared or violently excluded but are rather God's gifts to humankind. Hospitality is never simply more of "the same" but is rather a way of affirming difference and distinctiveness while also refusing to let such differences become grounds for violence and domination.

But, one might ask, would it not be a more helpful approach to hospitality to emphasize features that all humans share in common? Furthermore, is it not inherently antagonistic and even violent to define identities in

[6] Letty Russell, *Just Hospitality: God's Welcome in a World of Difference* (Louisville, KY: Westminster John Knox, 2009), 101.

[7] Ibid., 53–54.

[8] Letty Russell, "Encountering the 'Other' in a World of Difference and Danger," *Harvard Theological Review* 99.4 (2006): 458.

terms of contrast or opposition? In response to the first question, while it might be true that there are aspects of human nature or experience that are universal, in many cases differences (rooted in the particularities of embodiment and social location) are far more pronounced. It may be true that at least some minimal conviction about universal human nature is necessarily to hospitality. Nonetheless, basing one's practice of hospitality on a belief in ultimate similarities can lead either to the creation of a superficial gloss of "sameness" that covers over real differences between people or to the restriction of hospitality to those with whom such similarities are more readily apparent. By starting from the idea that hospitality invites—even requires—difference, a person or community is better prepared to attend to the distinctive voices of their guests and to extend a spirit of welcome even to those whose differences may be perplexing or unsettling. Moreover, a deeper and truer sense of partnership and common humanity actually comes through attention to and harmonization of difference rather than the assumption of sameness. With respect to the second question, it is precisely the antagonism of us-versus-them notions of difference and identity that hospitality seeks to avoid. Therefore, if they are to be hospitable limits, the boundaries of a space or a community cannot be based solely on opposition but must also be formed by their own distinctive and dynamic features and stories.

Hospitality and Identity

While the differentiation of spaces and of hosts and guests is a necessary condition of hospitality, other more positive aspects of identity are also crucial to ensuring that boundaries and differences are not the end of the story. When walls and boundaries exist primarily for the purpose of keeping out or defending against difference, they are not hospitable. Furthermore, because identities (especially those of groups) are not static or internally uniform, defining a space or community exclusively by what it is *not* may fail to account for the dynamism and difference within it. Hospitality involves the interaction of particular people, places, and identities—and therefore requires more than the mere crossing of boundaries. As suggested by Nouwen's conception of hospitality as an "articulate presence" that allows for "participation in plentitude" rather than an empty house, hospitality requires not simply the abstract roles of hosts and guests but their personal presence to one another. There must not only be spaces but also *places* of hospitality.

Although writers have different ways of understanding the difference between these two terms, for many the notion of space is neutral and abstract, whereas *places* are particular, concrete, and endowed with human meanings and values. A place, then, is not just about some specific geographic location but also involves a relationship with the events and personal narratives that have occurred or passed through there. The distinctive features and accumulated memories—whether of a house, a classroom, a neighborhood, or a church—not only differentiate it from other places but also *inhabit* it and give content as well as form to its hospitality (or, in some cases, its hostility). Just as human identities are formed by and move through places—I was born in such and such a place, went to school here and there, lived on this street or in that town—so too are places given identities and significance by the human events that have taken place there. Walter Brueggemann writes that

> place is space that has historical meanings, where some things have happened that are now remembered and provide continuity and identity across generations. Place is space in which important words have been spoken that have established identity, defined vocation, and envisioned destiny. Place is space in which vows have been exchanged, promises have been issued, and demands have been made. . . . Humanness, as biblical faith promises it, will be found in belonging to and referring to that particular locus in which the historicity of a community has been expressed and to which recourse is made for the purposes of orientation, assurance, and empowerment.[9]

The identity-in-place of hospitality intends to provide precisely such an orientation, assurance, and empowerment to both guests and hosts. Christine Pohl offers a lovely description of the sense of peace and restfulness that characterizes hospitable places, which are "comfortable and lived in," providing "shelter and sanctuary in the deepest sense." Hospitable places recognize the guest's separate identity without calling attention to the fact that she is an outsider. Although such places need not be beautifully maintained or decorated, they show both care and character: they express "an appreciation for life which has more to do with taking time than having money" and are "alive with particular commitments and practices."[10]

[9] Walter Brueggemann, *The Land: Place as Gift, Promise, and Challenge in Biblical Faith* (Philadelphia: Fortress, 1977), 10.

[10] Christine Pohl, *Making Room: Recovering Hospitality as a Christian Tradition* (Grand Rapids, MI: Eerdmans, 1999), 152–53.

It is not my intention here to provide a theory of personal and communal identity or an in-depth account of identity formation. Nonetheless, some such account is called for in light of the claim that hospitality involves the tension between stable identities and the dynamic indeterminacy of human encounters. I am quite aware of critiques of identity (not least from Derrida and others influenced by poststructuralism) and the potential for violence that can be—and historically often has been—a result of the desire to maintain a stable and homogenous identity in the face of difference. Rather than simply rejecting identity, however (or accepting it as something violent and oppressive yet inevitable), it seems important to cultivate understandings of identity that see an appreciation of difference and the evolution of people and communities as compatible with—perhaps even necessary to—a robust sense of identity.

Because they occur not only in space but also in time, human identities—whether individual or collective—are not so much fixed collections of attributes as they are the evolving and multiple narratives of struggle and celebration, affiliation and encounter, trauma and triumph. Our individual and collective identities are obviously not something that we choose and create *ex nihilo*, but neither are we entirely passive in their formation; rather, identity is a complex mixture of givenness and freedom. "We tell of who we are, of the 'I' that we are by means of a narrative. 'I was born on such and such a date, as the daughter of such and such . . .' etc.," explains Seyla Benhabib. Such narratives "are deeply colored and structured by the codes of expectable and understandable biographies and identities in our cultures . . . , but nevertheless we must still argue that we are not merely extensions of our histories, that vis-à-vis our own stories we are in the position of author and character at once."[11]

The notion of authorship is suggestive, for identity is a matter not only of concrete actions and affirmations but also of the way a person (or group) *tells* of such things, the ways in which particular significance is ascribed to some events or relationships while other engagements may be disavowed altogether. For this reason, self-deception is always a danger "as we systematically delude ourselves to maintain the story that has hitherto assured our identity. We hesitate to spell out certain engagements when spelling them out would jeopardize the set of avowals we have made

---

[11] Seyla Benhabib, "Feminism and Postmodernism: An Uneasy Alliance," in *Feminist Contentions: A Philosophical Exchange*, ed. Linda Nicholson (New York and London: Routledge, 1995), 21.

about ourselves."[12] Learning to tell a "truthful" story, which is essential to a nonviolent identity, requires the courage to "spell out" the things we do—that is, to name them as what they are rather than renarrating them to better cohere with an illusory sense of who we are—which comes from the belief that we are "constituted by a story given to us by a power beyond our will or imagination."[13] In many, if not most, circumstances, truthfulness also requires forgiveness, as we learn to honestly confess our faults before God and one another.

Furthermore, just as the interaction between characters in a story often does not destroy but rather deepens their own understanding of who they are—even if such interaction is adversarial or full of tension—so too can encounters with others in the context of hospitality deepen our own self-understanding. "My discovering my own identity doesn't mean that I work it out in isolation," writes Charles Taylor, "but that I negotiate it through dialogue, partly overt, partly internal, with others."[14] The identities of the self and the other thereby become a part of one another even as they maintain their distinctiveness. The stories we tell about ourselves—as individuals and as communities—help to provide us with a sense of orientation: they tell us not only *who* but also *where* we are, in both a literal and a metaphorical sense. Even within an enclosed and safe space, the experience of lostness and displacement—particularly when it is not embedded in any larger narrative that provides identity and meaning—can significantly limit the practice of hospitality. For this reason one might say that hospitality requires not only abstract (if bounded) space but also the places of meaning that our narrative-identity passes through or dwells within.

But is it really possible to create such places of meaning and hospitality today in an increasingly globalized and rootless world? In her writing on hospitality, Elizabeth Newman expresses concern over the way in which modern society—particularly in North America—is characterized by a "loss of place." This experience of a loss of place is not only a result of

---

[12] Stanley Hauerwas with David Burrell, "Self-Deception and Autobiography: Reflections on Speer's *Inside the Third Reich*," in *The Hauerwas Reader*, ed. John Berkman and Michael Cartwright (Durham, NC: Duke University Press, 2001), 206. Cf. Michael Goldberg, *Theology and Narrative: A Critical introduction* (Nashville: Abingdon, 1981), 104–9; Herbert Fingarette, *Self-Deception* (New York: Humanities Press, 1969).

[13] Ibid., 207.

[14] Charles Taylor, "The Politics of Recognition," in *Multiculturalism and the Politics of Recognition*, ed. Amy Gutmann (Princeton, NJ: Princeton University Press, 1994), 34.

the increased mobility (and virtual realities) of many contemporary individuals but also due to the homogeneity of airports, shopping malls, and housing subdivisions. While she acknowledges the ways in which attachments to places and traditions can be constraining and even oppressive, she is concerned that "with no concrete place of orientation, hospitality will be subject to the whims of the dominant economic and political forces."[15] Newman encourages Christian communities to reinvigorate their sense of the church as *oikos*—the Greek term meaning "household"—through a renewed understanding of worship as hospitality. In fact, the practice of hospitality not only flows out of but is a step toward the recovery of a sense of home and place, whether or not the individuals, households, and communities that practice it are themselves Christian. As the next section will show, the "place" of Christian identity *does* have a particular relationship to hospitality; wherever and however the practice of hospitality occurs, though, it can offer a foundation for a sense of place as human narratives converge and meaningfully reshape the spaces they occupy.

Hospitality and Christian Identity

The tensions that I have just described as limiting conditions (or perhaps conditional limits) of hospitality—between openness and boundaries, similarity and differentiation, identity and change—also apply in particular ways to the hospitality of Christians. As with hospitality in general, on one hand, Christian hospitality depends on the differentiation of Christian communities from society as a whole and on the distinct narratives and practices that orient and inform (i.e., provide positive identity to) that distinction. Critical of the notion that Christian worship is simply "inclusivity," Newman claims that "Christian hospitality disappears when the distinction between church and world is collapsed."[16] On the other hand, hospitality also requires that the boundaries of difference between church and world—the limits of identity—not be so definitive as to become hostile and unwelcoming.

Even as she is critical of some of the inhospitable ways that Christians have claimed a distinctive identity, Letty Russell forcefully articulates

---

[15] Elizabeth Newman, *Untamed Hospitality: Welcoming God and Other Strangers* (Grand Rapids, MI: Brazos Press, 2007), 35.

[16] Ibid., 43.

the relationship between the identity and hospitality of the Christian community:

> For Christians . . . hospitality is limited or finds its definition in the story of the One in whose name we gather. Therefore one of the limits of hospitality is commitment to Christ as the center of the life of the church. The stranger needs to be welcomed by a community that is able to practice hospitality. If a community has no sense of its identity in Christ as the center of its life, it will not have a great deal of generosity and compassion to share with others. Just as persons cannot give themselves away if they have no sense of self-worth to share, churches with no sense of identity and worth will have little to share. It is our identity in Christ who welcomes the stranger that leads us to join in the task of hospitality.[17]

Not unlike Nouwen's claim that hospitality is grounded in the experiences of solitude and prayer, Russell here points to the way in which the hospitality of the Christian community must have as its foundation the stories and practices that establish Christ as the center of its life. Many of these stories and practices have already been discussed in the previous chapters, although in what follows here I intend to offer a more sustained discussion of the vexing question of "Christian identity." Though most Christians would endorse Russell's statement that Jesus Christ is at the center of Christian identity, the proliferation of denominations and schisms within the church and the dramatically different understandings of the relationship between church and society testify to the way in which the concrete implications and limits of this center are far from self-evident.

Christian communities have long struggled with the nature of their relationship to the non-Christian world and the extent to which fidelity to the Gospel requires remaining separate—or at least distinct—from the cultures that surround them.[18] Citing the stories of Abraham and the

---

[17] Letty Russell, "Practicing Hospitality in a Time of Backlash," *Theology Today* 52.4 (Jan 1996): 483–84.

[18] H. Richard Niebuhr offers one classic discussion of the various approaches to this "enduring problem" in *Christ and Culture* (San Francisco: HarperSanFrancisco, 2001). I am aware of the complex and ambiguous set of meanings that have historically been ascribed to the word "culture"; insofar as in its contemporary usage "culture" has become "a ubiquitous synonym for identity, an identity marker and differentiator" (Seyla Benhabib, *The Claims of Culture: Equality and Diversity in the Global Era* [Princeton, NJ: Princeton University Press, 2002], 1), however, it is fitting to write of "cultures" in the context of a discussion of collective identity and difference.

apostle Paul, Miroslav Volf argues that the experience of *departure* marks Christian identity, that "at the very core of the Christian identity lies an all-encompassing change of loyalties, from a given culture with its gods to the God of all cultures."[19] As mentioned in the first chapter, Christian identity has long been shaped by the notion of being a people "on pilgrimage" with their true home to be found elsewhere. Yet this experience of departure should not become a flight from or abandonment of the world; rather, the "exculturation" of the Gospel message of God's love is necessary for its inculturation in ways that make "each people fruitful out of its own inner self."[20] It might be said that Christians are "against the world for the world"; that is, the church's "distance" from the culture that surrounds it and its distinctive identity ought not to arise out of enmity or a sense of superiority but rather from the desire to provide a sanctuary or oasis inhabited by a different spirit than that of the world. Rather than limiting Christian hospitality, a sense of pilgrim identity has often served to motivate it by fostering solidarity with others who may be on the margins of society.[21]

But does it really make sense to understand Christianity as a culture unto itself, a way of life and system of values distinct from others? Theologian Kathryn Tanner explains that Christianity is not—nor has it ever been—self-contained or self-sufficient as a culture; rather, Christian practices "are always forced to incorporate material from other ways of life if they are to constitute a whole way of life in themselves."[22] Tanner argues that Christianity borrows and transforms some symbols and practices and rejects others that are present in a surrounding culture, and it is through such interaction that Christian distinctiveness takes shape. Thus, "the distinctiveness of a Christian way of life is not so much formed by the boundary as *at* it: Christian distinctiveness is something that emerges in the very cultural processes occurring at the boundary, processes that construct a distinctive identity."[23] These processes might include Christians'

[19] Miroslav Volf, *Exclusion and Embrace: A Theological Exploration of Identity and Otherness* (Nashville: Abingdon, 1996), 40.

[20] Diego Irarrázaval, *Inculturation: New Dawn of the Church in Latin America*, trans. Phillip Berryman (Maryknoll, NY: Orbis, 2000), 3, 7.

[21] Christine Pohl, "The Significance of Marginality to the Practice of Welcome," *Annual of the Society of Christian Ethics* (1995). Cf. C. Leonard Allen, *The Cruciform Church: Becoming a Cross-Shaped People in a Secular World* (Abilene, TX: ACU Press, 2006), esp. 169–73; and Stanley Hauerwas, "The Servant Community," in *The Hauerwas Reader*, esp. 375–76.

[22] Kathryn Tanner, *Theories of Culture: A New Agenda for Theology* (Minneapolis: Fortress Press, 1997), 112.

[23] Ibid., 115.

particular ways of understanding work as a vocation rather than simply an occupation, ways of celebrating human events such as marriage and birth, distinctive perspectives on art, politics, sexuality, education, hospitality—as well as an overall orientation that is shaped by the elements of spiritual life that I described in the previous chapter. While there are (or ought to be) meaningful differences between Christian and non-Christian ways of life, these boundaries are often fluid and permeable.

Paul Hiebert's reflection on the category "Christian" offers insight into the nature of the "boundary" of Christian identity. Utilizing mathematical set theory, Hiebert explains that categories may be formed either intrinsically, by virtue of what they are "in themselves" (e.g., apples are round, edible fruits of the rosaceous tree), or extrinsically, by their relationship to other things or to a common point of reference (e.g., I am a sister to my brothers because of our relationship to common parents). He also explains that the boundaries of a category may be either "well-formed" or "fuzzy." Whereas in a well-formed set a thing either belongs to the set or is excluded from it by a clear boundary, fuzzy sets have no sharp boundaries—"day becomes night and a mountain turns into a plain without a clear transition."[24] Hiebert contends that Christianity has traditionally been understood as an intrinsically well-formed set, in which Christian identity is defined by believing in and doing certain things according to predefined standards. In this perspective, the boundary between Christian and non-Christian is "important and high, because boundaries define the ultimate nature of reality."[25]

In contrast to this, Hiebert argues that the category "Christian" should be understood as an *extrinsically* well-formed (i.e., "centered") set that is shaped by its members' common relation to something outside themselves. Although centered sets are not formed by drawing definitive boundaries, members of the category *can* be clearly distinguished from those outside of it. The difference between member and nonmember might be best envisioned as a matter of orientation or direction rather than members' intrinsic qualities: members of a centered set are facing or moving toward a common center; nonmembers are turned or moving away from it. The distinction between the church and the world is not some kind of intrinsic or metaphysical difference but rather a distinction between "the basic personal postures of men, some of whom confess and others of whom do not

---

[24] Paul Hiebert, "The Category *Christian* in the Mission Task," in *Anthropological Reflections on Missiological Issues* (Grand Rapids, MI: Baker Books, 1994), 110–11.

[25] Ibid., 116.

confess that Jesus Christ is Lord."[26] By describing Christian identity in this way, Hiebert maintains that the category "Christian" should be understood as inclusive of all those who make Jesus Christ the center or orienting point for their lives—regardless of the particular ways that this orientation shapes their practices. Although there is a clear distinction between Christian and non-Christian, the emphasis of Christian life should be on "exhorting people to follow Christ rather than on excluding others to preserve the purity of the set."[27]

Understanding the distinctiveness of Christian communities in terms of a common orientation—which I would suggest is maintained primarily through the sorts of practices I described in the previous chapter—rather than doctrinal orthodoxy or even moral performance means that the boundaries of such communities may be difficult to specify a priori and may allow for significant variation in Christian belief and practice. Whether or not such indeterminacy serves or undermines Christian hospitality is often precisely where discernment of limits comes in. Does the use of contemporary rock music in worship open a community's center in Christ to those who would find formal liturgy stuffy or unintelligible, or does it distort the community's worship by making it into a form of entertainment? Does affirmation of gay and lesbian relationships indicate a truer understanding of human dignity and divine welcome, or is it a harmful concession to a licentious culture? Does openness to the spiritual insights and practices of the world's religions reflect a humble recognition of God's transcendence, or is it a problematic watering down of Christian truth? Such questions are not always easily answered, but as Tanner suggests, the unity of the Body of Christ is "a unity of task and not necessarily of accomplishment."[28] That is to say, Christians may not understand the same thing by the claim that Jesus is the Son of God or that salvation comes through him, and they may not agree on the method or meaning of baptism in relation to those claims—but only for Christians are these matters of such crucial significance. "What unites Christian practices is not, then, agreement about the beliefs and actions that constitute true discipleship, but a shared sense of the importance of figuring it out."[29]

---

[26] John Howard Yoder, *The Original Revolution: Essays on Christian Pacifism* (Scottsdale, PA: Herald Press, 1971), 110.

[27] Hiebert, "The Category Christian in the Mission Task," 125–26.

[28] Tanner, *Theories of Culture*, 136.

[29] Ibid., 153.

Yet to say that there is indeterminacy in Christian identity is not to say that all claims to it are equally faithful to the center or that there are no parameters of true discipleship. Fidelity to Christ as a community's orienting center not only requires the practice of disciplines that invite the guidance of the Holy Spirit but also attention to the witness of Scripture. "Scripture," writes Stanley Hauerwas, "is the means the church uses to constantly test its memory." The authority of Scripture for the church means that it "sets the agenda and boundaries for a truthful conversation,"[30] but as Hauerwas also regularly emphasizes, an adequate reading of Scripture requires a community formed by particular practices and virtues such as humility, gratitude, courage, forgiveness, hospitality. An approach that looks to some of the orienting narratives of Scripture (e.g., creation/fall/redemption, covenant/idolatry/restoration, incarnation/cross/resurrection) rather than simply proof texting is most adequate for shaping the community's identity and hospitality and for making sense of its own ongoing story.

Thus, Christian hospitality does not simply invite strangers to an "outreach Sunday" service or Bible study or meal but rather welcomes them into the ongoing narrative of God's coming kingdom as proclaimed by Jesus and carried forward in the life of the church. They are also invited into the conversation about the meaning of Jesus' life for the lives of Christians today as that narrative continues to unfold in history in new and possibly surprising ways. Faithfulness to the living Word of God may mean that "as the church we have no right to determine the boundaries of God's kingdom, for it is our happy task to acknowledge God's power to make his kingdom present in the most surprising places and ways."[31] This "happy task" requires that Christian communities must become "three-dimensional" places of hospitality through their hospitality to God, hospitality to one another, and hospitality to strangers.

Three-Dimensional Hospitality

Even as a Christian community's hospitality is shaped by its identity—its center in the story of Christ—so too must its identity be shaped by the practice of hospitality. Christian communities, Christian homes, and Christian hearts ought to be identifiable as *places of hospitality*, spaces that are distinctively inhabited by stories of mercy and gratitude and where the

[30] Stanley Hauerwas, "The Servant Community," in *The Hauerwas Reader*, 373.
[31] Ibid., 377.

Spirit of God is invited to dwell. It may be helpful to think of the identity-forming hospitality of a Christian community as taking shape in three metaphorical dimensions, analogous to the depth, length, and width of a building or room. The foundation, the depth, and the height of Christian welcome is grounded in a community's hospitality to God, recognizing that human practices of hospitality always depend on God's prior invitation and grace. The length of a community's practice of welcome—its duration and sustainability through time—relies on its members' willingness to practice hospitality to one another, while its width points to the ways in which it is able to make room to welcome strangers. Each of these dimensions is necessary to shaping a habitable place, and each can impose crushing and violent limits if disregarded.

As the previous chapter explained in greater detail, through spiritual disciplines such as prayer, fasting, celebration, service, rest, and confession, communities make a place for God in their midst. Once again, this is not to suggest that Christian hospitality can exist independently of God's hospitality but rather that a community's openness to the living God requires deliberate attention to the new and strange ways that God may be speaking to its members, perhaps affirming their sense of identity, but perhaps calling them beyond doctrinal formulations or the comfort of tradition and more deeply toward their center in Christ. Rather than attending primarily to identity boundaries, a community's sense of itself and of the distinctive place into which it welcomes others should be shaped from that center outward. Because of Jesus Christ's identification with strangers and outsiders, moreover, deeper movement toward the center will also paradoxically draw a community's attention outward toward its margins, thus expanding the boundaries and limits, the depth and the height, of hospitality.

The opening of human hearts to God is the basic precondition for the opening of human hearts to one another. The second dimension of a place of hospitality involves reaching across difference within the household of Christian faith, which I am likening to the *length* of such a place. Of course, one might argue that it is fine for theoretical purposes to understand Christian identity as an "unfinished task" with Christ at its center, but what does this actually say to the highly particular and seemingly irreconcilable conflicts that often give rise to division and hostility within Christianity itself? How does a community's center in Christ help to resolve more specific concerns about who "we" are at the level of a local church or soup kitchen or even a Christian denomination? How does its hospitality to God address disputes over how a church should make use of its facilities or finances, the style of music or language used in worship, or who is entitled to preside at or receive the Lord's Supper?

In describing Christian identity as broadly as I did above, I do not mean to deny the significance of more particular and concrete identities that have been shaped by the history, context, needs, and gifts of a particular community. The ecumenism that underlies my perspective here is based not on a watered-down sense of the essence of Christianity, as if such an essence could be separated from its incarnation in very particular ways, but rather on the conviction that God both transcends and is present in many different communities' ways of following Christ. It is always through the "doorway" of a particular community that people are welcomed into God's love, and the different shapes that Christian community legitimately can assume are a way of speaking to different people and contexts in ways that are intelligible to them—a continuation of the spirit of Pentecost, in which "in our own languages we hear them speaking about God's mighty deeds of power" (Acts 2:11).

The pluralism of Christian expression can be a source of richness, beauty, and hospitality, but communities can also be at risk of subordinating their fidelity to the task of discipleship to their own particular fixed notions of identity. While they need not be timid in their judgments about what the Word of God requires at a particular place and time, Christians must also humbly remain aware of the limitations of their own perspective and willing to extend hospitality to other Christians with whom they differ. "United in the expectation that a purer witness will come of such efforts to work through their disagreements," Tanner writes, "participants must show a willingness to listen and be corrected if necessary by all others similarly concerned about the true nature of Christian discipleship. Others are worth listening to—if not ultimately agreeing with—to the extent that they have made the effort sincerely."[32]

When the differences within and between Christian communities become a source of hostility rather than ground for dialogue, they will find themselves significantly limited in their ability to be places of hospitality. Regardless of its ostensible desire to be welcoming to others, a household that is full of internal strife and animosity is unlikely to be hospitable to those outside (especially if the reasons for such fighting make little sense to those unacquainted with the history of the disagreement). Rather, "a

[32] Tanner, *Theories of Culture*, 125.

hallmark of the church should be the ability of believers to discuss, listen, encourage, and love. We should be able to disagree without acrimony. We should be known, of all people, as instruments of peace, as agents of reconciliation. We ought to love one another so profoundly, serve one another so aggressively, listen to each other so passionately, and respond to each other so humbly, that the Kingdom of God breaks in among us."[33]

One could certainly make a strong argument that peacemaking ought to be a distinguishing feature of followers of Jesus: "By this everyone will know that you are my disciples, if you have love for one another," he taught them (John 13:35). It requires no great stretch of biblical theology to claim that the central purpose of Jesus' life and death was to make peace between God and a hostile and estranged humanity, to heal divisions within humankind, and that for this reason the blessing upon peacemakers is that "they shall be called children of God" (Matt 5:9), participants in the same mission as Jesus Christ, the Son of God. Indeed, practicing love for enemies is especially reflective of the nature of God as revealed in Jesus (cf. Luke 6:35; Rom 5:10). If the identity and credibility of Christian communities as witnesses of God's truth and welcome to the world have been lost, it is at least in part because their members have grown accustomed to treating not only their enemies as enemies but in many cases their sisters and brothers as enemies. As stated in a report from a 1995 consultation of the National Council of Churches, "the divisions in the Body of Christ are a counter-witness to the Peace sought and proclaimed by the church as the follower of the Prince of Peace who prayed that his disciples might be one. . . . In the face of the fragmentation of the church we are agreed upon the importance of spiritual formation for unity in peacemaking."[34]

Such spiritual formation for peacemaking certainly involves the disciplines and virtues that I discussed in the previous chapter. Unity and peace—if not consensus on particulars—among believers are only possible to the extent that members of a community find their common dwelling place in God's unconditional love. Though there will still be distinctive practices and perspectives among different communities, many spiritual disciplines can contribute to a hospitable discernment of the limits of identity. For example, the practice of silent prayer—which means not only

---

[33] Jack Reese, The Body Broken: Embracing the Peace of Christ in a Fragmented Church (Siloam Springs, AK: Leafwood, 2005), 4.

[34] Quoted in Jeffrey Gros and John Rempel, eds., The Fragmentation of the Church and Its Unity in Peacemaking (Grand Rapids, MI: Eerdmans, 2001), 221, 223.

not talking but also learning to listen—can allow for the examination of one's own heart and motives and create space to truly hear the voices of others. An individual's desire to express herself and defend her opinions can sometimes be a barrier to fruitful dialogue, but "when we are able to be truly silent, to truly listen, then God can speak."[35] In contrast to the ways that the "world" deals with conflict—through taking sides, demonizing the opposition, breaking contact, giving the cold shoulder, or even overpowering the other through violence or deception—Christians must understand part of their distinctive identity to lie in their commitment to practices that promote hospitality and peace *within* the household of faith. At the same time, it may be important to include a note of caution about using "hospitality" to describe a commitment to peacemaking within the church, as it may suggest that some are insiders or hosts while others are guests. It is important to temper this tendency with the practice of *mutual* hospitality and the recognition that "it is not our table to which we welcome people; it is God's table to which we come as equals."[36]

This is perhaps an appropriate point to mention the issue of intercommunion or "eucharistic hospitality," that is, the question of whether members of different Christian denominations ought to share in the Lord's Supper, which is understood to be a sign of unity as well as an expression of divine hospitality. Although theologies of this sacramental meal vary widely, virtually all Christians are able to recognize the significance of these two features—namely, that the Lord's Supper is communion *among* the members of the Body of Christ as well as communion *with* Christ, who is ultimately the one who extends hospitality to those who come to the table. On one hand, the practice of intercommunion is supported by a belief in the unity created by baptism in Christ (1 Cor 1:10-17; 12:13; Eph 4:4-6), but for certain churches—particularly Eastern and Roman Catholic—their ecclesiological and sacramental theologies prohibit the extension of eucharistic fellowship to "separated sisters and brothers." While the Second Vatican Council's Decree on Ecumenism (*Unitatis Redintegratio*)[37] recognizes the existence of "some, though imperfect, communion with the Catholic Church" (3) among all baptized believers and fully supports efforts at dialogue, social cooperation, and prayer, it also maintains that "worship

[35] Johann Christoph Arnold, *Seeking Peace* (Farmington, PA: Plough Publishing House, 1998), 71.

[36] Pohl, *Making Room*, 157–58.

[37] Austin Flannery, ed., *Vatican Council II: The Basic Sixteen Documents* (Northport, NY: Costello Publishing Co., 2007).

in common (*communicatio in sacris*) is not to be considered as a means to be used indiscriminately for the restoration of unity among Christians" (8). While intercommunion may be acceptable in certain extraordinary circumstances, here the belief is that the Eucharist should express an *already-present* unity rather than striving to bring it about.

Here, as ever, there is a need for discernment. Certainly, it is possible to make a mockery of the Lord's Supper, a parody of the communion that it is intended to symbolize, when it is supposed that participation in a common ritual will by itself bring unity and heal divisions or when different parties come together in "bad faith," without any real desire for reconciliation and understanding. Such disregard for the significance of communion is of course equally likely (if not more so) among factions of a given church as it is between denominations; while there may be arguments for why eucharistic fellowship is appropriate in the former case and not in the latter, it is my opinion that thoughtful and sincere practices of intercommunion can be a profound and even necessary expression of Christians' hospitality toward one another. "If, as is the case, ecumenical dialogue is at a standstill," asks Pierre-François de Bethune, "is it not because we are fearful of . . . eucharistic hospitality[?]" He continues,

> When by common consent, Christians do dare to take that step, they discover that their doctrinal and traditional differences are no longer mutually exclusive, but can be considered within a framework that calls for equanimity and respect. . . . When it comes to spiritual and religious issues, we prefer to proceed with caution, a step at a time, gradually establishing areas of consensus. If, however, instead of thinking in territorial terms, we were to expand the concept of hospitality and welcome by extending it to what lies at the core of our spiritual life, might we not have a better chance of overcoming many of our inhibitions?[38]

Even—and perhaps especially—for those churches who find that their sense of identity places limits on eucharistic fellowship, there should be dedicated efforts made to ensure that these limits remain in some sense limits of hospitality, that even persons who are presently excluded from full participation are not excluded in principle. The practice of inviting non-Catholics forward to receive a blessing during the distribution of the Eucharist (which also requires acknowledging and providing explicit

---

[38] Pierre-François de Bethune, *Interreligious Hospitality: The Fulfillment of Dialogue* (Collegeville, MN: Liturgical Press, 2010), 155–56.

instructions to visitors, rather than allowing them to come forward only to be awkwardly denied communion) is one attempt to create a more hospitable boundary, indicating affirmation and gratitude for other individuals while also recognizing a distinctive Roman Catholic identity. Tokens of affirmation such as this must also be accompanied by "a careful and honest appraisal of whatever needs to be renewed and done in the catholic household itself" (UR 4) and "without prejudging the future inspirations of the holy Spirit" (UR 24) if they are truly to be in accordance with a spirit of hospitality, however. The tension between identity and indeterminacy within the life of the church may also therefore point beyond it, as a community extends hospitality to strangers.

Thus, just as each of the previous dimensions are related to each other in important ways, so also do they point to the third dimension of Christian communities as places of hospitality, namely, the width of welcome, as demonstrated in the practice of welcoming those who are more distant outsiders to a church or community. Of course, the practice of ecumenical hospitality can certainly involve a community's openness to others who differ greatly from it, and for this reason there is often blurring of the second and third dimensions of Christian hospitality. With some "strangers," differences (such as cultural or economic background) are so pronounced as to eclipse the Christian faith they hold in common. Such guests—for example, Christian immigrants and refugees as well as those who are homeless or very poor—may call for particular care in respecting both their particular proximity and distance from people or communities that extend hospitality to them. It is worth distinguishing "hospitality to one another" from "hospitality to strangers," however, in order to better discern what shape boundaries ought to take; hospitality to members of one's own community or tradition bears a different relationship to the limits of identity than hospitality to those of other religious traditions or none at all. In all cases, however, hospitality requires respect for the distinct identities of host and guest as well as openness to the possibility of transformation as a result of such an encounter.

Here, perhaps, it is necessary to distinguish between hospitality and evangelism by stating that the intention of hospitality is never to proselytize one's guest or host. To be sure, the line between these may be thin, insofar as both Christian hospitality and evangelism ought to flow from the desire to share the Good News of God's loving welcome to all people. If Christian communities are being faithful to their identity as places of hospitality and peace, this may be attractive to those people they welcome, much as it was for the first-century church. Historian Rowan Greer has written that "the example of Christian community life was probably more persuasive to unbelievers than the proclamation of the Christian message. It is impossible to resist the conclusion that . . . the church grew rapidly more because its common life acted as a magnet than because the Christians were effective in their public preaching."[39] While this may be true, it is not the point of hospitality, which must allow the stranger to remain a stranger, even as it extends the invitation to become a friend. As de Bethune explains in the context of interreligious hospitality, it is important not to gloss over the distinct and different nature of the stranger: "To assimilate him would be to do him dishonor. Regardless of whatever good intentions might motivate such an attempt . . . , if hospitality becomes a means toward the goal of assimilating another person into our world, it becomes repulsive to the one for whose 'benefit' it is orchestrated."[40]

In a church I am familiar with, one member's involvement in a program providing housewares to international graduate students has brought a significant number of these students—many of them Buddhists, Muslims, communists, or African Christians—into this small and relatively homogenous congregation. As far as I am aware, there is no deliberate attempt to convert these students to Christianity; the goal is only to welcome them into the life of this family-like community. While hospitality may give rise to mutual curiosity and enrichment—as it has in this case—the practice of hospitality is distorted if it becomes primarily an instrumental means to change people or if it assumes that they will eventually assimilate to a dominant identity.

This point is deeply important in the context of extending hospitality to immigrants and refugees, who in many ways represent paradigmatic strangers and who are often greeted with a highly ambiguous hospitality, if not with outright hostility, even among Christians. Though the United States has, in many ways, been a nation especially open to "huddled masses yearning to breathe free,"[41] its history has not been free of hostilities, and even in more hospitable moments there is an overall expectation that strangers will adopt characteristically American habits of life, language, family, and work. Immigrants have often been subject to exploitation and caricature by those

[39] Rowan Greer, *Broken Lights and Mended Lives: Theology and Common Life in the Early Church* (University Park, PA: University of Pennsylvania Press, 1986), 123.

[40] Ibid., 118–19.

[41] Emma Lazarus, "The New Colossus," at http://www.poets.org/viewmedia.php/prmMID/16111, accessed 11/04/2011.

who violently seek to maintain positions of privilege. Without a doubt, the issues involved in thinking about hospitality to immigrants and refugees can be complex due to their intersection with public policy and legislation (as well as the fact that assimilation to American culture is a desirable goal for some migrants), but this should not stand in the way of "a conversion of mind and heart which leads . . . to communion expressed through hospitality on the part of receiving communities and a sense of belonging and welcome" on the part of migrants and their families, who "should be able to find a homeland everywhere in the church."[42] The phantom of "national identity"—which is almost always an ideological construct used to justify violence and exclusion—should never be allowed to displace the spirit of hospitality within Christian communities.

Because hospitality to strangers may assume such an endless variety of forms, there is no sufficient way to summarize them here—or anywhere, for that matter—even for the sake of indicating their breadth. For this reason, once again, hospitality cannot be reduced to a rule but rather requires commitment to practices that form humble, grateful, and discerning hearts in those who seek to share God's welcome. The three dimensions of hospitality—its depth in hospitality to God, its length in hospitality within a community, and its width in hospitality to strangers—must expand concurrently in order to create hospitable places. Though differences between hosts and guests and the commitments and narratives that form their identities establish limits to hospitality, these must always be held in tension with indeterminacy if they are to remain limits of hospitality. As Miroslav Volf has argued, even if it is necessary to make judgments that exclude—often for the sake of the security of a particular community—the will to welcome others and even "to readjust our identities to make space for them, is prior to any judgment about others, except identifying them in their humanity."[43]

---

[42] Pontifical Council for the Care of Migrants and Itinerant Peoples, The Love of Christ Toward Migrants (Erga Migrantes Caritas Christi), 40–41, http://www.vatican.va/roman_curia/pontifical_councils/migrants/documents/rc_pc_migrants_doc_20040514_erga-migrantes-caritas-christi_en.html#Welcome%20and%20solidarity, accessed 11/04/2011.

[43] Volf, Exclusion and Embrace, 29; italics in original.

Chapter 4

The Limits of Security

I really couldn't write about hospitality and limits without writing about Sam and DayDay, two boys from New Haven, Connecticut, half brothers whom I sort of "inherited" from previous owners of the house on Mansfield Street. When I met them they were eleven and thirteen years old, and I believe they had been in the orbit of the house for at least five or six years by then. Sam, the elder, was pushing his five-year-old brother down the street in a grocery cart when a former resident of the house met them years ago. Another resident of the house who was an attorney helped their mother when the family was having trouble with their Section 8 arrangements around that time, and over the years that followed, others in the house maintained a relationship with the boys, amassing a pretty hilarious collection of stories as they brought them to church or on camping trips or had them over for dinner at the house.

At first, my connection was simply that of accompanying other members of the house when they took the boys for pizza or to youth group or to a movie, but when other residents who had been involved with them moved away, maintaining that relationship seemed to fall primarily to me. My involvement in their lives didn't seem to me to be particularly profound—I would treat them to Burger King or McDonald's about once a week ("Can't you at least feed them something *healthy*?" I often chided myself), and sometimes with the consent of other members of my household I would have them over for dinner or a movie night or let them check their Myspace accounts on my computer, or I would download the latest songs and burn CDs for them.

Though Sam and DayDay each bear a resemblance to their mother, Roberta, the boys could hardly be more different in terms of their character and temperament. Sam is almost unquenchably jovial, athletic, and hyperactive, with a great sense of humor and imagination. He has some significant learning disabilities and is virtually unable to read, but he is a hard worker, good-natured, and "smooth with the ladies" ("'Cause I got mad muscles, yo," he would explain, flexing his biceps). To this day Sam calls me "Jessica B"—B for "Brother"—when he calls me on the phone. Sam's father was in prison for a while, but I believe he now lives in a nearby town.

DayDay—whose given name is in fact Emmanuel—has never met his father. Although DayDay can be moody and disrespectful, he can be sweet and thoughtful and a lot of fun as well. At age thirteen he was diagnosed with bipolar disorder after he tried to commit suicide (I remember Sam showing up at our house that night, unusually serious, and telling us that "DayDay tried to kill hisself"). For as long as I've known him, DayDay has cross-dressed; when he was eight or nine, he started wearing a black T-shirt on his head (the neck of the shirt around his forehead) and pretending it was long hair, and by the time he was a teenager, he was wearing tight, skinny jeans, straightening or having extensions braided into his hair, and occasionally wearing makeup. Just after he turned fifteen years old, he was arrested for driving (a stolen car) without a license, and after a brief stay in a juvenile detention center, he went to live at the Children's Center—a residential facility in a nearby town for kids with emotional and behavioral problems—for a year. Though he missed his family, he recognized that the time at the Children's Center was helpful for him, providing greater structure and attention to his issues and needs as well as allowing him to meet other kids who were also different like him.

Particularly when they were younger, the boys were a *handful*: hyperactive, noisy, demanding, unruly, often fighting with each other over silly things as brothers tend to do. Their desires and needs were inexhaustible, and I felt unprepared to address many of their most significant needs due to the limits of my own time, energy, and skill. It was through my relationship with the boys, however, that I came to realize that—as with other disciplines—maintaining fidelity over time can be an extremely important way of ensuring that our limits are hospitable: that is, even if we can't give a person everything he or she needs due to our own finitude, or if we must set limits on a relationship because of his or her behavior, remaining committed to the relationship is a way of inviting the spirit of hospitality into those limits.

And so, for about four years I saw the boys almost weekly. Because he was allowed to come home on the weekends, every Friday during the year that DayDay was living at the Children's Center, I gave his mother a ride to pick him up and dropped him off on Sunday so they wouldn't need to take the bus. Again, for the most part these were small things, but I feel confident saying that their accumulation over time has had a lasting effect in each of our lives—perhaps mine most of all. The boys brought the gift of a different perspective—and with it often the gift of laughter—to my housemates and me.

There were certainly plenty of times along the way that Sam and DayDay both challenged and expanded the limits of my hospitality, however, not only beyond what was convenient but also beyond what was comfortable or "safe." Sam and DayDay could be risky guests: although there was never the slightest reason for any fear of violence from them, they certainly brought the security of one's possessions into question. Once DayDay stole a housemate's cell phone (off of the pew at church—ha!) and downloaded almost a hundred dollars of ringtones to his account before we realized what happened (housemates "sentenced" him to community service for his transgression). Another time, when I wasn't supervising him as closely as I should have, he completely crashed my computer.

Still another time, my neighbor Antonio—who also spent time with the boys and had warned me before that "they steal"—stopped by my house and asked if I was missing my iPod. Not really, I probably told him, and I wondered why he was asking. He explained that Sam had come over to his house earlier that day asking to use Antonio's computer to put music on his iPod, but when they hooked it up the computer identified it as "Jess's iPod." Sam was busted—they both knew who Jess was—but Antonio said that he denied stealing it from me, saying rather that he had taken it from his brother, who was the true thief. Sure enough, my iPod was missing out of the drawer where I had been keeping it, but when I confronted the boys about it, both denied their guilt and each blamed the other. I explained that I forgave them (whoever was in fact guilty), but if I couldn't trust them, I couldn't have them in my house—first and foremost because it wasn't only my possessions that I had to think of but also those of my housemates. Although the boys were not allowed into the house for the following year, I continued to see them and buy them food. Limits of hospitality, practiced over time . . .

I felt a kind of affirmation that such fidelity might have borne fruit—as well as deep agony at my helplessness—when Sam and DayDay's family (they lived with their mother and her boyfriend, their older sister and her sons) lost their apartment and called me for help a year or so after I moved away from New Haven. Roberta had been planning to move to another apartment but had not paid the deposit on time, so they had to leave their old apartment without another place to go. She had often complained to me about the conditions—drug dealers and users, pros-titutes, fighting, and noise—in and around their apartment building on Norton Street, saying that she just wanted a place where her boys would be safe, and it had broken my heart that I couldn't do more to help. Not only was my own house not entirely mine to give away, I realized, but to do so would also mean that hospitality (toward them or anyone else) would no longer be possible—hospitality is limited by a host's need to have a space to offer to others. After I moved and Sam called to tell me that his family was homeless, there was a part of me that wanted to buy him and his brother a Greyhound ticket and have them come live with me—eight hundred miles away from everything they knew—but I knew that was no real solution, for a host of reasons. I did all that I could to get in touch with friends who were still in New Haven and others from my house who had also moved away, hoping they might be able to help somehow. I prayed. Friends who knew them reminded me that "they are survivors" and would likely find a way for themselves even if I couldn't provide it. I let the boys know that they were always welcome to call me if they just wanted to talk. Within a few months, they had found a new apartment, but for DayDay, who had been particularly distraught at the thought of being without a home, being able to call and talk seemed to be an important form of hospitality—however limited it was.

Sam and DayDay were also challenging—yet delightful—guests simply because they were *so* different from me, a middle-class, West Virginia–born woman studying theology at Yale. Perhaps because they had the guileless and uninhibited curiosity of children, and perhaps because I was as strange to them as they were to me, the boys made me more aware of my own particular culture and social location—or, more to the point, my white-ness—than any other relationship in my life. Their music, their dress, their dialect were all totally foreign to the world in which I had lived most of my life, and for that reason they both expanded and allowed me to see that world more clearly for what it was. I remember when Sam showed up at our house looking for something to eat and loudly, laughingly asked, "How come all you got over here is white-people food, . . . like raisins . . . and nuts . . . and *books*?"

Because of my white privilege, I was beginning to see.

"Black-people food," he explained, consisted of things like fried chicken, Burger King, and pork chops. White people and black people, we discovered, both like Chinese food, pizza, and ice cream. In the paradox of all paradoxes, we realized that while "black-people bread" is white, white people eat brown bread. With nuts in it. In addition to food, regular references to "white-people music" or clothes or sports or speech made it clear that from Sam's perspective, scarcely a dimension of reality was not classifiable in black and white.

Though I have deliberately omitted reference to race in sharing my experiences of hospitality up to this point, the truth is that only a white person has the privilege of assuming that she is telling a colorblind story. Perhaps it should be noted that without exception every significant guest I have written about—Ani, John, JC, Lanay, Sam and DayDay—has been African American. This commonality in my own experience may be coincidental, but it nonetheless points to the pervasive injustice that has resulted in the violent dis-possession of dark-skinned people—not only in the legacies of slavery and racism that continue to shape black and white experience in the United States but also in the vastly unequal distribution of wealth on a global scale, which reinscribes the violent patterns of colonization (a violation of hospitality if ever there was one!). For a white person to remain silent or dismissive about the unfathomable violence that has been done to people of African descent on our own continent alone—not to mention the atrocities of colonialism, apartheid, and the "middle passage" of slaves to the Americas—is to be further implicated in the racism and guilt of those who have actively perpetuated the violence of white supremacy.

The term "white privilege" as I am using it here "attempts to make intelligible all the benefits that come simply from the fact that one is born with white skin."[1] Far more serious than the differences in our food or music choices are the differences in the opportunities and horizons that I have as a white woman in comparison with Sam and DayDay, two young, black men. I do not mean to ignore the role of economic as well as racial privilege here—as a West Virginian, it is abundantly clear to me that white poverty is also a diminishment of human potential—but I became strikingly conscious of the privilege that white skin entails when I went places in public with DayDay and Sam, who were often ignored or viewed with suspicion until I made it clear that they were with me. Experiences of other non-white friends confirm the way society continues to make assumptions about a person based on skin color. But furthermore, economic disparities actually show a striking correspondence with race. Recent census data

[1] Laurie Cassidy and Alex Mikulich, eds., *Interrupting White Privilege: Catholic Theologians Break the Silence* (Maryknoll, NY: Orbis, 2007), 2.

shows that the median wealth for white households in 2009 ($113,149) was approximately twenty times that of black households ($5,677), indicating a further widening of the gap between rich and poor, black and white, in America.[2]

It has been said that once you know, you can't not know. But what can one person *do* about the systemic violence of racial privilege?

Facing an unjust reality honestly and confessing one's implication in it—the benefits and privileges, possessions and security that I have enjoyed because of my whiteness—is a first step. And so here I must recognize that my own hospitality in the stories recorded in this book has been unjustly limited by the security I have enjoyed at the expense of others. Would it therefore have been better for me to have renounced hospitality altogether and relinquished my possession of a home, my ability to be a host, by *giving* my home to Sam and DayDay or JC or Lanay? Perhaps I am deceiving myself, but I am convinced that given the systematic nature of the injustice, maintaining the practice of hospitality with honesty about its limitations—continuing to pay the rent, to provide food, to build friendships—accomplishes more in these particular cases (for me and for society as well as for my guests) than giving it up. Not only was the practice of hospitality essential to opening my own eyes to the truth of racial privilege, but it can also be a step toward dismantling it by building authentic friendships and solidarity across racial boundaries.

While I cannot claim that my own hospitality has been free of the violence of white privilege, I still refuse to concede that hospitality as such involves or requires violence (I can recall many instances of hospitality in which the "need" of guests could not be linked to violence of any sort but rather was simply a function of our relationships to a particular place). It is important to raise this issue here because, when considering the need for a certain kind of possession and security as limits of hospitality in this chapter, it is essential to be on guard against using hospitality as a justification of the violence that often lies behind the fact that some have and others are without a home. Those in positions of privilege must strive to renounce the violence that has created and sustained it—even to the point of renouncing their own comfort and control—if hospitality is not to become a distortion of itself. Nonetheless, to make violence a *requirement*

---

[2] Hope Yen, "Wealth Gap between Whites, Minorities Widens to Greatest Levels in Quarter Century," *The Huffington Post*, July 7, 2011, http://www.huffingtonpost.com/2011/07/26/wealth-gap-whites-minorities_n_909465.html.

of hospitality removes grounds for critique as well as hope for change. There is, once again, a perennial need both to recognize the limits of our hospitality and to look beyond them.

Possession and Security

To be sure, a hospitable place requires limits of security—by which I mean the ability to provide for the needs of guests and hosts, as well as to offer reasonable assurance of safety within the space that is offered to them. For one thing, it is necessary for hosts to be in rightful possession of the space that they offer to others if their actions are to be recognizable as hospitality. Commenting on this feature, John Caputo notes that there is "only a minimum of hospitality, some would say none at all, involved in inviting a large party of guests to your neighbor's house (especially if you do not let the neighbor in on what is going on), or in inviting others to make themselves at home, say, in Central Park or the Grand Canyon or any other public place. A host is a host only if he owns the place, and only if he holds on to his ownership, if one limits the gift."[3] Thus, hospitality is shaped in an important way by a tension between gift—offering my home to another, free of charge—and possession. By "possession"—which comes from the Latin *posse*, "to have power" or "to be able"—I do not mean to refer solely to private ownership but rather to any legitimate claim and power over a space, whether that is the space of one's body and emotions, a home or facility that is shared with others, or a temporary "possession," as when a family rents a vacation home or a picnic pavilion. In addition to a host having sufficient control over a space to be able to offer it to others, the legitimacy of possession is also essential; the use of property acquired through unjust means—violence, deception, exploitation—undermines and limits hospitality.[4]

---

[3] John Caputo, ed., *Deconstruction in a Nutshell: A Conversation with Jacques Derrida* (New York: Fordham University Press, 1997), 110. Cf. his discussion of hospitality in *What Would Jesus Deconstruct? The Good News of Postmodernism for the Church* (Grand Rapids, MI: Baker Academic, 2007), 75–78.

[4] Once again, I recognize and am sensitive to the argument that *all* private property is violent due to the need for the force of law to maintain it and because of the inevitable injustices of inequitable distribution (not to mention the potential for injustice in the acquisition) of wealth. I find the perspective offered by Catholic Social Teaching compelling in this regard, however: though the "natural right" to provide for oneself and one's family does establish a provisional right to private property, there is nonetheless a "social mortgage" on all property—it must serve the common good (*Sollicitudo Rei Socialis* 42).

Hospitality is also shaped by tensions between comfort and sacrifice and between safety and risk. (Are there adequate [material and emotional] resources to provide for the needs of hosts and guests? Are we safe?) Certainly, there are ways in which the spirit of hospitality is a sacrificial spirit, willing to forgo certain comforts and make time and space for the sake of another, but when such sacrifices become resentful and forced, they introduce violence into hospitality; failure to set appropriate boundaries in *any* relationship can do harm to all involved. Hosts as well as guests have physical, emotional, and spiritual needs, and when the well is dry in any of these areas, it will be difficult to sustain the practice of hospitality. I imagine that this limitation—the finite resources and potentially endless needs of human men and women—is probably the first thing that comes to mind for most readers when hearing the title of this book, and it is true that in some ways these boundaries are the most straightforward; as finite creatures living in finite spaces, there are simply limits to what individuals and communities can provide for others—emotionally and physically—through their hospitality. A space can only accommodate a certain number of people, and there is only so much food and only so many hours in a day to spend serving or visiting with guests. Furthermore, human finitude also involves vulnerability to physical and psychological harm, and providing for the safety of those who are in situations of particular vulnerability is an important part of offering them hospitality. It is quite reasonable for hosts to be concerned for their own safety as well as for the safety of their household as a limit to the welcome they extend to "risky" outsiders. The presence of a threatening or violent guest (or host) can easily destroy the possibility of a hospitable place for all others involved, and securing a space against violence would seem to be one of the most basic requirements—that is, conditions or limits—of hospitality.

And yet, upon deeper consideration, the limits of security are not straightforward or clearly defined. Needs—both material and emotional—vary considerably between different people and cultures: an action that one person intends to be hospitable may be uncomfortable or perplexing to another, just as time and resources that are easily given by one person may be an overwhelming burden to someone else. Furthermore, it is necessary to recognize the variety of contexts in which hospitality occurs and the fact that hospitality that intends to address the basic needs of the poorest of the poor will look different than hospitality in the context of material comfort. This is not to justify withholding resources from a particular class of people (as if minimal hospitality is good enough for the poor), nor to justify material excess, nor to say that one or the other is a better or truer form of hospitality, but rather to indicate, once again, that there is no fixed rule that can define the limits of human resources and needs. Although an involuntary or resentful sacrifice can entirely undermine hospitality, there may be ways in which sacrificial giving can sometimes open up new forms of abundance as time and treasures are "offered up" with gratitude. Furthermore, the legitimate need for safety can become so exaggerated that it builds walls of suspicion and hostility in place of limits of hospitality—a problem that Nouwen identified as one of the greatest obstacles to the practice of hospitality in society. To again quote Caputo, "the only way to eliminate the risk built into hospitality is to eliminate hospitality itself by screening the guests so carefully in advance that every trace of welcoming the other has been extinguished. There is always a risk in everything worthwhile. We are put at risk whenever we love or trust or believe in someone, and the greater the love or the hospitality, the greater the risk."[5] While a measure of security is necessary for the creation of safe and friendly spaces, making the need for security absolute can also become idolatrous as the need for control over all of life replaces surrender and openness to the Spirit of God.

Love and Limits

He said to him, "'You shall love the Lord your God with all your heart, and with all your soul, and with all your mind.' This is the greatest and first commandment. And a second is like it: 'You shall love your neighbor as yourself.'" (Matt 22:37-39)

When Jesus explained the greatest commandments to the lawyer in Matthew 22, he opened as many questions as he answered for those who have desired to follow him. The first commandment is challenging enough—but what, one might ask, does it mean to say that the "second is like it"? Is the love of neighbor *subordinate* to or *equal* to love of God? Or perhaps it is another way of saying the same thing? Does loving your neighbor *as* yourself mean loving neighbors *in the same way* as you love yourself (implying the goodness of *some* amount of self-love) or *in place* of yourself? In addition to questions such as these, the relationship between agape—divinely inspired, other-regarding, overflowing, selfless love—and human love has been a perennial concern in Christian ethics.

[5] Caputo, *What Would Jesus Deconstruct?*, 77.

In a world marked by suffering and virtually infinite need, is it ever legitimate to limit care and concern for others for the sake of one's own needs and desires? Is self-concern always a manifestation of violence? To what extent are Christian hosts called to sacrifice material comfort, time, and even safety for the sake of their guests? Certainly, many prominent voices in the history of Christianity have recommended total self-sacrifice as the purest expression of love—indeed, the death of Christ points in this direction—though others have offered compelling defenses of love as mutuality and have provided sound reasons for placing limits on what is due to others out of love.

In a significant contemporary philosophical treatment of these questions, Gene Outka not only offers an analytical account of the content of human agape but also draws upon this account in a consideration of the relationship of self-regard and regard for others.[6] Outka proposes the term "equal regard" to describe the universal scope and unconditional nature of agape, which loves the neighbor *as such*, simply because of his or her existence as a human person. While showing commitment to the other that is independent of any of her particular attributes or actions, agape as equal regard also authorizes legitimate self-regard and concern for third parties. In his discussion of the problem of the "blank check," Outka asks how it is possible to differentiate between legitimate attention to another's needs (and the possibility of sacrificing one's own comfort in order to meet them) and harmful submission to exploitation and injustice. He concludes that agape itself, understood as equal regard, potentially offers three reasons to refrain from responding to a neighbor's inordinate needs or demands: the good of the neighbor, the welfare of third parties, and the good of the self.

In the first place, in some circumstances, resisting rather than giving in to the sinful or self-destructive desires of another may be the more loving thing to do; that is, "for the neighbor's own sake I should not conflate his or her legitimate needs and actual wants."[7] Citing Kierkegaard, Outka notes the contrast between a "misplaced caressing indulgence" and earnest

---

[6] My discussion here draws primarily from Gene Outka, *Agape: An Ethical Analysis* (New Haven, CT, and London: Yale University Press, 1972), although Outka's later treatment of issues related to agape and self-love are also illuminating; see, for example, "Universal Love and Impartiality," in *The Love Commandments: Essays in Christian Ethics and Moral Philosophy*, ed. Edmund Santurri and William Werpehowski (Washington, DC: Georgetown University Press, 1992).

[7] Outka, "Universal Love and Impartiality," 40.

neighbor love that does not give in to "particular weakness and turpitude."[8] In the context of hospitality, this may mean that issuing a "blank check" to the guest—for example, failing to set limits on what is permitted in the home, what service is offered, and the length of the stay—enables destructive and irresponsible behavior that is harmful to both host and guest.

As I briefly mentioned in the introduction to this book, at one point members of my household in New Haven agreed to offer temporary shelter to a man they knew who was addicted to crack cocaine and who had been on and off the streets for the previous seven years. While John[9] is as gentle and earnest a soul as one might imagine and there was no question of him using drugs in our home, the issue of whether or not to give him a ride to a "friend's" house—where we knew he would get high—sometimes did arise. Here we saw a limit to hospitality that arose from the nature of hospitality itself. John's sincere desire was to get clean, and yet often the pressures of life and society and his own wounds and addictions were greater than his will. For us to enable his self-destructive behavior would have been a distortion, not an extension, of hospitality.

Ultimately, after going to great lengths to get John into a treatment program that he soon dropped out of, we decided that it would not be in his own best interest to continue to provide him with assistance. The help that he needed was beyond our capacity, and it seemed that he might have to hit bottom in order to get it. At the same time, however, there was extensive effort made to ensure that this limit was a limit of hospitality rather than simply a result of frustration or giving up on him. John remained—and, through ongoing cycles of struggle, success, and relapse, all bathed in prayers of gratitude and mercy, he remains—a part of our community, even when he wasn't living at the house on Mansfield Street. He continued to come to dinner at our house occasionally and regularly met for breakfast with one of the members of the house. Even after I left town, we continued to pray for one another aloud on the phone—John loves and craves prayer—and he sent me handwritten letters of encouragement and friendship. When I went back to visit several months after graduation, he insisted on treating me to lunch, and there have been many times when John's joy and trust in God were an inspiration and comfort to me. As of the time that I am writing this, he is once again in a treatment program.

[8] Outka, *Agape*, 22.
[9] This name has been changed.

Outka's second reason for love's refusal to issue a blank check stems from concern for the welfare of third parties; that is, as a consideration of justice, I must limit what I will permit or give to one neighbor out of a concern for still other neighbors who might be harmed by my action. At certain points, it may be necessary to limit my hospitality to one guest out of a sense of fairness to others or of "comparative justice." For example, at the soup kitchen I wrote about in chapter 2, we offered only a limited portion until all had been served to ensure that there was enough to go around, even though there was usually plentiful food to allow for multiple helpings to all who wanted them. This second consideration is particularly important in the context of *shared* spaces, where there are multiple people in the roles of host or guest. While sharing spaces and possessions can be a way of expanding limits imposed by the needs and resources of individuals, there are also particular responsibilities that go along with holding spaces in common. It is important not only to recognize the different (and potentially competing) needs and vulnerabilities of different people but also to adjudicate between the needs of those *within* a household and those *outside* it and to pay attention to the distribution of benefits and burdens in the practice of hospitality. Hospitality must account for the requirements of justice and benevolence within as well as outside the boundaries of a household or community, and it is important to recognize the ways that some members might be disproportionately affected by unlimited hospitality.

The gendered analysis of household relationships provided by feminists offers helpful insight into how this second limitation might function. In many if not most cultures (including our own), the host or "master of the house"—he who stands at the door to welcome or to turn away guests, who decides and defines the limits of hospitality—is paradigmatically male, while the responsibility for much of the practical labor of hospitality (e.g., preparing food or keeping a home clean and orderly) often falls to women. In some cultures, it is even considered a form of hospitality to offer a wife or daughter to a male guest for his sexual pleasure—clearly a violation of just hospitality. Although less dramatically unjust, many women I have had the chance to speak with about these issues express the difficulty that arises when husbands or children invite guests home with little awareness of the additional work this creates.

While insisting that they too wanted to be welcoming, these women recognized the need to draw limits to hospitality based on concern for its effect on *all* members of a household. While not writing from a feminist point of view, Dorothy Day signals the disparity that exists in men's and women's experiences of household life as she writes about the disciplines of Pythagoras[10] and the solitude necessary for listening to God. Reflecting on this in light of her own experience, she writes:

> But I am a woman, with all the cares and responsibilities of a woman, and though I take these words of Père Gratry and St. Augustine to heart, I know that what I write will be tinged with all the daily doings, with myself, my child, my work, my study, as well as with God. God enters into them all. He is inseparable from them. I think of Him as I wake and as I think of Teresa's daily doings. Perhaps it is that I have a wandering mind. But I do not care. It is a woman's mind, and if my daily written meditations are of the people about me, of what's going on—then it must be so. . . . Because I am a woman involved in practical cares, I cannot give the first half of the day to these things, but rather must meditate, when I can, early in the morning and on the fly during the day. Not in the privacy of a study—but here, there, and everywhere—at the kitchen table, on the train, on the ferry, on my way to and from appointments and even while making supper or putting Teresa to bed.[11]

Elsewhere in her writing Day sometimes observes her male coworkers' oblivion to the practical tasks involved in practicing hospitality as a way of life.[12] My discussion here is not intended to essentialize male and female experience (as Day admittedly does—often in a way that would not please many feminists), but only to indicate one common way that unlimited hospitality can lead to a kind of violence if the experiences and needs of all are not taken into consideration. Ideally, recognition of disparities ought to prompt internal reconfiguration or redistribution of labor, which in many cases will allow for an expansion of a household's capacity to be hospitable. Those engaged in the practice of hospitality must remain aware of how it can become a source of oppression or resentment rather

---

[10] "Pythagoras used to divide his disciples' days into three parts: the first was for God and spent in prayer, the second for God and spent in study and meditation, and the third for men and the business of life. Thus, all the first two-thirds of the day was for God. And as a matter of fact, it is in the morning, before the distraction of our intercourse with men, that we must listen to God." Père Gratry, *The Well Springs*, quoted in Dorothy Day, *House of Hospitality* (New York and London: Sheed & Ward, 1939), 1.

[11] Day, *House of Hospitality*, 2–3.

[12] See, for example, Dorothy Day, *Loaves and Fishes* (Maryknoll, NY: Orbis, 1997), 99.

than of welcome and gratitude when burdens are inequitably distributed or involuntarily imposed.

Of course, the line between burdens that are unjustly imposed and those that are assumed voluntarily (if nonetheless unjustly) is not always so clear, which points to the third reason that Outka offers for placing limits on one's obligations to others: that is, concern for oneself as a person worthy of care and possessing dignity. "If whatever characterizes my being as a human person as such falls under equal regard," he writes, "this may justify resistance to certain kinds of demands and encroachments."[13] Basic self-respect implies resistance to abuse from others, just as every person's finitude requires that her own needs be met if she is to be able to give freely to others. In some cases, it is clear when boundaries must be drawn for the sake of self-preservation. As the following section will show, however, even when it is clear that a boundary ought to be drawn and the needs or desires of others should be refused, this is not always so easy to do, and people often fail to set limits for all the wrong reasons.

God beyond *Boundaries*

"This is THE most life-changing book I've ever read, apart from the Bible," writes one Amazon.com reviewer quoted on the first pages of Henry Cloud and John Townsend's best-selling book *Boundaries: When to Say Yes, How to Say No to Take Control of Your Life*.[14] Bill Hybels, the wildly successful senior pastor of Willow Creek Community Church, is also quoted on the back of the book, saying that "the whole trajectory of my life would have been different and better had I read this twenty years ago." The book, which boasts of "Over 2 Million Copies Sold" on its cover, has also spawned the follow-up volumes *Boundaries in Marriage*, *Boundaries in Dating*, *Boundaries with Kids*, and *Boundaries with Teens*, as well as several editions of resources and study guides for churches. Clearly, Drs. Cloud and Townsend, both clinical psychologists, are saying something that resonates with American Christians. Beginning from questions such as "Can I set boundaries and still be a loving person?" and "How do boundaries relate to submission?" the book claims to help its readers to "see the deeply biblical nature of boundaries as they operate in the character of God, his universe, and his

---

[13] Outka, *Agape*, 24.

[14] Henry Cloud and John Townsend, *Boundaries: When to Say Yes, How to Say No to Take Control of Your Life* (Grand Rapids, MI: Zondervan, 1992).

people."[15] They argue that part of Christian responsibility entails knowing what is one's job and what is not. It is essential for all people to recognize healthy physical, mental, emotional, and spiritual boundaries and to set limits when appropriate. They offer the example of an overworked and emotionally undernourished Christian mother who is unable to say no to some of the overwhelming demands of her mother, her husband, her children, her coworkers, her church, and her friends. Not only does "Sherrie" find that she is lonely, exhausted, and resentful, but her ability to give to these relationships and responsibilities also suffers.

Throughout the book, the authors draw from their clinical and counseling experience to provide examples of other people who have different problems with boundaries, and they provide insight into the ways that relational boundaries are formed—and deformed—throughout a person's life. While some people have trouble respecting others' boundaries, other people set too few boundaries or do so for the wrong reasons. Rather than acting out of freedom and concern for others, such people are motivated by guilt or by fear—fear of abandonment or fear of the anger or disapproval of others—and often end up replicating the unhealthy relational dynamics that gave rise to such guilt and fear in the first place. Cloud and Townsend adamantly affirm the legitimacy of the boundaries imposed by human finitude, identifying the ways in which healthy and appropriate relational boundaries actually *increase* rather than diminish people's ability to care for one another, since "our loving heart, like our physical one, *needs an inflow as well as an outflow of lifeblood*."[16] Failing to set appropriate boundaries can lead to hostility and depression as exhaustion and resentment build.

The authors helpfully distinguish between the "hurt" that our boundaries might cause other people and the "harm" that can be done to ourselves and others when we fail to acknowledge these limits: being confronted with certain challenges and truths can be hurtful and uncomfortable, even if it is good for us, just as enjoyable things can sometimes be very harmful. They attempt to dispel the myth that setting boundaries is selfish or aggressive, arguing that appropriate boundaries are not an offensive weapon but rather a defensive tool, defining us and showing us "where I end and someone else begins, leading me to a sense of ownership" of my life and gifts.[17] The metaphors of "ownership" and one's life

[15] Ibid., 28.
[16] Ibid., 49; italics in original.
[17] Ibid., 31.

and self as "property" are dominant throughout the book, and the authors argue that just as we are not responsible for taking care of someone else's yard or home, neither are we responsible for others' basic well-being. Yet Cloud and Townsend are also quite clear that boundaries are not walls that cut us off from others but must have "gates" that help to "keep the good in and the bad out."[18] They explain that boundaries are not opposed to but rather for the sake of relationships, and their persistent advocacy of support groups and networks acknowledges the ways in which "relational problems can only be solved in relationships, for that is the context of the problems themselves, and the context of spiritual existence."[19]

One of the book's most profound contributions is its emphasis on the truth as a guideline for setting healthy relational boundaries. "There is always safety in the truth," they write, "whether it be knowing God's truth or knowing the truth about yourself. Many people live scattered and tumultuous lives trying to live outside their own boundaries, not accepting and expressing the truth of who they are."[20] The authors discuss numerous ways in which failure to accept and express the truth of our desires, feelings, and limitations can have disastrous personal and relational consequences. Ironically, it is often a fear of the consequences of telling the truth that causes people to deny it: we fail to acknowledge our fatigue or our resentment or our true desires because we fear the loss of a friendship, the disapproval of a parent, the anger or contempt of coworkers or other Christians. Or we well-meaningly want to spare others (and ourselves!) the hurt and discomfort that telling the truth may involve. But to reiterate the distinction above, hurt is not necessarily harm. There is no violence in truth.

Boundaries contains numerous other insightful discussions of how and why setting appropriate boundaries can be challenging, and it is no wonder that so many people have found this book helpful and transformative. Without denying the valuable contributions that Cloud and Townsend make to a proper understanding of human boundaries, a theological critique of their work here is desperately needed. Attempting to ground their discussion of boundaries in "the nature of God," they write that "God defines himself as a distinct, separate being, and he is responsible for himself. He defines himself and takes responsibility for his personality by telling us what he thinks, feels, plans, allows, will not allow, likes and

---

[18] Ibid., 33–34.
[19] Ibid., 103.
[20] Ibid., 37.

dislikes. He also defines himself as separate from his creation and from us. He differentiates himself from others. He tells us who he is and who he is not."[21] They state that God "is a good model for how we should respect our property,"[22] because like any responsible property owner, "God also limits what he will allow in his yard."[23] God "sets standards" and "limits his exposure to evil, unrepentant people, as should we."[24] Successfully taking control of one's life, they claim, means that "we need to develop boundaries like God's."[25]

But what kind of God is this? A finite and bounded God, separate from us and fully comprehensible to us? A God without mystery, grace, or power? Rather, in the words of the prophet Isaiah, God rebukes human beings who believe that they can comprehend or master God's absolute, unfathomable, and infinite mystery:

> For my thoughts are not your thoughts,
>   nor are your ways my ways, says the LORD.
> For as the heavens are higher than the earth,
>   so are my ways higher than your ways
>   and my thoughts than your thoughts. (Isa 55:8-9)

Contrary to Cloud and Townsend's god of boundaries and control, any God who can be fully understood by humans and who exists on a par with other beings, "separate from his creation," is no God at all. God is not a "distinct, separate being" but rather the condition of the possibility of any and every and all being, always and everywhere. God created the whole earth and all the people who inhabit it, marking out "the times of their existence and the places that they would live, so that they would search for God and perhaps grope for him and find him," and yet God "is not far from each one of us. For 'in [God] we live and move and have our being'" (Acts 17:26-28).

[21] Ibid., 35. Though I do not intend to belabor the point here, it is noteworthy—though also no wonder—that Cloud and Townsend use masculine pronouns for God so pervasively and unconsciously throughout their book; any finite and defined God is going to be gendered, and of course the humans who have traditionally assumed responsibility for such definition have also assumed that God is male like them. Here as much as anywhere, however, it is crucial to recognize that God both encompasses and transcends the limits of gender, that God is both Father and Mother, as well as both host and guest.

[22] Ibid., 240.

[23] Ibid., 35.

[24] Ibid., 45.

[25] Ibid., 35.

An *infinite* God is—by definition—*unbounded.* One of the reasons for human finitude, the apostle Paul tells us here, is precisely so that human people might gropingly strive for the love and the truth that lie eternally beyond them.

Every attempt to define and delimit God will invariably yield an anthropomorphic projection of human desires, prejudices, aspirations, and idolatries that serves to sacralize our own limited perspectives and decisions. C. Leonard Allen offers a helpful description of the human tendency to form God in our own image:

> Not only do we form God into our own personal image, we also form God in the image of the social grouping to which we belong. . . . God becomes to some degree a projection of the economic and social values we hold dear and thus serves as the legitimator and preserver of those values. So the God of middle-class white Americans views America as Number One, or perhaps as the elect nation chosen to lead the world in the paths of righteousness. God sanctions the American work ethic where prosperity and affluence become signs of divine favor and poverty becomes a sign of moral failure. God becomes an ardent capitalist, a supporter of the nuclear arms race, a proponent of the "American dream." This God may even lend cautious support to the credo that happiness is measured by pleasure and secured by material accumulation. God, in short, begins to sound a lot like successful, patriotic, upwardly-mobile, church-going Americans.[26]

This tendency is nowhere more evident than in Cloud and Townsend's depiction of God as a suburban property owner who assumes responsibility for his own house and yard. In the spiritual realm as well as the physical, they claim, "the owner of the property is legally responsible for what happens on his or her property. Non-owners are not responsible for the property."[27] Like any good middle-class home owner, God takes care of his own clearly defined property and allows his neighbors to respect or neglect or destroy theirs as they see fit: "God sets standards," they write, "but he lets people be who they are and then separates himself from them when they misbehave, saying in effect, 'You can be that way if you choose,

---

[26] C. Leonard Allen, *The Cruciform Church: Becoming a Cross-Shaped People in a Secular World* (Abilene, TX: ACU Press, 2006), 104–5.

[27] Cloud and Townsend, *Boundaries,* 31.

but you cannot come into my house.'"[28] As long as humans do not make trouble for God, he also "respects our boundaries."[29]

In many—perhaps most—cultures outside the United States, however, this conception of private property and individual responsibility would be completely unintelligible. Even in many other industrialized and democratic societies, there is a far more robust notion of social solidarity and the common good that serves as a basis for politics and personal responsibility. This is generally even truer for the cultures of developing societies. The delightful movie *The Gods Must Be Crazy* (1980) offers a glimpse into the ways that exclusive ownership is a culturally particular phenomenon—and perhaps not a particularly good one. In this movie (which admittedly offers an overly idealistic picture of tribal life), the harmony and contentment of a community in rural Botswana is ruptured when a Coke bottle drops unbroken from an airplane flying overhead. The introduction of a scarce commodity—the Coke bottle—brings with it the experiences of envy, discontentment, and violence. The African proverbs affirming "I am strong if you are strong" or even "I am because we are" also indicate that Cloud and Townsend's sense of individual responsibility and autonomy is nowhere written into the laws of the universe. Inscribing the notion of legal entitlement to private property onto the nature of reality as Cloud and Townsend do serves to provide unwarranted divine sanction to an American ethic of possessive individualism.

Such individualistic and libertarian notions of personal property not only are entirely foreign to many cultures but also fail to recognize the dynamic nature of personal boundaries, which are shifting, variable, and often only recognizable in the context of concrete interactions with others. Although the authors do stipulate that "you own your boundaries. They do not own you," and hence we are able to "renegotiate" the boundaries we set with others when that is appropriate,[30] their guiding metaphor of exclusively owned property and their claim that boundaries "define your soul . . . , leading to a sense of ownership"[31] is far too static. Contrary to the idea that "we [alone] have to deal with what is in our soul, and boundaries help us to define what that is,"[32] a person is formed not by fixed boundaries like a parcel of land but rather *at* the boundaries of the

---

[28] Ibid., 45.
[29] Ibid., 236; cf. 55.
[30] Ibid., 124.
[31] Ibid., 31.
[32] Ibid., 32.

loves that both center and draw her beyond herself in important ways. In her discussion of human persons as "embodied spirits" or "inspirited bodies"—that is, both finite and transcendent—Margaret Farley describes how "when we open ourselves to relationship through knowledge and love, we transcend what we already are. To step into relation is to step out of a center that holds only ourselves. We open ourselves radically, whether minimally or maximally, to come into union by knowing and loving. . . . Our center is now both beyond ourselves and within ourselves."[33] Farley is by no means denying the importance of personal autonomy and boundaries, but her statement points to the way that authentic personhood is not only about defining our boundaries and living within them but also about expanding and reaching out beyond them by inviting others in— including, perhaps most importantly, the Spirit of God.

Yet the Christian God is almost entirely absent from *Boundaries*. There is no entry for "Christ," "Cross," "Spirit," or "Holy Spirit" listed in the book's index, and the two occurrences of the idea of God as Trinity serve primarily to reinforce the notion of three bounded persons having their own distinct responsibilities.[34] If a God beyond the limits of human culture and comprehension causes trouble for *Boundaries*, however, the God of cross and resurrection creates greater problems still for the idea that "we need to develop boundaries like God's" as a means of defense and self-preservation.[35] The Christian story is not the story of a God who "limits his exposure to evil, unrepentant people" but rather the story of a God who "welcomes sinners and eats with them" (Luke 15:1-2; cf. Matt 9:10-11) and who proves his love by dying for human beings while we were still sinners (Rom 5:8). Although Cloud and Townsend recognize that human boundaries exist for the sake of love, they fail to consider Jesus' words that "no one has greater love than this, to lay down one's life for one's friends" (John 15:13). Furthermore, the apostle Paul tells us, though Christ was in the form and nature of God, "he became obedient to the point of death—even death on a cross" (Phil 2:8).

While Boersma makes the mistake of interpreting the cross as a place of divine rather than human violence, Cloud and Townsend deny the cross altogether—not only for humans, who they claim can successfully "take

---

[33] Margaret Farley, *Just Love: A Framework for Christian Sexual Ethics* (London: Continuum, 2006), 129.

[34] Cloud and Townsend, *Boundaries*, 35, 269.

[35] Ibid., 35.

control" of their lives by setting appropriate boundaries, but also for God: "Whenever God decides that 'enough is enough' and he has suffered long enough, he respects his own property, his heart, enough to do something to make it better. He takes responsibility for the pain and moves to make his life different. He lets go of the rejecting people and reaches out to some new friends," they write.[36] In an almost embarrassingly anthropomorphic passage on God's forgiveness (and an oblique reference to the cross), Cloud and Townsend state that "God did not deny what we did to him. He worked through it. He named it. He expressed his feelings about it. He cried and was angry. And then he let it go."[37]

But such a limited view of God denies both God's mercy and God's power, for if God's mercy is not broad enough to embrace those who are sinful and suffering, then neither is his power great enough to save them. Rather, as the words of Frederick William Faber's hymn gratefully sing,

> There's a wideness in God's mercy
> like the wideness of the sea;
> there's a kindness in God's justice
> which is more than liberty.
> There is welcome for the sinner
> and more graces for the good;
> there is mercy with the Saviour;
> there is healing in his blood.
>
> There is no place that earth's sorrows
> are felt more than in heaven;
> there is no place where earth's failings
> have such kind judgment given.
> There is plentiful redemption
> in the blood that has been shed;
> there is joy for all the members
> in the sorrows of the Head.
>
> For the love of God is broader
> than the measure of man's mind;
> and the heart of the Eternal
> is most wonderfully kind.
> If our loves were but more faithful,
> we should take him at his word;

[36] Ibid., 241.
[37] Ibid., 269.

and our lives would be thanksgiving
for the goodness of the Lord.

But it does not actually seem that God or God's Spirit have much of a role to play in saving, sanctifying, and healing human lives according to Henry Cloud and John Townsend. Aside from a few passing mentions of grace and prayer throughout the book, the authors' practical advice focuses solely on "horizontal" and therapeutic strategies for recognizing and expressing boundaries consistent with a person's own feelings and personal goals—from losing weight to saving money to becoming free from parasitic friends and family members.[38] While their advice in this realm is sound and they do identify the church as a potential part of a "support network," they make no room for inviting the Spirit of God into the process of discerning—and more importantly, empowering the transformation of—our boundaries. For all their insightful emphasis on truth, Cloud and Townsend fail to acknowledge that even the truth of our own lives often lies beyond us. "This is the Spirit of truth," Jesus told his disciples, "whom the world cannot receive, because it neither sees him nor knows him. You know him because he abides with you, and he will be in you" (John 14:17). Not only our limited cultural perspectives and our self-deceptive blindness to our sin but also our lives' unforeseeable possibilities and untold potential require us to look to God—beyond our own perception of our boundaries—to help us define them. That is, not only our limitations as finite beings but also our possibilities as transcendent, spiritual creatures made in God's image should be defined by God, not us.

Though I realize that the critiques I have just articulated may seem harsh, I truly do not mean to discount the value of Boundaries as a study in human psychology. The authors' insight into the ways that most people's "boundary issues" stem from their experiences as young children, and their perceptive questions for reflection are very helpful for understanding human boundaries and limits. Self-awareness and self-preservation are both important, and despite their questionable theology, Cloud and Townsend offer valuable guidance for understanding human boundaries. It is true, as they say, that it is better to say a clear and honest "no" to what we do not desire or are not prepared to welcome than to invite hostility by making resentful and dishonest sacrifices. Nonetheless, it is absolutely crucial that we recognize

---

[38] See, for example, advice given on pages 228–32, 260–67, and 291 of Cloud and Townsend, Boundaries.

that these are our boundaries—and not God's—in order to avoid turning our own limits of security into idols of comfort, success, and control. A more helpful theological basis for approaching the question of boundaries might ground its insights in not only human *likeness to* but also human *difference from God*—for although we are given life by the breath of God, we are also creatures of dust, and to dust we shall return (Gen 2:7; 3:19). And yet recognizing the way that human finitude differentiates us from God also indicates that our limitations are only one pole of our spiritual lives. We must also recognize that through practicing hospitality to the infinite and unbounded Spirit of Truth, we are empowered to live beyond what limits us.

Beyond the Economics of Scarcity

Contrary to the way it may seem in light of such repeated calls to look beyond ostensible human boundaries, the *affirmation* of finite, material existence is in fact one of the underlying goals of this book. From the accounts of creation in Genesis to the incarnation of Christ to the institution of the sacraments, there is solid ground for such affirmation within the Christian tradition. Our particularity as embodied and historical men and women should not be understood as something evil or regrettable in itself but should rather be seen as an opportunity to contribute in a distinctive way to a specific place, community of people, or moment in history. There may also be, in Martha Nussbaum's words, a "particular beauty of human excellence" found precisely in its vulnerability.[39] The practice of hospitality, which I have argued *requires* a definite place and time, is a way of affirming this particular reality precisely by opening it to others. And yet, without a doubt, there is a tragic dimension to finite existence, an unavoidable clash of competing goods: not only are we unable to do all the good we might like to (or perhaps ought to) do, but sometimes distance and inevitably death also separate us from people we love. Our limited perspectives can cause us to make unjust choices, often in relation to the finite, material resources at our disposal. As Charles Camosy states in his book on this topic, however, "though we must live in this *tragic* situation, we need not live in an *unjust* situation"[40]—even in life's most tragic circumstances, it is possible to opt for truth, nonviolence, and gratitude.

[39] Martha Nussbaum, *The Fragility of Goodness* (Cambridge: Cambridge University Press, 1986), 2.

[40] Charles Camosy, *Too Expensive to Treat? Finitude, Tragedy, and the Neonatal ICU* (Grand Rapids, MI: Eerdmans, 2010), 1.

Even so, beyond the economics of finitude and scarcity, there is, in John Koenig's words, "a secret abundance [built] into the scheme of things, an abundance that can more than fill our needs when we seek to form partnerships for the kingdom." Based on his exegetical study of New Testament hospitality, Koenig identifies an "economics of the Spirit" that "presumes a reciprocity between God's abundance and human acts of sacrifice."[41] Although the idea of "sacrifice" has become almost synonymous with tragedy, deprivation, and resentment—as in Cloud and Townsend's statement that "God wants us to be compliant from the inside out (compassionate), not compliant on the outside and resentful on the inside (sacrificial)"[42]— Koenig specifies that he takes sacrifice in its original sense of "making something sacred by offering it up to God."[43] Thus, it is not deprivation as such but rather willing and intentional renunciation for the sake of the kingdom that is the mark of a true sacrifice.

Once again, Cloud and Townsend are quite right to say that it may be better for a person to be honest with herself and others about what she is not able or willing to do than to make a resentful and dishonest sacrifice. But we are not freed from our hostility and resentment simply by drawing clearer boundaries. Disciplines of gratitude must invite God into our boundaries so that *God empowers a grateful sacrifice*—not only in the sense of enabling us find joy in giving up what may be rightfully ours for the sake of another but also in the sense of empowerment in that just as God multiplied the loaves and the fishes in the hands of Jesus, God miraculously multiplies things that are offered up with gratitude. Men and women can willingly and even joyfully forgo some of their legitimate interests for the sake of another person or a higher good and find that their sacrifice yields far more than it cost them. As Jesus told his disciples, "there is no one who has left house or brothers or sisters or mother or father or children or fields, for my sake and for the sake of the good news, who will not receive a hundredfold now in this age" (Mark 10:29-30)—although he also explains that with such abundance will come persecution.

---

[41] John Koenig, New Testament Hospitality: Partnership with Strangers as Promise and Mission (Eugene, OR: Wipf and Stock, 2001), 130.

[42] Cloud and Townsend, Boundaries, 54. Here the authors claim to be commenting on Jesus' words in Matthew 9:13 stating that God desires compassion (NASB)—also translated "mercy"—and not sacrifice, but they neglect the second half of this verse, which reveals what Jesus meant by this statement: "For I have come to call not the righteous but sinners."

[43] Koenig, New Testament Hospitality, 131.

As the following chapter will show, accounts of ministry among the poor often testify to God's miraculous provision and protection in circumstances of extreme need. In her accounts of their truly radical ministry among the orphans of Mozambique, charismatic missionary Heidi "Mama Ida" Baker often tells of such divine provision. Since 1980, Heidi and her husband, Rolland Baker, have served thousands of orphaned children from the streets and trash dumps of Maputo, Pemba, and rural villages of Mozambique, which they chose precisely because it was one of the poorest and most violent nations on earth at the time. She explains how at one point, when she and her husband were overwhelmed with the desperate need around them,

> We didn't know how to cope. We had nowhere near the food or the cooking and sanitation facilities we needed. . . . Everyone was exhausted; everything was in complete chaos. And more children kept gravitating toward our gate. . . . We weren't prepared in any way to feed all those children. A precious woman from the US embassy came over with food. "I brought you chili and rice for your family!" I opened the door and showed her all our children. "I have a big family!" I pointed out tiredly, but in complete and desperate earnest. My friend got serious. "There's not enough! I need to go home and cook some more!" but I just told her to pray over the food. . . . We began serving, and right from the start I gave everyone a full bowl. I was dazed and overwhelmed. I barely understood at the time what a wonderful thing was happening. But all of our children ate, the staff ate, my friend ate, and even our family of four ate. Everyone had enough. Since then, we have never said no to an orphaned, abandoned, or dying child. Now we feed and take care of more than one thousand children. They eat and drink all they want of the Lord's goodness. Because he died, there is always enough.[44]

Stories of miracles—food multiplication, healing, protection, and guidance—are generally dismissed by most contemporary Westerners (including those who claim to believe in the story of Jesus, replete as it is with stories of the miraculous) as craziness or kooky superstition that can be explained away by modern science. But as Shane Claiborne (author and founder of the Simple Way community) explains, perhaps such people live at too great a distance from real sacrifice or insecurity to experience the economics of the spirit: "We have insulated ourselves from miracles,"

[44] Heidi and Rolland Baker, *There is Always Enough* (Kent, UK: Sovereign World, 2003), 52.

he writes. "We no longer live with such reckless faith that we need them. There is rarely room for the transcendent in our lives. If we get sick, we go to a doctor. If we need food, we go to a store and buy it."[45] Yet Claiborne and many others who have adopted voluntary poverty as a sacrifice for the sake of the kingdom point to the way that sacrifices made in faith and gratitude introduce God's abundance into finite lives. Dorothy Day, whose work will be the focus of the following chapter, explains that "we must often be settling down happily to the cornmeal cakes, to the last bit of food in the house, before the miracle of the increase comes about"—but the increase *does* come, and "somehow everything works out," and "there will be enough."[46] Indeed, the limits of security—in the sense that a host must himself be materially secure in order to provide for others—are called into question by the poor themselves. One can find countless literary and anecdotal accounts that identify the way in which faith in God's provision and generous compassion for others is necessary for survival in poverty in ways that are unknown to those in positions of greater affluence.

The faith and generosity of the poor were made clear to me in abundant ways during a trip to San Diego a number of years ago when I was in town to present a conference paper on hospitality and borders. One afternoon while I was there, I decided to take the trolley to the Mexican border, and it did not take long for the environment outside the trolley window to change from the impressive and immaculate streets of downtown San Diego to a dirtier, wearier, more industrial landscape. Just past the 12th and Imperial transfer station, an African American man and woman sat down across from where I sat and began talking to a Mexican woman with purple hair in the seat beside me. They were telling her about a homeless Mexican man who was often on the streets near where they lived, who was in the United States illegally, and who had recently disappeared. The man sitting across from me—Bryson, as he later introduced himself—wore a large gold cross prominently around his neck. He expressed hope that the homeless man had simply returned to Mexico, although he feared that the man had been kidnapped. "We try to do what we can for the people on the streets," he explained when it became obvious that I was listening to their conversation. "We get them some food, take them home, and get them cleaned up. It's not much, and you can't help everyone, but we try

---

[45] Shane Claiborne, *The Irresistible Revolution: Living as an Ordinary Radical* (Grand Rapids, MI: Zondervan, 2006), 48, cf. 180–82.

[46] Dorothy Day, *House of Hospitality*, 60.

to do what we can," he said, describing how they had been homeless for several months when they first came to San Diego years ago. They also told of how their faith in Christ informed their practice of hospitality, enthusiastically sharing Bible verses about how Jesus was homeless.

Later that afternoon I met Toby, a young man who had come to Tijuana from Louisiana with his disabled father because they could get more affordable medical care and prescription drugs in Mexico than in the United States. Toby and his father were providing hospitality to two brothers (whom I also met) who had recently lost their home in the fires outside San Diego. Back in the city that evening, I encountered an elderly woman in a wheelchair who was begging for change on the street. She had a beautiful light in her face, and when I stopped to give her what was in my pocket and offered a brief "Bless you" along with a few quarters and dimes, she told me, "Oh, I *am* blessed!" and explained to me how God was her best friend: "He gives me everything I need."

None of this is meant to deny the reality of finite resources or the harshness of poverty or to imply that acknowledging limits entails a lack of faith. But even aside from those things that one might consider miracles of a supernatural sort, there are a variety of straightforward ways that the limits of resources can be extended. One of these is *practicing* hospitality, plain and simple: it gets much easier to say yes to one or two or eight more dinner guests when you have had some practical experience cooking for a large group and learning how to make a meal go a little further when necessary (by making more rice or pasta, more salad or vegetables or bread) or how to throw something together with whatever happens to be on hand. As shown by the description of Marge Hughes, whom Dorothy Day describes as "the epitome of hospitality," it is often possible for someone with a bit of skill to make a lovely meal out of very little:

> When there is nothing in the house but rice and a few vestiges of vegetables, she can produce a delicious dinner consisting mainly of fried rice and onions. Hers is a joyous and uncomplaining spirit, never perturbed, always welcoming. . . . Like the widow of Zarephath, she does not hesitate to use "the last of her meal and oil" for the needy and hungry guest, and somehow there is "always enough for one more."[47]

---

[47] Day, *Loaves and Fishes*, 143.

Sometimes a person's practical skill and her hospitable disposition are in fact her most important resources, far more significant than material abundance.

Yet another way of extending scarce resources involves *sharing* them with others—including extending resources of time and energy by sharing in the practice of hospitality as a community. As with the example of Weather Amnesty that I offered in the first chapter—in which the hospitality of the extended community was significantly greater than what an individual or family or even those living at the Catholic Worker could have provided by themselves—sharing in the practice of hospitality not only multiplies the finite material and human resources needed to sustain it but can also expand a sense of security by finding safety in solidarity with others. It is quite understandable for human hosts to be overwhelmed and insecure if they feel like they are going it alone in their sacrifices and attempts to welcome strangers, as Ana María Pineda explains: "Hospitality is made up of hard work undertaken under risky conditions, and without structures and commitments for welcoming others, fear crowds out what needs to be done. . . . In the face of overwhelming human need for shelter and care, and in the face of our own fear of strangers, we need to develop ways of supporting one another in the practice of hospitality."[48]

Pineda describes how St. Peter's parish, a church in the Mission District of San Francisco, is deeply committed to the practice of hospitality to meet the needs of the surrounding community. "In spite of its limited resources," she writes, "this parish continually looks for ways to extend hospitality, helping both guests and hosts to grow stronger in the many aspects and richness of this practice. Here, hospitality extends beyond feeding the hungry and sheltering the homeless; here, it also involves creating space where people can learn how to receive and give."[49] This dynamic of giving and receiving—the economy of gift—allows people to look beyond scarcity and possessiveness to the needs of those around them.

Beyond the Idolatry of Security

Just as the limits of hospitality are formed by the tension between material comfort and sacrifice, possession and gift, so also are they shaped

---

[48] Ana María Pineda, "Hospitality," in *Practicing Our Faith: A Way of Life for a Searching People*, ed. Dorothy Bass (San Francisco: Jossey-Bass Publishers, 1997), 35.

[49] Ibid., 36.

by the tension between safety and vulnerability. As I explained earlier in this chapter and in numerous ways throughout this book, it is necessary for a space to be safe for both hosts and guests if it is to be a place of hospitality rather than a place of violence, hostility, and fear. And yet the legitimate need for security and control can easily become inhospitable and even idolatrous when these needs are made absolute, crowding out openness even to God. Once a host or guest finds it necessary to employ violence for the sake of security, hospitality is significantly limited, if not altogether lost. Here, many of the well-worn lines of argument about the legitimacy of just war or pacifism as expressions of Christian responsibility are relevant to the context of hospitality and the limits of security. While "realists" emphasize the intractability of sin and Christians' obligation to use violence if necessary to defend the vulnerable against evil, Christian pacifists maintain that discipleship requires following in the nonviolent footsteps of Jesus and trusting God for ultimate outcomes. My point in this section is not primarily concerned with the question of armed international conflict but rather with the ways that human "illusions of immortality" and control can lead people to make their own security into an idol that commands the violent exclusion of the spirit of hospitality.

The contest for human worship and allegiance between the true God and idols is an important theme throughout the narratives of the Old Testament. Time and time again, Israel turns from the covenant with YHWH to worship the gods of other cultures or even images that they themselves created. The story of the prophet Hosea powerfully identifies how "they keep on sinning and make a cast image for themselves, idols of silver made according to their understanding, all of them the work of artisans" (13:2) but also tells of the truth of God's merciful love: "I will not execute my fierce anger . . . ; for I am God and no mortal, the Holy One in your midst, and I will not come in wrath" (11:9). Such is the pattern throughout the stories of the judges, prophets, and kings. It is crucial to recognize, however, that idolatry need not be as primitive or blatant as bowing down before a golden calf; in several places throughout his letters, the apostle Paul identifies greed with idolatry (e.g., Eph 5:5; Col 3:5), indicating that an idol may be "anything that people devote their lives to, place their trust in, make sacrifices for, or invest with ultimate significance,"[50] whether that something is wealth or accomplishments or personal relationships or national security.

[50] C. Leonard Allen, *The Cruciform Church*, 99.

As a number of theologians and scholars have pointed out, despite the veneer of transcendence, all idolatry is in fact a projection of human self-interest, an "allegiance to something beyond ourselves that we view as ultimately good (or as God) but which, in reality, we use to serve our own purposes" and which attempts to make God "less elusive, less sovereign, less free, more at the beck and call of human interests."[51] In many ways, the more noble the end or object of one's devotion—justice or freedom or family or church—the deeper is the temptation to identify God with it and thereby subordinate God to it. For this reason, security—whether of one's own life or possessions or the safety of one's family or nation—is a particularly subtle and tenacious idol, which is closely related to human illusions of immortality. As Nouwen explains in Reaching Out, even though humans claim to be aware of their mortality, they often behave in ways that "eternalize" their lives and property and thereby justify the construction of violent defenses to protect these as ultimate values that must be maintained at any cost. "Our human relationships easily become subject to violence and destruction when we treat our own and other people's lives as properties to be conquered or defended and not as gifts to be received," he writes.[52] Moving beyond hostility to hospitality therefore requires unmasking illusions of immortality and entering into prayer, which involves the grateful recognition that God, not us, is ultimately responsible for our lives. This movement is difficult but worthwhile, "since it leads us from false certainties to true uncertainties, from an easy support system to a risky surrender, and from the many 'safe' gods to the God whose love has no limits."[53]

Indeed, as Stanley Hauerwas has repeatedly affirmed throughout his writing, "when we try to live securely rather than well, our world begins to shrink,"[54] and we are in fact mastered by our own illusions of control. "Living well," in contrast, involves the recognition that the unexpected—including the unexpected visitor—is often our greatest resource. Hauerwas explains that the cross reveals to Christians that they must "seek not so much to be effective as to be faithful" and must learn to "live out of control

---

[51] Ibid. Cf. Daniel Groody, *Globalization, Spirituality, and Justice* (Maryknoll, NY: Orbis, 2009), 43–47.

[52] Henri Nouwen, *Reaching Out: The Three Movements of the Spiritual Life* (New York: Doubleday/Image Books, 1975), 116, 119.

[53] Ibid., 126.

[54] Stanley Hauerwas, "The Servant Community," in *The Hauerwas Reader*, ed. John Berkman and Michael Cartwright (Durham, NC: Duke University Press, 2001), 381.

in the sense that we must assume God will use our faithfulness to make his kingdom reality in the world."[55] This does not mean that Christians should not work to promote justice in the world or that they should seek out martyrdom but rather that the ends of self-preservation and even justice do not legitimate the use of violent means for their attainment. Hauerwas makes it clear that those who are violent must be resisted, but "on our terms"—that is, in accordance with the story of Jesus and the ongoing presence of the Holy Spirit in the church. The "marks of the church" as he outlines them in this particular essay involve not only the celebration of the sacraments and the discipline of prayer—in which "we learn to make ourselves open to God's presence" and "let God loose in the world"[56]—but also hospitality to the stranger. Because they have been formed by God's love, Christians know that they need not fear the stranger: "We must be a people who have hospitable selves," he writes, and "we must be ready to be stretched by what we know not."[57]

But, one might ask, does our hospitable willingness to be stretched and challenged extend to the point that we are willing to be subject to the violence of others? Does it require that we forfeit the safety of those who are vulnerable for the sake of openness to the stranger? What do we do when openness and trust result in betrayal and hostility? Once again, both discernment and courage are in order: although prudence may suggest that we close our doors to some people so as not to invite harm to ourselves, our children, and our other guests, the virtues of patience and courage can help to ensure that this is a limit of hospitality rather than one of fear, paranoia, or prejudice. Even when exclusion and harm occur, the spirit of hospitality strives to affirm relationships—perhaps through extending forgiveness, seeking dialogue and understanding, or simply refusing to dismiss a person as unworthy of concern—when and however possible. Such a spirit of loving affirmation can only proceed from looking beyond the idolatry of security to find one's refuge in God, declaring with the Psalmist,

> The LORD is my light and my salvation;
>   whom shall I fear?
> The LORD is the stronghold of my life;

---

[55] Ibid., 380–81.

[56] Ibid., 384.

[57] Hauerwas, "Jesus and the Social Embodiment of the Peaceable Kingdom," in *The Hauerwas Reader*, 137.

of whom shall I be afraid?
Though an army encamp against me,
   my heart shall not fear;
though war rise up against me,
   yet will I be confident.
One thing I asked of the LORD,
   that will I seek after:
To live in the house of the LORD
   all the days of my life.
For he will hide me in his shelter
   in the day of trouble.
Wait for the LORD;
   be strong, and let your hearts take courage;
   wait for the LORD! (Ps 27:1, 3-5, 14)

Without such confidence, which comes as a result of dwelling with God in prayer, hospitality remains limited by human illusions and fears. In fact, for some people who have suffered trauma and violence, it may seem impossible to move beyond fears to extend hospitality to certain strangers—and I believe it would be unjust to suggest that they must do so—but it is also important to seek healing in supportive relationships and communities and to find hope in remembering that "with God all things are possible" (Mark 10:27).

Chapter 5

Radical Hospitality: Challenging Limits

We need Houses of Hospitality
  to give to the rich
  the opportunity
  to serve the poor.
We need Houses of Hospitality
  to bring the scholars
  to the workers
  or the workers
  to the scholars. . . .
We need Houses of Hospitality
  to show
  what idealism looks like
  when it is practiced.

—Peter Maurin[1]

The Catholic Worker

To those who are familiar with the Catholic Worker—and perhaps even to those who are not—its influence on this book has likely been obvious from its first pages. The movement's commitments to personalism, community, nonviolence, and works of mercy have shaped my own thought in important ways. And yet, on the surface of it, the Catholic Worker certainly seems like a strange place to look for guidance concerning the limits of hospitality. With respect to the material and psychological security

[1] Peter Maurin, "Houses of Hospitality," in *Easy Essays* (New York: Sheed & Ward, 1936), 46, http://www.catholicworker.org/roundtable/easyessays.cfm.

of hosts and guests, Catholic Worker Houses of Hospitality operate well beyond the average American's sense of boundaries and limits. Of his time at the Catholic Worker in New York City, historian Marc Ellis writes that "everyone was welcome . . . ; craziness and violence were part of the life Worker people had learned to accept,"[2] and virtually anyone with some experience in a Worker House of Hospitality can share similar stories of feeling overwhelmed and overworked, made hostile or humbled by the needs and demands of their guests (and fellow hosts). Nonetheless, as the writing of founder Dorothy Day and the testimonies of many others within the movement bear witness, even here there are limits—limits that I will argue correspond to those identified in the previous two chapters. Just as Day affirmed that "it is important that we not tell the world to follow us or tell the world that our way is the way to go, to be,"[3] I do not intend to present the Catholic Worker as a normative model for every practice of hospitality. Rather, by offering it as a radical and prophetic challenge to complacency and comfort, I hope to demonstrate further the tension that is ever present at the limits of hospitality, as well as the spirit of nonviolent affirmation at its heart.

The Catholic Worker Movement began in the season of Advent, 1932, with an encounter between French peasant Peter Maurin and Dorothy Day, a young journalist who had been active in the socialist movements of her time and who had converted to Catholicism several years before meeting Maurin. Day had just returned from a trip to Washington, DC, where she had prayed "with tears and with anguish, that some way would open up for me to use what talents I possessed for my fellow workers, for the poor,"[4] when Maurin came to her to present his three-part vision for "building a new society in the shell of the old . . . , 'a society in which it is easier for people to be good.'"[5] Maurin's vision, which was based on the principles of the Sermon on the Mount and the philosophy known as personalism, consisted of roundtable discussions and a newspaper for the "clarification of thought," houses of hospitality to provide food and shelter to those in need, and farming communes. Within months, the first issue of *The Catholic Worker* was distributed at a penny per copy, and by the

[2] Marc Ellis, *A Year at the Catholic Worker: A Spiritual Journey among the Poor* (Waco, TX: Baylor University Press, 2000), 23.

[3] Quoted in Robert Coles, *Dorothy Day: A Radical Devotion* (Reading, MA: Perseus Books, 1987), 113.

[4] Dorothy Day, *The Long Loneliness* (New York: Harper & Brothers, 1952), 166.

[5] Ibid., 170.

end of 1933, it had a circulation of one hundred thousand, and news of the incipient movement rapidly spread around the country. Shortly after the paper was released, people began to come to the offices of *The Catholic Worker* to seek food and shelter, and the first Houses of Hospitality and breadlines began. "We were just sitting there talking when lines of people began to form, saying 'We need bread,'" Day writes in the postscript to *The Long Loneliness*. "We were just sitting there talking and people moved in on us. . . . And somehow the walls expanded."[6]

It was in such Houses of Hospitality—which soon sprang up not only in New York City under Day and Maurin but also in numerous other cities around the United States—that the Catholic Worker's commitment to personalism and the works of mercy became most concrete. Both the corporal works of mercy (feeding the hungry, giving drink to the thirsty, clothing the naked, sheltering the homeless, visiting the sick, ransoming the prisoner, and burying the dead) and the spiritual works of mercy (instructing the ignorant, counseling the doubtful, rebuking the sinner, bearing wrongs patiently, forgiving injuries, and praying for the living and the dead) were central to the identity of the movement and were seen as a form of direct action against the dehumanizing forces of industrial capitalism and the impersonal nation-state. As I mentioned briefly in chapter 1, one of the key elements of the philosophy of personalism is an emphasis on personal responsibility: every person should take responsibility for the good of his or her neighbors rather than assuming that this is the duty of the state or some other organization. In one of his "Easy Essays" written to disseminate the philosophy of the movement, Maurin wrote that

> People no longer
> consider hospitality to the poor
> as a personal duty.
> And it does not disturb them a bit
> to send them to the city. . . .
> But the hospitality that the "Muni"
> gives to the down and out
> is no hospitality
> because what comes from the taxpayer's pocketbook
> does not come from his heart.[7]

[6] Ibid., 285.
[7] Quoted in Harry Murray, *Do Not Neglect Hospitality: The Catholic Worker and the Homeless* (Philadelphia: Temple University Press, 1990), 52.

As Michael Baxter has explained, this emphasis on direct action and personal responsibility marks the Catholic Worker as a radical movement in contrast to its liberal counterparts: "Liberals say, 'Hey! The homeless aren't being fed. Let's march on the city hall.' Radicals say, 'The homeless aren't being fed. Let's feed them.' . . . Getting down to the basics means I've got to do it. We've got to do it. We've all got to make this thing concrete in our lives. . . . We say, 'Let's return to the heart of the Gospel, to the Beatitudes. Let's really live this life as the early Christians did.'"[8] Indeed, despite persistent allegations of communism from its critics, the Worker's communitarian vision of property as well as its pacifism sprang directly from the New Testament's account of the teachings of Jesus and the early Christian community. Maurin, Day, and others involved in the movement have sought to live out the words of the gospels—"Whoever has two coats should share with anyone who has none; and whoever has food must do likewise" (Luke 3:11)—and the belief that "whatever we have beyond our own needs belongs to the poor."[9]

Although Maurin's vision and Day's leadership and prolific writing continue to shape the Catholic Worker in decisive ways, the very personalism that informed the movement's aims and purposes (as well as the anarchism of some of its members) has encouraged a considerable amount of variation among the numerous communities around the country. While some offer daily meals, others give short- or long-term shelter to those who need a place to live, while still others help to provide clothing or housewares or offer after-school programs for children or are engaged in a host of other activities, from war resistance to community gardens and grocery cooperatives. Even within particular communities, adherence to the Worker's personalist norm often means that there are only the most minimal rules governing community life (e.g., no fighting, no drugs or drinking), and even these are not always strictly enforced. Rather, those in positions of responsibility are often told to use their judgment when deciding whether to allow a particular guest to stay or when dealing with a problem.[10] For all these reasons, the Catholic Worker is not a movement that is easy to pin down—particularly when it comes to some of the limits

---

[8] Quoted in Rosalie Riegle Troester, ed. *Voices from the Catholic Worker* (Philadelphia: Temple University Press, 1993), 517.

[9] Dorothy Day, *Loaves and Fishes* (Maryknoll, NY: Orbis, 1997), 92.

[10] See, for example, Murray, *Do Not Neglect Hospitality*, 94, though it should be noted that the extent of rules and methods of deciding who stays or leaves vary considerably between different communities.

and practices that concern us here—and it is not my intention to do so; as one observer has noted, "trying to define the Catholic Worker is like trying to bottle morning fog."[11] Nonetheless, insofar as Day represents a paradigmatic voice of the Catholic Worker Movement, it is possible to trace several key features that are present to some degree in most communities. I have already mentioned personalism and the works of mercy, but it is also important to recognize a commitment to voluntary poverty and to nonviolence in the life of the Catholic Worker. Furthermore—at least in the life of Dorothy Day, if not that of every person who has followed her—devotion to prayer and to other spiritual disciplines was essential to the Worker's active practice of hospitality to the poor.

Poverty and Precarity

"Poverty is a strange and elusive thing," Dorothy Day writes in her book *Loaves and Fishes*. "I condemn poverty and I advocate it; poverty is simple and complex at once; it is a social phenomenon and a personal matter. . . . Yes, the poor will always be with us—Our Lord told us that—and there will always be a need for our sharing. . . . But I am sure that God did not intend that there be so many poor."[12] Yet from the Catholic Worker's beginnings through its operations today, Day and others have been committed not only to providing for the needs of the poorest of the poor—"the least of these"—but also to sharing in the poverty and precariousness of their existence. For a number of reasons, the Catholic Worker refused financial assistance from the government and official church agencies and instead relied exclusively on goodwill donations from neighbors and supporters, so that "there is never anything left over, and we will always have a few debts to keep us worrying, to make us more like the very poor we are trying to help."[13] Indeed, as I have mentioned in previous chapters, it was explicitly part of the aims of the Catholic Worker not only to meet the needs of the poor—which could perhaps be done more effectively through impersonal charity—but also to foster solidarity across social classes by blurring the line between Worker and guest. As Harry Murray observes of one house in particular, "Workers wore clothes from the same clothing room that supplied the guests. . . . An observer can be at a house for days

---

[11] Riegle Troester, *Voices from the Catholic Worker*, xvii.
[12] Day, *Loaves and Fishes*, 71, 74.
[13] Ibid., 91.

and still not be sure who is Worker and who is guest."[14] Of course, the extent of Workers' voluntary poverty differs from place to place, as does the nature of the distinction between guests and Workers, but in general the movement strives to narrow the distance between those who offer and those who receive hospitality.

For this reason, there is no mistaking the sense of living "on the edge" that characterizes accounts of life at the Worker ("just how to pay for the supply of food we need is an exercise in faith and hope"[15]), although Day also writes of the "little miracles" that fill a life lived for the sake of the kingdom of God and the ways in which—as if in direct response to prayer—their needs were met. "During this last cold snap, one of the girls from the apartment came in to tell us they could use four more blankets," she writes, "and that very afternoon a car drove up to the office and four blankets—beautifully heavy ones—were brought in by a chauffeur."[16] On another occasion, she describes how, when they had overdrawn their bank account by two hundred dollars, she and her companions stopped at a church to pray. Upon returning to the Catholic Worker's offices, they served tea and toast to a woman who had come to visit and who left them a check for the exact amount of the overdraft—though they had not mentioned their need to her.[17] While she expresses great gratitude for such miraculous provision and for the many simple joys that can be found even in a life of poverty, Day also makes clear that giving up one's possessions and dignity "are hard, hard things; and I don't think they get any easier."[18]

The economics of the spirit—that "secret abundance" born of human acts of sacrifice made in faith—that marks Day's accounts of the Worker certainly serve to deconstruct conventional limits of security. While she is keenly aware of the material (and emotional) resources necessary to provide hospitality to those in need, it often seems that Day and others at the Worker extend hospitality beyond what seems possible given their lack of material security. "God seems to intend us to depend solely on Him," she writes. "We must live this lesson of dependence on Him that we preach in these pages. Economic security, something every reader and

---

[14] Murray, *Do Not Neglect Hospitality*, 109. "Where does the staff begin and where does it leave off?" Day asks in a chapter of *Loaves and Fishes* entitled "Editors also Cook."

[15] Day, *Loaves and Fishes*, 89.

[16] Dorothy Day, "Another Miracle, Please, St. Joseph," in *Selected Writings: By Little and By Little*, ed. Robert Ellsberg (Maryknoll, NY: Orbis, 2009), 60.

[17] Day, *Loaves and Fishes*, 91.

[18] Ibid., 84.

we ourselves would like to have, is not for us."[19] And yet, she also points to the deeper reality of how ephemeral every instance of material security is and how true security can only come through following the precepts of the gospels[20] and living "so close to the bottom that when you fall you do not have far to drop, you do not have much to lose."[21] Such advice seems strikingly pertinent—perhaps as much now as when Day wrote these statements more than seventy-five years ago.

But it was not only the inadequacy of their material resources that made life at the Worker so precarious—it was also the immensity of need. Beginning in Lower Manhattan during the Great Depression when millions of working-age adults were unemployed and many who came to them were mentally ill or addicts—"the undeserving poor," Day sometimes remarks—it seemed that there was *always* more to do, others to feed or shelter. "It sometimes seemed that the more space we had, the more people came to us for help, so that our quarters were never quite adequate," Day writes. "But somehow we managed. Characters of every description and from every corner of life turned up—and we welcomed them all."[22] And yet, both in Day's accounts of life at the Worker and in those of others, it is clear that the limits of finite spaces and resources necessitate drawing boundaries for the sake of all involved.

In one "roundtable discussion" recorded in Rosalie Riegle Troester's *Voices from the Catholic Worker*, Workers from around the country discuss the perennial tension between an emphasis on the *quantity* versus the *quality* of hospitality that a house provides: "One theory is that when a stranger comes to the door, it's Christ and you let him in," Fr. Richard McSorley comments. "And the other theory is that if you're going to let Christ in, you don't want to have Christ sleep under the sink, and you don't want Christ to crowd out all the other Christs that are already in there."[23] Others who took part in the discussion affirm that beyond a certain point, one can scarcely speak of hospitality in any meaningful way. "I'm not really

---

[19] Day, "Thank You!" in *Selected Writings*, 61.

[20] "Why they think a weekly wage is going to give them security is a mystery. Do they have security on any job nowadays? If they try to save, the bank fails; if they invest their money, the bottom of the market drops out. . . . They have no security and they know it. The only security comes in following the precepts and counsels of the Gospels." Day, "Security," in *Selected Writings*, 69.

[21] Day, *Loaves and Fishes*, 86.

[22] Ibid., 37.

[23] Riegle Troester, *Voices from the Catholic Worker*, 164.

offering a home to anybody . . . by taking in another ten families and hanging them on hooks" or by having people sleeping on the landings of the stairways, says one Worker.[24] That is, offering hospitality—even to those in situations of desperate poverty—requires recognizing the human dignity of one's guests as well as their need. Discerning such limits is seldom easy, and a sense of tragedy and hopelessness may sometimes accompany the need to set boundaries—but these very limits can also be the ground for creativity and growth.

In numerous accounts of life at the Catholic Worker, one theme that regularly occurs is the way in which every effort is made to do what could be done for people, even when there is an inability to provide food or shelter. Even to offer as little as a piece of buttered bread to a person in need could be a sign of affirmation, of hospitality, despite the limits imposed by finite resources. Is it possible, while recognizing one's own limits, to leave a person even just a little better off than they were before? Day's own approach to limits was significantly informed by this question, as she recalls in *Loaves and Fishes*, "I kept remembering how St. Thérèse of Lisieux said that when you had to say no, when you had to refuse anyone anything, you could at least do it so that the person went away a bit happier."[25] Although doing even this much can be challenging at times, the only conditions of such limits of hospitality are genuine attention to the needs of another and gratitude for their presence.

Violence and Vulnerability

The precariousness that characterizes life for many in Catholic Worker Houses of Hospitality is not only a product of voluntary poverty and scarce resources but is also due to the Worker's commitment to nonviolence in contexts where violence is often the norm. At both an international[26] and an interpersonal level, the Worker strives to promote hospitality and to live out the Gospel demand to love enemies by resisting "a culture that resolves conflict and threat by destroying that which is threatening."[27]

---

[24] Ibid.

[25] Day, *Loaves and Fishes*, 84.

[26] The Catholic Worker's active opposition to war and the arms race is an important part of its commitment to nonviolence, though this will not be a focus of my discussion here.

[27] Angie O'Gorman and Patrick Coy, "Houses of Hospitality: A Pilgrimage into Nonviolence," in *Revolution of the Heart: Essays on the Catholic Worker*, ed. Patrick Coy (Philadelphia: Temple University Press, 1988), 241.

This commitment to nonviolence is necessary not only in situations when guests threaten violence toward Workers but also in adjudicating disputes between guests and, possibly most importantly, in dealing with the inevitable conflicts that arise among a staff of people who live and work together under intense pressure day after day.

Here may be as good a place as any to acknowledge, without any kind of thesis or conclusion, the relationship between violence and mental illness. The violence of war and the violence of sexual abuse both contribute to the number of our society who, from trauma and terror, suffer these things recurrently—and may even be compelled to revisit them on others. Day suffered much from these—or rather, suffered from and with those people who suffered them. In a diary entry of 1945, she tells of a mentally ill man who insisted that she get him back in the seminary from which he had been dismissed five years before:

> He would come in and stand over me with livid face—sweat rolling down his face—call down curses from heaven upon me, damning my soul to hell for interfering, as he said, with his vocation. . . .
>
> A few months before [there was] another mental case whose mother joined in abusing me in my lack of charity for not keeping her. . . . Thief, hypocrite, lacking in hospitality, charity, and brotherly love, lazy, a malingerer, expecting others to do all the work while I went traveling around the country, a liar, cheat, deceiver, perverter of Peter's teaching. People have so trembled with rage as they approached me, shaking their fists, shouting, beating on the table, that I have literally expected to be assaulted, beaten.
>
> One night I dreamt that I was struck. I have a haunting memory of having read somewhere about a woman being torn to pieces by a mob, and I am so surrounded by human hatred that I was afraid. . . .
>
> How fearful a work this is. I wonder at my presumption and yet I have to go on. I pray for love—that I may learn to love God, and I am surrounded by such human hatred and dislike that all natural love and companionship is taken from me. . . . I can only comfort myself by remembering that vines must be pruned to bear fruit. Love is being cut away to bear more love.[28]

The question of whether those who are mentally ill ought to be held responsible for the violence—verbal as well as physical—that they inflict on

---

[28] Dorothy Day, *The Duty of Delight: The Diaries of Dorothy Day*, ed. Robert Ellsberg (Milwaukee: Marquette University Press, 2008), 90.

others is a question that I am not able to answer here. Nonetheless, as is clear to anyone who has worked among the poor, the challenge of responding to violence once or twice removed is no less difficult or complicated than that of responding to it in its most obvious forms.

Though it may be unlikely that the staff of a Catholic Worker House would be *physically* violent with one another, the violence of thoughts and words is an ever-present danger in this context: "We're able to discipline ourselves into listening to some absolute lunatics and treating them with dignity and respect," one person explains. "Then when we're completely exhausted, one of our co-workers does something to disappoint us, and we berate them like we're probably tempted to do to the lunatic. . . . That displaced anger is one of the perennial problems of the Catholic Worker."[29] It is for this reason that Angie O'Gorman and Patrick Coy advocate the importance of "disarming one's heart" as part of a pilgrimage to nonviolence:

> It is one thing to speak of nuclear disarmament between world powers and another to actively disarm one's heart when the missiles of anger or revenge are ready to fire. The Catholic Worker provides a context in which a different sort of "preparedness" is learned. One can begin to understand that self-preservation requires reconciliation rather than self-defense, and that security, whether personal or national, is impossible until it is available to all. Life at the Worker reveals that people can be firm in their need for personal security without jeopardizing the security of another. . . . Hospitality houses are on the front lines in the battle for a peaceful world.[30]

Not only in the relationships among staff members but also in their relationships with very poor and often desperate and disturbed guests, Workers' commitment to nonviolence is put to the test on a daily basis. "We've had some very troubled people here," Day explains in an interview with Robert Coles. "Some were dangerous. They came armed. They had knives and guns. They had been drinking a lot." She goes on to share the story of a situation in which "a very drunk sailor, who was a notoriously angry man, came to us, and he told all the people in the room to shut up, and he told a few of the men if they didn't get out of the room, he'd kill them." Day explains how she remembered Paul's admonition in Romans 12 to "overcome evil with good," and she thanked the man for his visit, offering him soup and bread despite his hostile behavior. After a few tense exchanges, the man eventually accepted the food that he was offered and sat down to eat peacefully. The next day the man returned with bags full of carrots and celery and potatoes, and soon he became one of the regulars at the house.[31] Other accounts also indicate how a staff member's vulnerability and refusal to meet a hostile guest on his or her terms can be essential to dealing with a violent or potentially violent situation. "The more liberated a person can become from the need to win, to dominate, the freer she is to base her response in a desire for the well-being of everyone involved in a crisis situation, to root her actions in the love the Christian gospel calls for, even of one's enemies."[32]

Although nonviolence is not always successful in defusing a tense or threatening situation—despite Workers' best efforts, sometimes fights break out and individuals are physically or emotionally injured—every effort is made to intervene in ways that do not cause an escalation of violence (indeed, many houses express reticence in resorting to the "lawful violence" of the police for this reason). Because what works in one set of circumstances can cause disaster in another, dealing with threatening or tense situations requires "a grace of immense sensitivity to the relational moment,"[33] which often can only be acquired through preparation and practice. "The art of intervention, especially when blows are being exchanged, is a hard-won skill. There is a range of possibility between the . . . extremes of standing back and allowing someone to be hurt, or rushing into a situation shoving and swinging while verbally threatening the troublemaker."[34] That is—to reiterate one of the major claims of this book—in many cases it *is* possible to set limits and restrain evil without mirroring the violence that one intends to exclude. Yet often there can be no substitute for the virtues acquired through practical experience to allow for a courageous and nonviolent response in the moment; theories and strategies can only take a person so far before a kind of practical know-how is needed.

And indeed, it is important to face up to the fact that the commitment to nonviolence *does* entail greater vulnerability than a readiness to employ violence to repel a threat—but, to reiterate, hospitality accepts a certain

[31] Coles, *Dorothy Day: A Radical Devotion*, 123–25.
[32] O'Gorman and Coy, "Houses of Hospitality," 257.
[33] Ibid., 253.
[34] Ibid., 258.

amount of risk as the price of a deeper security than that which can be attained through violence. "The act of hospitality posits vulnerability, allowing others access to one's life space," writes one person familiar with life at the Catholic Worker. "Hospitality means vulnerability embraced day by day."[35] As the website for the Los Angeles Catholic Worker (serving the area around LA's "Skid Row") explains,

> when one of your values is precarity, anything can happen. Our cars get stolen, our houses get broken into, our bank account runs dry, people die, get sick, lose their jobs, get arrested, or rip us off, but these are, hopefully, balanced by the times that we are divinely surprised by that one thousand dollar check, the angry person who caused a fight yesterday coming back today to apologize, the person who once ate at the soup kitchen coming back after ten years of sobriety to thank us for our work, or finding a wonderful gift of brie cheese in the food donation. By definition, being vulnerable to God's grace and goodness means that we must be equally vulnerable to chaos and disaster as well.[36]

But is such a life actually sustainable? Is this commitment to challenging limits not, in fact, opening the door to greater injustice and violence, as Boersma suggests? Does the Catholic Worker offer anything to "normal" practices of hospitality beyond a sense of insufficiency and guilt? Even more to the point of this book, does the Worker have anything of value to say about the limits of hospitality? And do the spiritual disciplines that I have presented as foundational to the practice of hospitality have a role to play in the radical hospitality of the Catholic Worker?

The question of sustainability is a difficult one and is inextricably tied up with the intensely personal question of vocation—a point I will consider in the final section of this chapter. For many people, it is true that the precariousness and vulnerability of the Worker may not be a sustainable way of life over the course of a lifetime. But this does not mean that all it offers is a sense of insufficiency and guilt to those whose practices are less radical. On one hand, as I stated above, Dorothy Day was always clear about the fact that "the houses of hospitality we have going now . . . are not meant to be a reason for anyone to feel 'inadequate' or 'selfish.' . . . It

---

[35] Daniel DiDomizio, "The Prophetic Spirituality of the Catholic Worker," in *Revolution of the Heart*, ed. Patrick Coy, 222.

[36] "Los Angeles Catholic Worker," at http://lacatholicworker.org/who-we-are, accessed 10/17/2008.

is not selfish to realize that this kind of living . . . is not for everyone."[37] On the other hand, however, the Worker can stand as both an affirmation and a challenge; in many ways, as the following section will show, the limits of hospitality (identity, security) are shaped by the same tensions in the context of the Worker as in any other context of the practice of hospitality. In this sense they affirm that even here limits are necessary. At the same time, the Worker offers a prophetic challenge to ordinary human limits—a challenge that one might choose to interpret as an inspiration rather than an indictment of other practices of hospitality—especially if one attends to the spiritual practices that empower such work.

Limits Even Here

Although it may appear that there are few limits to the hospitality of the Catholic Worker, even here hospitality cannot exist as total openness or surrender. While the limits of Catholic Worker hospitality generally fall well outside what most people would find tolerable, limits are by no means absent. In many ways these limits reflect the same concerns for identity and security that I have articulated in the previous chapters: there is, ultimately, a distinction between hosts and guests, just as there must be lines drawn "for staff survival" as well as for the safety of all involved.[38] "Knowing your limits is your life jacket here," writes Marc Ellis of his year at the Worker,[39] and a number of people (including Day herself) have pointed to how Day "drew boundaries very quickly"[40] and "was quick to stand up for her personal requirements, which to her were compatible with the idea of community."[41] Furthermore, in addition to these, a commitment to personalism also introduces certain limits of its own by insisting that hosts not simply go through the motions of hospitality without being present and attentive to the *person* they are meeting. "When it became all automatic, when my heart wasn't there, that was an indication that I needed to hit the road," one Worker comments. "I needed something else, so that I could come back and do it well, not just do it."[42]

[37] Coles, Dorothy Day: A Radical Devotion, 113.
[38] Riegle Troester, Voices from the Catholic Worker, 167; cf. 175.
[39] Ellis, A Year at the Catholic Worker, 103.
[40] Riegle Troester, Voices from the Catholic Worker, 167.
[41] Coles, Dorothy Day: A Radical Devotion, 130.
[42] Riegle Troester, Voices from the Catholic Worker, 179.

In the first place, however open or egalitarian the practices of the Catholic Worker may be, there remains a distinction between those who are "at home" in a house and those who are guests. "The line between [Worker and guest] is often vague," Murray observes, "but it does exist."[43] Despite a theoretical commitment to leveling such distinctions, one Worker notes that "the fact is that one person is having to come to others for food because he doesn't have any money, because he doesn't have a job, because he drinks heavily."[44] Another person explains,

> There's no getting around it. I decide whether they stay here. They don't decide whether I stay here. . . . There's no way [the relationships will be any different] unless we change and this becomes a house where everybody lives here permanently and guests have the responsibility for saying who stays and who doesn't. Unless it becomes completely their house, too, and then we can't do hospitality anymore. I realize the power, but I also realize I don't have the right not to exercise it. With the people we have who are mentally ill and absolutely unable or unwilling to make decisions, it would be less Christian and less loving not to exercise it.[45]

At the same time, of course, many guests who come to the Catholic Worker out of need are quite capable of taking on responsibility for the community, and as I have mentioned in previous chapters, sometimes such people become the most indispensible members of a particular household. In other cases—particularly in houses that offer long-term hospitality—the duration of a person's stay at a house can make functional distinctions problematic. "The people who come because of Catholic Worker philosophy tend to spend shorter times," one staff member of Maryhouse in New York observes. She recalls laughing when a volunteer referred to one of the long-time residents as a guest—"Sandra's lived here for twelve years, and you've lived here for about twelve days. And you're the host?"[46] But even in this case, the speaker is not so much contesting the *existence* of a distinction between hosts and guests as she is the criteria for determining who is who. Here, as in other practices of hospitality, the limits of identity are informed by hosts' and guests' relationship to a particular space—even as the ambiguity of that relationship introduces indeterminacy into such distinctions.

---

[43] Murray, *Do Not Neglect Hospitality*, 109.
[44] Riegle Troester, *Voices from the Catholic Worker*, 168.
[45] Ibid., 181.
[46] Ibid., 171.

Perhaps the distinction between hosts and guests—the limits of identity—becomes most clear in light of the question of security. Once again, both in terms of physical safety and material comfort, life at the Worker may seem incredibly insecure. At the end of the day, however, as indicated by the quote above, *someone* holds the keys to the door and is able—more or less—to use that power for the sake of others' safety. One Worker from St. Elizabeth's House in Chicago explains the implementation of a rule that requires men to leave the house between nine and five each day, whereas women and children are permitted to stay: "We wanted women to feel safe and secure, and we wanted it to be a nice place for them."[47] Members of this community found that this goal was best met by asking the men to leave during the day—a decision that could be seen as a preferential concern for more vulnerable members of a community and also as a limit of hospitality. A person from another community tells how she did spot-checking for drugs and other contraband: "I didn't like playing policewoman. . . . It was a hard role, but it had to be done for the safety of people here."[48] In these and other ways—despite significant vulnerability—the hospitality of the Catholic Worker involves a strong recognition of the need for safety and a willingness to draw boundaries in order to maintain a measure of security.

Beyond the limits of identity and security, however, the personalism of the Catholic Worker presents another aspect of hospitality that can serve as both a limit and a challenge. At the most basic level, personalism refers to a philosophical perspective that affirms the dignity, freedom, and particularity, as well as the relational nature, of human persons. It resists a one-size-fits-all approach to human needs, recognizing the ways in which a concern for effectiveness can sometimes get in the way of true hospitality. "Sometimes," one Worker comments, "we were so stretched out trying to meet all the needs that we lost track of the personalism," and she explains the situation of an older woman with severe emphysema who once came to their house. The staff was busy trying to accommodate her needs and to schedule appointments with doctors and the like, but suddenly the woman started crying and said, "Everyone is so willing to *do* everything for me. All I really want is someone to sit down with me and have a cup of coffee."[49] Another person explains how "the *doing* closes you

---

[47] Ibid., 169.
[48] Ibid., 175.
[49] Ibid., 171.

off to being really present to the people who are here. . . . That's the core of it. . . . If you lose that, then no matter how many people you're feeding, no matter how many diapers you're giving out, . . . it just doesn't make sense anymore."[50] When physical and emotional strain makes it difficult to act out of freedom and care for others, when one's heart is not in it, a personalist perspective may require a host to take a step back and acknowledge the limits of her hospitality. Dorothy Day acknowledges that

> you must know when to find your own, quiet moment of solitude. But you must know when to open the door to go be with others, and you must know *how* to open the door. There's no point in opening the door with bitterness and resentment in your heart. . . . I remember one day realizing that the best, the very best, I could do for everyone in the community, including our guests, was to stay away, to not fight staying away, which I might have done successfully. There are times when one's generosity is a mask for one's pride: what will "they" do without me?[51]

As Day's statement here recognizes, hospitality is not always a matter of simply opening a door; it also requires the host's ability to discern when and how to close it in order to respect others—and herself—as *persons* rather than simply providers and recipients. This does not mean that there are not times when it is appropriate to extend oneself beyond what is comfortable or convenient—Day's diaries make clear that she often worked through experiences of emotional exhaustion and physical discomfort, and such times of challenge may also be important times of growth—but even in those moments, personal challenges must be grounded in personal freedom rather than compulsion.

This ideological commitment to encouraging the free acceptance of personal responsibility facilitates Catholic Worker hospitality in certain ways while limiting it in others. On the one hand, when members of a household willingly contribute to the work in ways that meaningfully use their gifts, this can allow hospitality to flourish in unforeseeably abundant ways. Observing the "rules and regulations and red tape" of the prison system when she was imprisoned for protesting the Civil Defense Act in 1959, Day states that this "made me see how much more we accomplish

[50] Ibid., 178.
[51] Coles, *Dorothy Day: A Radical Devotion*, 130–31.

at the Catholic Worker . . . by cultivating a spirit of trust."[52] On the other hand, because some houses do not assign mandatory duties to residents, the lack of organization can lead not only to inefficiency but also to frustration and even hostility. While efficiency may be a price worth paying for personal freedom, one Worker explains how "it was difficult to come in from wherever and want to help out because people would just say, 'Well, whatever you see that needs to be done, you know, just whatever you see, you do it.'. . . And so things would get done by three or four people . . . because they didn't want to tell anybody else to do anything. It was very frustrating."[53] Just as in society at large, some people in a community may be more willing or able or differently abled than others.

Nonetheless, when asked whether it would not be better "to have more rules to facilitate the work" or "to kick out those who do not help," Day responds that "things might run a little more smoothly on the surface . . . but the criticisms and the lack of cooperation would go on. Let your abundance supply their want. There are always those who can do more work or who can do one thing better than they can do other things." She realizes that some people will take advantage of this, but "don't we take advantage of God? . . . Does not God put up with us?"[54] Ultimately, it is gratitude for the abundance of God's mercy that grounds and empowers the challenging limits of Catholic Worker hospitality. While I am certainly not trying to claim that all who come to the Worker (even those who come voluntarily) do so out of an explicit theological or spiritual motive, I do think that it is impossible to understand the enduring success of the movement as a whole without attending to the spirituality of Day and others who have shaped it.

Spirituality, Vocation, and the Gift of Hospitality

One cannot read far in Day's many descriptions of her life without recognizing her sustained commitment to spiritual growth and discipline as well as to the day-to-day concerns of the Worker and to sharing its vision through her writing and travel. Day's accounts of the struggles and achievements of the Worker are regularly punctuated by mention of attending Mass or saying the rosary or by reflections on the devotional material she was reading at the time. Particularly for a person whose

---

[52] Day, *Loaves and Fishes*, 177.

[53] Murray, *Do Not Neglect Hospitality*, 222.

[54] Dorothy Day, *House of Hospitality* (New York and London: Sheed & Ward, 1939), 124.

practical responsibilities could be so intense, Day's life demonstrates an impressive commitment to spiritual practices. As her own writing makes clear, however, such practices were not experienced as an additional burden but rather as a "duty of delight" that helped to sustain her other activity. This phrase, which appears numerous times in Day's writing, "served as a reminder to find God in all things—the sorrows of daily life and the moments of joy, both of which she experienced in abundance," according to Robert Ellsberg.[55] Ellsberg, who has edited several collections of Day's letters, diaries, and other writings, observes that "her daily life was spent in continuous reference to God. As she writes, 'Without the sacraments of the church, I certainly do not think that I could go on.'"[56] When asked how she would like her life to be described in one interview, Day quoted a former archbishop of Paris who stated that to be a witness to Christ "means to live in such a way that one's life would not make sense if God did not exist."[57] Day's own fascinating life—which baffled relatives and friends and involved an agonizing separation from her "natural happiness"[58]—is certainly a mystery without reference to God.

In addition to attending Mass daily and regularly going on spiritual retreats, Day maintained a robust practice of prayer and study even when her schedule ("working from seven [in the morning] until twelve at night, or traveling fifteen hours by bus"[59]) would scarcely seem to permit a moment's reflection. In 1936, Day recorded the following as part of a "rule" for the year:

> Morning prayers, in my room before going to Mass. . . .
> Around the middle of the day to take, even though it be to snatch, fifteen minutes of absolute quiet, thinking about God and talking to God. . . .
> The rosary daily.

[55] Dorothy Day, *The Duty of Delight*, xxi.

[56] Ibid., xvii.

[57] Coles, *Dorothy Day: A Radical Devotion*, 160.

[58] Day uses this phrase in *The Long Loneliness* to describe her life with Forster Battterham, with whom she lived and had a child but left because he was unwilling to get married when she converted to Catholicism: "I was happy," she writes, "but my very happiness made me know that there was a greater happiness to be obtained from life than I had ever known. I began to think, to weigh things, and it was at this point that I began consciously to pray more" (116).

[59] Day, *The Duty of Delight*, 14.

I do plenty of spiritual reading to refresh myself and to encourage myself so I do not have to remind myself of that.

The thing to remember is not to read so much or talk so much about God, but to talk to God.

To practice the presence of God.[60]

In fact, not only in Day's life but also in those of many other extremely active figures—from Mohandas Gandhi to Martin Luther King Jr. and even in what we know of the life of Jesus—there seems to be a paradoxical correlation between the intensity of emotional and practical demands and the necessity of maintaining space for spiritual life: that is, the more demanding a person's active responsibilities are, the more important it is to find guidance and refreshment in prayer, reflection, and the support of a community.

Yet despite Day's deep commitment to the sacramental life of the church—and, arguably, her sense that the vitality of the movement rested on this foundation[61]—the Catholic Worker's relationship to the Roman Catholic Church has always been somewhat ambiguous. For one thing, the Worker has no official ties to the institutional church, from which it has received both admiration and skepticism (largely due to its pacifism and alleged communist sympathies). Critiques of the church from within the Worker have also made for a tense relationship at times. At least as far as I am aware, neither Catholic faith nor Catholic practice has ever been a condition of the hospitality of Catholic Worker communities, either for those who come as Workers or for those who come as guests.

At the same time, however, while not all share Day's strong commitment to the Catholic Church and its spiritual traditions and practices, a significant number of sources testify to Workers' recognition of the importance of spiritual disciplines to their practice of hospitality. On its website, the Los Angeles Catholic Worker explains how "we have over the years tried to build a structure that forces us to take time for regular prayer, reflection, Bible study, and dialog because as Thomas Merton once wrote, 'He who attempts to act and do things for others or for the world without deepening his own self-understanding, freedom, integrity and capacity

---

[60] Ibid., 15.

[61] Fr. Richard McSorley notes that "before [Day] died, I asked her: 'Do you think it's necessary for Catholic Worker houses to publicly express and live out their affiliation with the Catholic faith?' And she said, 'Absolutely!' And the proof of that is that those that don't do it, don't continue." Riegle Troester, *Voices from the Catholic Worker*, 521.

to love, will not have anything to give others.'" Elsewhere on the website, they explain that "because our days can be pretty exhausting, we have had to force ourselves to create the time to be reflective" through prayer, Bible study, and communal liturgy. Through such practices, members of the community are able to "renew our understanding and commitment to the work we do."[62]

Even in houses that are less defined by traditional Christian beliefs and practices, there is often recognition of the necessity of spiritual disciplines that complement and empower a community's active work. A Worker from Seattle who describes his community as "real ecumenical" also recognizes this need:

> Every week we try to take a "Mindfulness Day." That's a day, or at least half a day, where each person as an individual doesn't work at the Family Kitchen, or do any other of the things we do. Instead they stay pretty much alone and do reflection or meditation in any way they see fit. . . . The spiritual practice for almost all of us here is meditation. . . . Gradually we left some of the Catholic stuff and just did meditation. . . . I don't think we've quit being Catholic. It's just that we don't pray in the traditional Catholic way.[63]

While there may be no way to conclusively prove a correlation between dedication to spiritual life and expansiveness of one's hospitality, the testimonies of those who have lived lives of radical hospitality bear witness to the ways in which attentiveness to God's Spirit empowers one's ability to see and love Christ in every guest.

Throughout her life, Day always remained humbly aware that the good she accomplished came from a source that was beyond her, and this humility made her confident that the same grace that empowered her work is available to any who seek it. She encourages her readers:

---

[62] "Los Angeles Catholic Worker," at http://lacatholicworker.org/who-we-are, accessed 11/04/11.

[63] Riegle Troester, *Voices from the Catholic Worker*, 512. I am aware of the complications that arise for my earlier formulation of spiritual disciplines as "hospitality to God" with the incorporation of interreligious practices that make no explicit reference to God; in many ways this opens up a discussion of truth and pluralism that is not only unresolvable but also peripheral to my overall concern here. My own conviction on this matter is that every practice that seeks to invite wisdom, compassion, and peace into human hearts and communities also makes space for the power of God's Spirit, who "intercedes with sighs too deep for words" (Rom 8:26) in every human prayer.

> Do what comes to hand. Whatever thy hand finds to do, do it with
> all thy might. After all, God is with us. It shows too much conceit
> to trust to ourselves, to be discouraged by what we ourselves can
> accomplish. It is lacking in faith to be discouraged. After all, we are
> going to proceed with his help. We offer him what we are going
> to do. If he wishes it to prosper, it will. We must depend solely on
> him. Work as though everything depended on ourselves, and pray as
> though everything depended on God, as St. Ignatius says. . . . I do
> know how small I am and how little I can do and I beg you, Lord,
> to help me, for I cannot help myself.[64]

Day's conviction that it was the Spirit of God who empowered the successes
of the Catholic Worker led, on the one hand, to a sense that anyone could
do what she was doing and, on the other hand, to an awareness that not
everyone is called to the same sort of work. Despite Day's extraordinary
commitment to the Worker, for which she was recognized as "Servant of
God" by the Vatican in 2000 (a first step toward possible canonization),
she is famous for her quote, "Don't call me a saint. I don't want to be
dismissed that easily"—meaning that she "didn't want recycling food
from dumpsters, sleeping on a stinky prison cell floor, and getting to mass
every afternoon to be dismissed as being for only special people. . . .
She practiced the Pauline understanding that *all* people of God are called
to be saints—not just those with a Vatican imprimatur."[65] Day's faith that
God would take small human gifts and multiply them for the good of the
world gave her confidence that *everyone* had a role to play—a vocation—in
building the kingdom of God. "God has given us our vocation," she writes,
"as He gave it to the small boy who contributed his few loaves and fishes
to help feed the multitude, and which Jesus multiplied so that He fed five
thousand people."[66]

   To recognize that every person has a calling or vocation is not, of course,
to say that all are called to the same thing; in the words of the apostle Paul,
"there are varieties of gifts, but the same Spirit; and there are varieties of
services, but the same Lord; and there are varieties of activities, but it is the
same God who activates all of them in everyone. To each is given the manifestation of the Spirit for the common good. . . . Indeed, the body does not
consist of one member but of many" (1 Cor 12:4-7, 14). It is important to

[64] Day, "Small Things," in *Selected Writings*, 64.
[65] Rose Marie Berger, "Don't Call Me a Saint," *Sojourners Magazine* 29.4 (July/Aug 2000).
[66] Day, *Loaves and Fishes*, 215.

recognize, as Day herself did in keeping with a spirit of personalism, that the form of hospitality practiced by the Catholic Worker is not for everyone. Pondering the question of why people leave, Day acknowledges the ways that the Catholic Worker has given many young people a springboard for work in other fields: "Social work, editing, labor organizing and politics, teaching, writing, nursing—in all these fields there are Catholic Workers or former Catholic Workers." Ultimately, she writes, "the reasons for leaving are as diverse as the reasons which prompt them to come."[67] Indeed, many people who come to the Worker out of ideological commitments or curiosity stay for only a short time (often a year or less) and come to find that the precariousness of life there is not sustainable for them over the long term. Particularly as people feel called to raise children, concern for security may lead them away from the sort of vulnerability that tends to characterize life in Houses of Hospitality.[68]

While the Worker's commitments to voluntary poverty and nonviolence lived out in community offer a radical and important witness to the demands of the Gospel (e.g., loving neighbors as oneself, loving enemies), it is not the only way in which faithfulness to a calling in the service of God's kingdom might be incarnated. Day and others in the movement have been eager to affirm the value of other ways of life as a manifestation of Christian vocation. Fr. Tom Lumpkin of the Detroit Catholic Worker explains the need for discernment of vocation based on one's natural gifts and inclinations: "You pray about it, certainly. Talk to other people, people you respect as having a certain amount of holy wisdom, if you will. And then if it's possible, you try it out tentatively. Also, I think even more basically, there's something to say about God's call in some way corresponding to the particular gifts you've been given. . . . It's a question of particular gifts and talents."[69] As with most activities in our lives, the practice of hospitality will come more easily to some people than to others. Certain individuals may be said to have a gift of hospitality—just as other people are gifted as teachers, writers, physicians, counselors, scientists, or

---

[67] Ibid., 136.

[68] Of course, many families *do* raise children in Worker communities, and often both kids and parents express the richness as well as the challenges of this kind of upbringing (see, e.g., Riegle Troester, *Voices from the Catholic Worker*, 312–32). Other communities, such as Kalamazoo's Peace House (which focuses on after-school programs for at-risk children rather than hospitality to adults), have shaped their work in ways that are more conducive to family life.

[69] Riegle Troester, *Voices from the Catholic Worker*, 516.

musicians—and may find that the limits of their hospitality are naturally more flexible and expansive than others'. Much like the reality that not everyone has the capacity to become a professional athlete or pianist or poet, regardless of how diligently they practice, not everyone is called to live the kind of radical hospitality of the Catholic Worker.

Yet this diversity of gifts and vocations should not be taken in such a way as to dull the challenge presented by the Catholic Worker or the many saints who have done God's work through the ages. Though I may never run a marathon, I still have the ability—and, arguably, the obligation—to exercise and train my body in accordance with the gifts I have been given. It is my deep conviction in writing this book that the ability to open one's heart in hospitality to God and to other people is not only a challenge but also a gift given to all—a gift that allows us to move beyond loneliness and hostility into the life of the Spirit of Peace—and that our capacity to receive this gift grows in proportion to our gratitude for it. Dorothy Day, whose life was marked by "a gratitude so large only God could receive it," also wrote in her diary that "gratitude makes you love people."[70] And in every true practice of hospitality, however challenging or joyous, miraculous or mundane, "the final word is love":

> At times it has been, in the words of Father Zossima, a harsh and dreadful thing, and our very faith in love has been tried through fire.
>
> We cannot love God unless we love each other, and to love we must know each other. We know Him in the breaking of bread, and we are not alone anymore. Heaven is a banquet, and life is a banquet, too, even with a crust, where there is companionship.
>
> We have all known the long loneliness and we have learned that the only solution is love.[71]

[70] Day, *The Duty of Delight*, xiv, 51.
[71] Day, *The Long Loneliness*, 285–86.

Afterword

Having been away from South Bend for a while due to holiday and work-related travel, I made a point of asking JC how he had been when I saw him at a First Friday—a celebration of Eucharist, a potluck dinner, and a speaker and discussion for the "clarification of thought" held every month at Our Lady of the Road—just before I moved to another town. "Oh, . . . things are all right," he said in his slow, deliberate way. But he told me that he was no longer JC. His name was now IC—as in "I *see*," he explained, with a knowing nod of his head.

I am sure he does.

He certainly helped me to better see and understand the limits of hospitality, not only through the episode I shared at the beginning of this book but also through the way that it continues to shed its light on a variety of thoughts and events that have followed. Perhaps, as I said in the first chapter, JC was too big of a guest for me. But I am certain that the "stretching" I experienced by giving serious consideration and prayer to the possibility of him staying in my house was essential to creating the space in my heart and home to welcome Lanay (who was also a pretty big guest in some ways). It is also important, I realize, to recognize how relationships of hospitality are embedded in communities: just as it is unlikely that I would have gotten to know JC (or Lanay, for that matter) without the hospitality of Our Lady of the Road, that community also remained necessary to support and provide space for my relationship to him. Through taking part in a community's practice of hospitality, not only were the time and gifts that I could offer multiplied, but I also found strength and joy in the friendships that grew out of that practice.

In sum, my central point in this book has been that each of us must begin our practice of hospitality from an honest recognition of our limits—our abilities and identities and resources and hostilities—but that hospitality really begins to grow and flourish as we strive to make room for what lies beyond these limits, holding identity in tension with openness to difference, possession in tension with gift, security in tension with risk. Rather than fortifying limits around what is comfortable or convenient, the Spirit of Christ invites us to explore ways of living and loving that may feel precarious but that in fact enlarge the space available in hearts and homes for the abundant life that God has promised. In his book *The Company of Strangers*, Parker Palmer writes that

> the way of the cross challenges us not to remove tensions from our lives by avoiding the places where tension is found, or by abandoning the convictions that cause us to feel tension. Instead, the cross points another way, a way of "living the contradictions," a way of taking tension into our lives and transforming it from a *force* of destruction to an *energy* of creation. . . . There is a tendency to want to resolve all dilemmas neatly, to draw back from situations that are ambiguous. We imagine, sometimes, that our faith requires us to lead tightly controlled lives, and this means placing ourselves only in those relationships which we can shape and form into some sense of propriety. But by doing so, we deny God the opportunity to work miracles in our lives, to draw us beyond what we think we can do.[1]

That God calls a person beyond what she thinks she can do is not to say that she must perpetually live on the brink of exhaustion or self-annihilation, however. The key to inhabiting tensions creatively is rather to honor the finitude of human gifts while acknowledging the infinite—even impossible—possibilities that are opened up by God's love. We can each start to stretch and expand beyond the limits of possessiveness and fear, of prejudice and resentment, and even of exhaustion and poverty to the extent that we allow ourselves to be filled to overflowing with a spirit of gratitude and peace.

Before concluding, I would like to note that an earlier version of this book also contained a sixth chapter on "The Limits of Politics," dealing with questions surrounding the limits of hospitality in the context of national immigration and economic policy. Though I decided that the issues raised in that context warrant a much more extensive treatment than could be addressed in a single chapter, in closing here I would like to make a few gestures in this direction in light of recent political events.

---

[1] Parker Palmer, *The Company of Strangers: Christians and the Renewal of America's Public Life* (New York: Crossroad, 1981), 116–17.

As I write these final pages, the United States has just passed through weeks of "reckless and divisive"[2] partisan wrangling over the nation's debt, resulting in a historic downgrade of its credit rating from Standard & Poor's. Spokespeople for the ratings agency and other commentators have stated that at its heart this is a political decision rather than an econometric one, indicating a lack of confidence in the United States' political leadership rather than in its economic viability. Felix Salmon, quoted on *The Economist's Free Exchange* blog, writes that "America's ability to pay is neither here nor there: the problem is its willingness to pay. And there's a serious constituency of powerful people in Congress who are perfectly willing and even eager to drive the US into default. The Tea Party is fully cognizant that it has been given a bazooka, and it's just itching to pull the trigger. There's no good reason to believe that won't happen at some point."[3] Other commentators have noted that a nation can survive its economic troubles—of which the United States has plenty—so long as its democratic institutions continue to function. If the recent dysfunction of Congress is any indication, it seems that the trouble may be just beginning.

Lest this seem superfluous to the focus of this book, allow me to point out that the word "economy" comes from the Greek word *oikos*, which is generally translated "household" in English. The concept of an "economy" originally referred not to abstract figures about the vitality of markets but rather to the management of household affairs: what goods are produced internally for the provision of household needs, what resources are acquired through trade, who is responsible for which tasks on a day-to-day basis. On this small, domestic scale, it seems fairly obvious that a household is more likely to flourish (and to be hospitable) if—as I described in chapter 4—the resources and burdens of its maintenance are equitably distributed[4] among its members. Perhaps even more important than such

---

[2] *The Economist*, "Downgrading Our Politics," *Free Exchange* (blog), August 6, 2011, http://www.economist.com/blogs/freeexchange/2011/08/sps-credit-rating-cut, accessed 8/10/2011.

[3] Ibid.

[4] Note that I do not necessarily consider *equitable* to be *equal* distribution in a strict and literal sense; not only do some people have greater or different needs and abilities than others, but it seems only just that there should be some incentive for ingenuity and hard work. Nonetheless, the current state of the US economy—in which the wealthiest 1 percent of its citizens control 40 percent of the nation's wealth, while nearly 15 percent live in poverty—spits in the face of justice and equity. See Dave Gilson and Carolyn Perot, "It's the Inequality, Stupid," *Mother Jones*, February 7, 2001, http://m.motherjones.com/politics/2011/02/income-inequality-in-america-chart-graph, accessed 8/12/2011.

equitable distribution, however, is a commitment among its members to the common good of the household. If each member of a family were to deny responsibility to and for the others and seek rather to secure his or her own interests apart from the whole, it is unlikely that this would be a healthy—or hospitable—environment for anyone, including those members themselves.

Obviously, there are a great many complications that arise when this domestic analogy is extended to a national scale. Nonetheless, the growth of an ideology that blatantly denies not only society's obligations to its most vulnerable members but also citizens' responsibility to one another is corrosive and destructive at any level. The Christian personalism of Peter Maurin and Dorothy Day was, in its own way, far more strongly opposed to "big government" than the free-market ideology of the Tea Party: the Catholic Worker has been outspoken and active not only in its critique of military spending but also in its claim that it is a *failure* on the part of society—that is, on the part of *Christians*—when the poor must be cared for at the expense of taxpayers. Yet Maurin and Day never denied the need for social responsibility and solidarity between the wealthy and the poor. They did not seek an expansion of "entitlements" or the "welfare state" but rather a reinvigoration of the conviction, especially among followers of Jesus, that we *are* our brother's keeper and are called to care for "the least of these" at our *own* personal expense. I cannot help but think that many of Maurin's *Easy Essays* seem even more appropriate to our current historical moment than to his own. With characteristic simplicity, he writes,

> In the first centuries
>   of Christianity
>   the hungry were fed
>   at a personal sacrifice,
>   the naked were clothed
>   at a personal sacrifice,
>   the homeless were sheltered
>   at personal sacrifice.
> And because the poor
>   were fed, clothed and sheltered
>   at a personal sacrifice,
>   the pagans used to say
>   about the Christians
>   "See how they love each other."

In our own day
> the poor are no longer
> fed, clothed, sheltered
> at a personal sacrifice,
> but at the expense
> of the taxpayers.
And because the poor
> are no longer
> fed, clothed and sheltered
> the pagans say about the Christians
> "See how they pass the buck."[5]

I cannot help but fear for the least of my sisters and brothers if these latest trends in government "downsizing" and partisan politics are not accompanied by a robust revolution of hospitality among American people. After all, the greatest limit to hospitality is the hardness of heart that denies responsibility for others and closes people off not only to one another but also to God. The greatest challenge of our age, writes Dorothy Day—even greater than rising unemployment or the volatility of the stock market or wars overseas—is this:

> How to bring about a revolution of the heart, a revolution which has to start with each one of us? When we begin to take the lowest place, to wash the feet of others, to love our brothers with that burning love, that passion, which led to the Cross, then we can truly say, "Now I have begun." Day after day we accept our failure, but we accept it because of our knowledge of the victory of the Cross. . . . How much we owe to God in praise, honor, thanksgiving![6]

Indeed, we owe *everything* to God—and it is precisely this recognition that moves and empowers us to share our time and possessions with others. As I have stated throughout this book, the limits of hospitality must be informed by gratitude and humility as well as faith and love, recognizing that all we have to give has been given to us.

That said, I am sure that for some people who read this book, its stories of soup kitchens and teenage boys and all-night vigils and living in community may seem well beyond their current or imaginable limits,

---

[5] Peter Maurin, "Feeding the Poor at a Sacrifice," http://www.catholicworker.org/roundtable/easyessays.cfm.

[6] Dorothy Day, *Loaves and Fishes* (Maryknoll, NY: Orbis, 1997), 215.

while to others, the perspectives and experiences that I have shared remain mired in and limited by bourgeois mediocrity. To the extent that there is truth to the latter view, I can only ask for the hospitality of forgiveness and pray that ongoing practice will eventually allow me to move past these limitations. For those who feel themselves as part of the first category, however, I encourage you to begin to grow from where you are, with small steps, like inflating a balloon—one breath at a time. Stretch yourself: invite someone you don't know well[7] to dinner, or reach out to a neighbor, or make a commitment to service in your community or to a spiritual discipline that you find challenging. Just as few people would attempt to run a marathon without training (lest they meet the same fate as the first marathon runner!); a deep and sustained practice of hospitality also requires the development of human virtues and capacities. Seek out fellowship in communities that are committed to and shaped by their practice of hospitality, in recognition of the fact that the diverse gifts that we have been given are often multiplied when shared.

Perhaps most importantly, remember the inevitability of weakness, failure, and folly, not only in the practice of hospitality but also in the spiritual life more generally. Always wary of "paralyzing self-criticism," Day recalls Peter Maurin's advice to her: "We can't expect to run to meet the world with our message and not fall flat on our faces. We've got to take the risk. We've got to get up after we fall and keep moving. If we say no, no more moving, because we've made a mistake, ten mistakes, a hundred, we're all washed up."[8] Trust that God not only knows your weaknesses, but that God's boundless power "is made perfect in weakness" (2 Cor 12:9).

To be sure, the spiritual life, the life of hospitality to God and neighbor, "is no easy task," writes Letty Russell. "This is why I continue to reiterate the concept of impossible possibility: we are called beyond what we believe are our limitations to live into a greater possibility."[9] While acknowledging that human hospitality will always face limitations, Russell argues that rather than dwelling on these, humans need to be open to the gifts of God: "We know that what we do is inadequate, but we include God in the relationship, confident that the mending [of creation] can be brought about by God. Hospitality is a gift of God to us, one that we need

---

[7] Or someone whom you *do* know well—as even this much can be a challenge sometimes!

[8] Robert Coles, *Dorothy Day: A Radical Devotion* (Reading, MA: Perseus Books, 1987), 120.

[9] Letty Russell, *Just Hospitality: God's Welcome in a World of Difference* (Louisville, KY: Westminster John Knox, 2009), 116.

to practice, so that we are more open to its blessing."[10] With gratitude, humility, discipline, and joy, human men and women are called by God to dwell within the love that has no limit.

I pray that, according to the riches of his glory, God may grant that you may be strengthened in your inner being with power through his Spirit, and that Christ may dwell in your hearts through faith, as you are being rooted and grounded in love. I pray that you may have the power to comprehend, with all the saints, what is the breadth and length and height and depth, and to know the love of Christ that surpasses knowledge, so that you may be filled with all the fullness of God.

Now to him who by the power at work within us is able to accomplish abundantly far more than all we can ask or imagine, to him be glory in the church and in Christ Jesus to all generations, forever and ever. Amen. (Eph 3:16-20)

[10] Ibid., 117.

Selected Bibliography

Allen, C. Leonard. *The Cruciform Church: Becoming a Cross-Shaped People in a Secular World.* Abilene, TX: ACU Press, 2006.

Arnold, Johann Christoph. *Seeking Peace.* Farmington, PA: Plogh Publishing House, 1998.

Arturbury, Andrew. *Entertaining Angels: Early Christian Hospitality in Its Mediterranean Setting.* Sheffield, England: Sheffield Phoenix, 2005.

Baker, Heidi and Rolland. *There is Always Enough.* Kent, England: Sovereign World, 2003.

Bass, Dorothy. *Practicing Our Faith: A Way of Life for a Searching People.* San Francisco: Jossey-Bass Publishers, 1997.

Behdad, Ali. *A Forgetful Nation: On Immigration and Cultural Identity in the United States.* Durham, NC, and London: Duke University Press, 2005.

Bellah, Robert, et al. *Habits of the Heart: Individualism and Commitment in Public Life.* Berkeley: University of California Press, 1985.

Benhabib, Seyla. "Feminism and Postmodernism: An Uneasy Alliance." In *Feminist Contentions: A Philosophical Exchange*, edited by Linda Nicholson. New York and London: Routledge, 1995.

————. "Hospitality, Sovereignty, and Democratic Iterations." In *Another Cosmopolitanism.* Edited by Pobert Post. Oxford: Oxford University Press, 2006.

Benveniste, Emil. "*L'hospitalité.*" In *Le vocabulaire des institutions indo-européennes* I. Paris: Minuit, 1969.

Berger, Rose Marie. "Don't Call Me a Saint." *Sojourners Magazine* (July/Aug 2000).

Berry, Hugh. *Being a Welcoming Congregation.* Louisville: National Ministries Division, Presbyterian Church, 1996.

Beumer, Jurjen. *Henri Nouwen: A Restless Seeking For God.* Translated by David Schlaver and Nancy Forest-Flier. New York: Crossroads, 1997.

Boersma, Hans. "Irenaeus, Derrida, and Hospitality: On the Eschatological Overcoming of Violence." *Modern Theology* 19.2 (2003).

————. *Violence, Hospitality, and the Cross: Reappropriating the Atonement Tradition.* Grand Rapids, MI: Baker Academic, 2004.

Bolchazy, Ladislaus. *Hospitality in Early Rome: Livy's Conception of Its Humanizing Force.* Chicago: Area Publishers, 1977.

Bretherton, Luke. *Hospitality as Holiness: Christian Witness amid Moral Diversity.* Aldershot, England: Ashgate, 2006.

Brown, Wendy. "Wounded Attachments." *Political Theory* 21.3 (1993).

Browner, Jesse. *The Duchess Who Wouldn't Sit Down: An Informal History of Hospitality.* New York: Bloomsbury, 2003.

Brueggemann, Walter. *The Land: Place as Gift, Promise, and Challenge in Biblical Faith.* Philadelphia: Fortress Press, 1977.

Byrne, Brendan. *The Hospitality of God: A Reading of Luke's Gospel.* Collegeville, MN: Liturgical Press, 2000.

Camosy, Charles. *Too Expensive to Treat? Finitude, Tragedy, and the Neonatal ICU.* Grand Rapids, MI: Eerdmans, 2010.

Caputo, John. *The Prayers and Tears of Jacques Derrida: Religion without Religion.* Bloomington, IN: Indiana University Press, 1997.

————. *What Would Jesus Deconstruct? The Good News of Postmodernism for the Church.* Grand Rapids, MI: Baker Academic, 2007.

Caputo, John, and Michael Scanlon, eds. *God, the Gift, and Postmodernism.* Bloomington, IN: Indiana University Press, 1999.

Carroll R., M. Daniel. *Christians at the Border: Immigration, the Church, and the Bible.* Grand Rapids, MI: Baker Academic, 2008.

Cassidy, Laura, and Alex Mikulich, eds. *Interrupting White Privilege: Catholic Theologians Break the Silence.* Maryknoll, NY: Orbis Books, 2007.

Claiborne, Shane. *The Irresistible Revolution: Living as an Ordinary Radical.* Grand Rapids, MI: Zondervan, 2006.

Cloud, Henry, and John Townsend. *Boundaries: When to Say Yes and When to Say No to Take Control of Your Life.* Grand Rapids, MI: Zondervan, 1992.

Coakley, Sarah. "Deepening Practices: Perspectives from Ascetical and Mystical Theology." In *Practicing Theology: Beliefs and Practices in Christian Life,* edited by Miroslav Volf and Dorothy Bass. Grand Rapids, MI: Eerdmans, 2002.

Coles, Robert. *Dorothy Day: A Radical Devotion.* Reading, MA: Perseus Books, 1987.

Cooke, Bernard. "Ecclesiology: Implicit but Influential." In *Tensions between Citizenship and Discipleship,* edited by Nellie Slater. New York: The Pilgrim Press, 1989.

Coy, Patrick, ed. *Revolution of the Heart: Essays on the Catholic Worker.* Philadelphia: Temple University Press, 1988.

Crisp, Roger, and Michael Slote. *Virtue Ethics.* New York and Oxford: Oxford University Press, 1997.

Day, Dorothy. *The Duty of Delight: The Diaries of Dorothy Day.* Edited by Robert Ellsberg. Milwaukee, WI: Marquette University Press, 2008.

————. *House of Hospitality.* New York and London: Sheed & Ward, 1939.

————. *Loaves and Fishes.* Maryknoll, NY: Orbis Books, 1997.

————. *The Long Loneliness.* New York: Harper & Brothers, 1952.

————. *Selected Writings: By Little and by Little*. Edited by Robert Ellsberg. Maryknoll, NY: Orbis Books, 1992.

de Bethune, Piérre-François. *Interreligious Hospitality: The Fulfillment of Dialogue*. Collegeville, MN: Liturgical Press, 2010.

Derrida, Jacques. *Acts of Religion*. Edited by Gil Anidjar. New York and London: Routledge, 2002.

————. *Adieu to Emmanuel Levinas*. Stanford, CA: Stanford University Press, 1999.

————. "Hospitality, Justice, and Responsibility." In *Questioning Ethics: Contemporary Debates in Philosophy*, edited by Robert Kearney and Mark Tooley. London: Routledge, 1999.

————. "Hostipitality." Translated by Barry Stocker. *Journal of the Theoretical Humanities* 5.2 (December 2000).

————. *Negotiations: Interventions and Interviews, 1971–2001*. Edited and translated by Elizabeth Rottenberg. Stanford, CA: Stanford University Press, 2002.

————. *Of Hospitality: Anne Dufourmantelle Invites Jacques Derrida to Respond*. Stanford, CA: Stanford University Press, 2000.

————. *On Cosmopolitanism and Forgiveness*. New York: Routledge, 2001.

————. "Perhaps or Maybe." In *Responsibilities of Deconstruction*, vol. 6 of PLI: *The Warwick Journal of Philosophy* (1997).

————. "The Principle of Hospitality." *Parallax* 11.1 (2005; reprinted from *Le Monde*, December 2, 1997).

Derrida, Jacques, and John Caputo. *Deconstruction in a Nutshell*. New York: Fordham University Press, 1997.

Dooley, Mark. "The Politics of Exodus: Derrida, Keirkegaard, and Levinas on 'Hospitality.'" In *Works of Love*, vol. 16 of *International Kierkegaard Commentary*, edited by Robert L. Perkins. Macon, GA: Mercer University Press, 1999.

Dykstra, Craig, and Dorothy Bass. "A Theological Understanding of Christian Practices." In *Practicing Theology: Beliefs and Practices in Christian Life*, edited by Miroslav Volf and Dorothy Bass. Grand Rapids, MI: Eerdmans, 2002.

Ellis, Marc. *A Year at the Catholic Worker: A Spiritual Journey among the Poor*. Waco, TX: Baylor University Press, 2000.

Epp-Stobbe, Eleanor. "Practicing God's Hospitality: The Contribution of Letty M. Russell Toward an Understanding of the Church." ThD diss., University of Toronto, 2000.

Farley, Margaret. *Just Love: A Framework for Christian Sexual Ethics*. London: Continuum, 2006.

Fingarette, Herbert. *Self-Deception*. New York: Humanities Press, 1969.

Flannery, Austin, ed. *Vatican Council II: The Basic Sixteen Documents*. Northport, NY: Costello Publishing Co., 2007.

Ford, Michael. *Wounded Prophet: A Portrait of Henri J.M. Nouwen*. New York: Doubleday, 1999.

Foster, Richard. *Celebration of Discipline:The Path to Spiritual Growth.* San Francisco: Harper-SanFrancisco, 1998.

Fry, Timothy, ed. *The Rule of Saint Benedict 1980.* Collegeville, MN: Liturgical Press, 1981.

Goldberg, Michael. *Theology and Narrative: A Critical Introduction.* Nashville: Abingdon, 1981.

Greer, Rowan. *Broken Lights and Mended Lives:Theology and Common Life in the Early Church.* University Park, PA: University of Pennsylvania Press, 1986.

———. "Hospitality in the First Five Centuries of the Church." In *On Hospitality and Other Matters.* Monastic Studies 10. Pine City, NY: Mount Savior Monastery, 1974.

Groody, Daniel. *Globalization, Spirituality, and Justice.* Maryknoll, NY: Orbis Books, 2009.

Gros, Jeffrey, and John Rempel, eds. *The Fragmentation of the Church and Its Unity in Peacemaking.* Grand Rapids, MI: Eerdmans, 2001.

Hallett, Garth. *Priorities in Christian Ethics.* Cambridge: Cambridge University Press, 1998.

Hallie, Philip. *Lest Innocent Blood Be Shed:The Story of theVillage of Le Chambon and How Goodness Happened There.* New York: Harper & Row, 1979.

Hastings, James, et al. "Hospitality." In *Encyclopedia of Religion & Ethics.* New York: Scribner, 1928.

Hauerwas, Stanley. *The Hauerwas Reader.* Edited by John Berkman and Michael Cartwright. Durham, NC: Duke University Press, 2001.

———. *The Peaceable Kingdom.* Notre Dame, IN: University of Notre Dame Press, 1977.

Heal, Felicity. *Hospitality in Early Modern England.* New York: Oxford, 1990.

Hernandez, Wil. *Henri Nouwen: A Spirituality of Imperfection.* New York: Paulist Press, 2006.

Hershberger, Michele. *A ChristianView of Hospitality: Expecting Surprises.* Scottsdale, PA: Herald Press, 1999.

Hiebert, Paul. "The Category Christian in the Mission Task." In *Anthropological Reflections on Missiological Issues.* Grand Rapids, MI: Baker Books, 1994.

Holder, Arthur, ed. *The Blackwell Companion to Christian Spirituality.* Oxford: Blackwell, 2005.

Homan, Daniel, and Lonni Collins Pratt. *Radical Hospitality: Benedict's Way of Love.* Brewster, MA: Paraclete Press, 2002.

Inge, John. *A Christian Theology of Place.* Burlington, VT: Ashgate, 2003.

Irarrázaval, Diego. *Inculturation: New Dawn of the Church in Latin America.* Translated by Phillip Berryman. Maryknoll, NY: Orbis Books, 2000.

John Paul II. *Sollicitudo Rei Sociali: On Social Concern.* In *Catholic Social Thought:The Documentary Heritage,* edited by David O'Brien and Thomas Shannon. Maryknoll, NY: Orbis Books, 1992.

Koenig, John. *New Testament Hospitality: Partnership with Strangers as Promise and Mission.* Eugene, OR: Wipf and Stock, 2001.

LaNoue, Deirdre. *The Spiritual Legacy of Henri Nouwen.* New York: Continuum, 2000.

Lebacqz, Karen. "Paul Revere and the Holiday Inn: A Case Study in Hospitality." In *Tensions Between Citizenship and Discipleship,* edited by Nellie Slater. New York: The Pilgrim Press, 1989.

Lévinas, Emmanuel. *God, Death, and Time.* Translated by Bettina Bergo. Stanford, CA: Stanford University Press, 2000.

————. *Totality and Infinity: An Essay on Exteriority.* Translated by Alphonso Ligis. Pittsburgh, PA: Duquesne University Press, 1969.

MacIntyre, Alasdair. *After Virtue: A Study in Moral Theology.* Notre Dame, IN: University of Notre Dame Press, 1981).

Malherbe, Abraham. *Social Aspects of Early Christianity.* Philadelphia: Fortress Press, 1983.

Massignon, Louis. *L'hospitalité sacrée.* Paris: Nouvelle Cité, 1987.

Mathews, John Bell. "Hospitality and the New Testament Church: An Historical and Exegetical Study." ThD diss., Princeton Theological Seminary, 1964.

Maurin, Peter. *Easy Essays.* New York: Sheed & Ward, 1936.

McGinn, Bernard, and John Meyendorff, eds. *Christian Spirituality I: Origins to the Twelfth Century.* New York: Crossroads, 1985.

Meilaender, Gilbert. *The Theory and Practice of Virtue.* Notre Dame, IN: University of Notre Dame Press, 1984.

Merton, Thomas. *Faith and Violence: Christian Teaching and Christian Practice.* Notre Dame, IN: University of Notre Dame Press, 1968.

Miles, Margaret. *Practicing Christianity: Critical Perspectives for an Embodied Spirituality.* New York: Crossroad, 1988.

Murray, Harry. *Do Not Neglect Hospitality: The Catholic Worker and the Homeless.* Philadelphia: Temple University Press, 1990.

Naas, Michael. "*Alors, êtes-vous?* Jacques Derrida and the Question of Hospitality." *SubStance* 34.1 (2005).

Newlands, Goerge, and Allen Smith. *Hospitable God: The Transformative Dream.* Burlington, VT: Ashgate, 2010.

Newman, Elizabeth. *Untamed Hospitality: Welcoming God and Other Strangers.* Grand Rapids, MI: Brazos Books, 2007.

Nouwen, Henri J. M. *Clowning in Rome: Reflections on Solitude, Celibacy, Prayer, and Contemplation.* Westminster, MD: Christian Classics, 1979.

————. *The Genesee Diary: Report from a Trappist Monastery.* New York: Doubleday/Image Books, 1981.

————. "Hospitality." In *On Hospitality and Other Matters.* Monastic Studies 10. Pine City, NY: Mount Savior Monastery, 1974.

————. *Life of the Beloved: Spiritual Living in a Secular World.* New York: Crossroad, 1992.

————. *Making All Things New: An Invitation to the Spiritual Life.* San Francisco: Harper & Row, 1981.

————. *Peacework: Prayer, Resistance, Community.* Maryknoll, NY: Orbis Books, 2005.

————. *Reaching Out: The Three Movements of the Spiritual Life.* New York: Doubleday/ Image Books, 1975.

————. *Return of the Prodigal Son: A Story of Homecoming.* New York: Continuum, 1995.

————. *Spiritual Journals: Genesee Diary, ¡Gracias!, The Road to Daybreak.* New York: Continuum, 1997.

————. *The Wounded Healer: Ministry in Contemporary Society.* New York: Doubleday/ Image Books, 1979.

Norris, Kathleen. *Amazing Grace: A Vocabulary of Faith.* New York: Riverhead Books, 1998.

Oden, Amy. *And You Welcomed Me: A Sourcebook on Early Christian Hospitality.* Nashville: Abingdon Press, 2001.

————. *God's Welcome: Hospitality for a Gospel-Hungry World.* Cleveland, OH: Pilgrim Press, 2008.

Ogletree, Thomas. *Hospitality to Strangers: Dimensions of Moral Understanding.* Louisville: Westminster John Knox, 2003.

Outka, Gene. *Agape: An Ethical Analysis.* New Haven, CT, and London: Yale University Press, 1972.

————. "Universal Love and Impartiality." In *The Love Commandments,* edited by Edmund Santurri and William Werpehowski. Washington, DC: Georgetown University Press, 1992.

Palmer, Parker. *The Company of Strangers: Christians and the Renewal of America's Public Life.* New York: Crossroad, 1981.

Pineda, Ana María. "Hospitality." In *Practicing Our Faith: A Way of Life for a Searching People,* edited by Dorothy Bass. San Francisco: Jossey-Bass Publishers, 1997.

Pohl, Christine. "A Community's Practice of Hospitality: The Interdependence of Practices and of Communities." In *Practicing Theology,* edited by Miroslav Volf and Dorothy Bass. Grand Rapids, MI: Eerdmans, 2002.

————. "Hospitality from the Edge: The Significance of Marginality in the Practice of Welcome." *Annual of the Society of Christian Ethics* (1995).

————. "Hospitality: Mysterious and Mundane." *Reformed Review* 57.2 (2004): 1–14.

————. *Making Room: Recovering Hospitality as a Christian Tradition.* Grand Rapids, MI: Eerdmans, 1999.

————. "Responding to Strangers: Insights from the Christian Tradition." *Studies in Christian Ethics* 19.1 (2006): 81–101.

Pontifical Council for the Care of Migrants and Itinerant Peoples. *Erga Migrantes Caritas Christi (The Love of Christ towards Migrants).* Issued 2004.

Reese, Jack. *The Body Broken: Embracing the Peace of Christ in a Fragmented Church*. Siloam Springs, AR: Leafwood, 2005.

Riegle Troester, Rosalie, ed. *Voices from the Catholic Worker*. Philadelphia: Temple University Press, 1993.

Russell, Letty Mandeville. *Church in the Round: Feminist Interpretations of the Church*. Louisville: Westminster John Knox, 1992.

———. "Encountering the 'Other' in a World of Difference and Danger." *Harvard Theological Review* 99.4 (2006): 457–68.

———. "Hot-House Ecclesiology: A Feminist Interpretation of the Church." *Ecumenical Review* 53.1 (2001): 48–56.

———. *Household of Freedom: Authority in Feminist Theology*. Philadelphia: Westminster, 1987.

———. *Just Hospitality: God's Welcome in a World of Difference*. Edited by Shannon Clarkson and Kate Ott. Louisville: Westminster John Knox, 2009.

———. "Postcolonial Challenges and the Practice of Hospitality." In *A Just and True Love: Feminism at the Frontiers of Theological Ethics: Essays in Honor of Margaret A. Farley*, edited by Maura Ryan and Brian Linnane. Notre Dame, IN: University of Notre Dame Press, 2007.

———. "Practicing Hospitality in a Time of Backlash." *Theology Today* 52.4 (1996): 476–84.

———. "Toward a Trinitarian Language of Hospitality." *Living Pulpit* 8.2 (1999): 26–27.

Schneiders, Sandra. "Theology and Spirituality: Strangers, Rivals, or Partners?" *Horizons* 13.2 (1986).

Spohn, William. "Spiritual Theology and Christian Ethics." In *Blackwell Companion to Christian Spirituality*, edited by Arthur Holder. Oxford: Blackwell, 2005.

Stählin, Gustav. "ξένος." In *Theological Dictionary of the New Testament*, translated and edited by Gerald Bromiley. Grand Rapids, MI: Eerdmans, 1964–76.

Steindl-Rast, David. *Gratefulness, the Heart of Prayer: An Approach to Life in Fullness*. New York: Paulist Press, 1984.

Sutherland, Arthur. *I Was a Stranger: A Christian Theology of Hospitality*. Nashville: Abingdon Press, 2006.

Swan, Laura. *Engaging Benedict: What the Rule Can Teach Us Today*. Notre Dame, IN: Ave Maria Press, 2005.

Tanner, Kathryn. *Theories of Culture: A New Agenda for Theology*. Minneapolis: Fortress Press, 1997.

Taylor, Charles. "The Politics of Recognition." In *Multiculturalism and the Politics of Recognition*. Edited by Amy Gutmann. Princeton, NJ: Princeton University Press, 1994.

United States Conference of Catholic Bishops and Conferencia del Episcopado Mexicano. *Strangers No Longer: Together on the Journey of Hope; A Pastoral Letter Concerning Migration*. Issued January 22, 2003.

Vanden Busch, Roger. "The Value of Silence in Christian Spirituality." *Spirituality Today* 37 (1985).

Volf, Miroslav. *Exclusion and Embrace: A Theological Exploration of Identity, Otherness, and Reconciliation.* Nashville: Abingdon, 1996.

Volf, Miroslav, and Dorothy Bass. *Practicing Theology: Beliefs and Practices in Christian Life.* Grand Rapids, MI: Eerdmans, 2001.

Voskamp, Ann. *One Thousand Gifts.* Grand Rapids, MI: Zondervan, 2010.

Vosloo, Robert. "Identity, Otherness, and the Triune God: Theological Groundwork for a Christian Ethic of Hospitality." *Journal of Theology for South Africa* 119 (2004): 69–89.

Weir, Alison. *Sacrificial Logics: Feminist Theory and the Subversion of Identity.* New York: Routledge, 1996.

Westerhoff, Caroline. *Good Fences: The Boundaries of Hospitality.* Harrisonburg, PA: Morehouse Publishing, 1999.

Willard, Dallas. *Spirit of the Disciplines: Understanding How God Changes Lives.* San Francisco: HarperSanFrancisco, 1988.

Yoder, John Howard. *The Original Revolution: Essays on Christian Pacifism.* Scottsdale, PA: Herald Press, 2003.

Yong, Amos. *Hospitality and the Other: Pentecost, Christian Practices, and the Neighbor.* Maryknoll, NY: Orbis Books, 2008.

Young, Iris Marion. *Justice and the Politics of Difference.* Princeton, NJ: Princeton University Press, 1990.

Index

Made in the USA
Columbia, SC
17 May 2024

35808389R00102